WITHDRAWN

HOSPITAL CHAPLAINCY IN THE TWENTY-FIRST CENTURY

Issues of faith and spirituality have been resurgent in the UK since the opening of the twenty-first century. This book charts the impact of shifting attitudes towards spirituality through the experiences of health care chaplains. Rooted in a new and challenging interpretation of the chaplain's work in the past, the book moves on to describe a current crisis in the nature of spiritual care. Using the tools of practical theology to analyze these experiences, fundamental problems are identified for chaplains as they work within the culture of 'evidence based practice'.

As the National Health Service struggles to balance its books in the face of national economic uncertainty, chaplains will continue to come under increasing levels of scrutiny. Some chaplains have faced the prospect of redundancy or cuts to their budgets, while a growing number of NHS Trusts no longer offer chaplaincy to patients out of hours. In this context the nature of chaplaincy itself has come into question, and rival models of the profession have emerged. Is chaplaincy a new and distinct profession within health care, based on evidence and available to all? Or is it State-funded religious activity, theoretically open to all but in practice utilized chiefly by the faithful few? In responding to these questions the book concludes with a vision of how chaplaincy can both maintain its integrity – and be a valued part of twenty-first century health care.

Explorations in Practical, Pastoral and Empirical Theology

Series Editors: Leslie J. Francis, University of Warwick, UK
and Jeff Astley, Director of the North of England
Institute for Christian Education, UK

Theological reflection on the church's practice is now recognised as a significant element in theological studies in the academy and seminary. Ashgate's new series in practical, pastoral and empirical theology seeks to foster this resurgence of interest and encourage new developments in practical and applied aspects of theology worldwide. This timely series draws together a wide range of disciplinary approaches and empirical studies to embrace contemporary developments including: the expansion of research in empirical theology, psychological theology, ministry studies, public theology, Christian education and faith development; key issues of contemporary society such as health, ethics and the environment; and more traditional areas of concern such as pastoral care and counselling.

Other titles in the series include:

Theology without Words
Theology in the Deaf Community
Wayne Morris
978-0-7546-6227-3

Reconstructing Practical Theology
The Impact of Globalization
John Reader
978-0-7546-6224-2

The Bible and Lay People
An Empirical Approach to Ordinary Hermeneutics
Andrew Village
978-0-7546-5801-6

Inspiring Faith in Schools
Studies in Religious Education
Edited by Marius Felderhof, Penny Thompson and David Torevell
978-0-7546-6031-6

Hospital Chaplaincy in the Twenty-first Century
The Crisis of Spiritual Care on the NHS

CHRISTOPHER SWIFT
Leeds Metropolitan University, UK

ASHGATE

Published by
Ashgate Publishing Limited
Wey Court East
Union Road
Farnham
Surrey, GU9 7PT
England

Ashgate Publishing Company
Suite 420
101 Cherry Street
Burlington
VT 05401-4405
USA

www.ashgate.com

British Library Cataloguing in Publication Data
Swift, Christopher
    Hospital chaplaincy in the twenty-first century : the crisis of spiritual care on the NHS. –
    (Explorations in practical, pastoral and empirical theology)
    1. Chaplains, Hospital – Great Britain
    I. Title
    259.4

Library of Congress Cataloging-in-Publication Data
Swift, Christopher, 1965–
    Hospital chaplaincy in the 21st century : the crisis of spiritual care on the NHS / Christopher Swift.
        p. cm. – (Explorations in practical, pastoral, and empirical theology)
    Includes bibliographical references (p.   ).
    ISBN 978-0-7546-6416-1 (hardcover : alk. paper)
    1. Great Britain. National Health Service–Chaplains. 2. Chaplains, Hospital–Great Britain. I. Title.

    BV4335.S95 2009
    259'.4110941–dc22

    2009000410

ISBN 978 0 7546 6416 1

Mixed Sources
Product group from well-managed
forests and other controlled sources
www.fsc.org Cert no. SA-COC-1565
© 1996 Forest Stewardship Council
FSC

Printed and bound in Great Britain by
MPG Books Ltd, Bodmin, Cornwall.

For Stanley and Marjorie

Contents

Illustrations

Both sets of photographs are by John Sherbourne

Foreword

This is an important book. Health care chaplaincy is currently undergoing a rapid transformation. An inherited and accepted service, embedded in the National Health Service since its inception, it is inevitably caught up in the changes that affect both the service as a whole and the wider social context.

From the NHS comes the demand for managerial efficiency, based on 'value for money', evidence-based practice and patient choice. So the chaplaincy service is being asked how its presence is justified and how it can be quantified. Moreover, this is given a sharper edge in an increasingly secularized body politic where there is considerable suspicion about the public place of religion. Yet, at the same time, the recognition that British society is increasingly pluralistic and culturally diverse suggests that any such provision being offered should be multi-faith in form. Then again, ironically, some branches of medicine, notably palliative care and nursing, pressing for a 'holistic' approach to patient care, have responded to the current interest in 'spirituality', seeing this as a vital dimension, but without a necessary reference to religion. In all these ways the chaplaincy service, always small but curiously growing in recent times, finds itself under threat.

It is also true that chaplains have often found themselves marginal to the life of the Churches in whose name they minister. This gap is increased as they find themselves more and more having to find an identity within the health service and conform to its norms and expectations.

What Chris Swift here provides is a much needed and comprehensive study of health care chaplains today. Its focus, inevitably, given that they are the largest contingent, is on the Anglicans, but a careful eye is given to Roman Catholic and Free Church and other chaplains. It is rooted in history but gathers together the small but growing research and writing around these contemporary debates. He also brings his own extensive pastoral experience and research (there is a PhD lurking in the background) and teaching (in Cardiff and Leeds), together with a deep involvement in the life of the College of Health Care Chaplains and working with various levels of the health service. He thus offers a well informed, sharp and critical slant on the story to which we all should pay attention.

The result is a valuable resource which will stand the test of time. His colleagues will find it a constant point of reference as they wrestle with the issues both locally and nationally. Health care professionals, especially managers, will find a way into the heart and mind of this schematic oddity with which they have to work. Many others, too, could find this a way of being informed about a key area of health care. Moreover, and perhaps most importantly, there is a challenge here to the Churches to take chaplaincy seriously as the frontier ministry it is. It needs active support, both for the practitioners and within the deliberations of the Churches;

but it is also necessary to listen to the experiential and theological wisdom that can emerge from this ministry to enrich the wider community of faith. But there is a corollary. Practitioners do not find it easy to report back but this is essentially two-way traffic. For practical theologians this is a welcome and accessible case study of a vital sector of ministry, useful for reflection and teaching.

It is a pleasure, therefore, heartily to commend the work of one who has been, over a number of years, a valued colleague.

Paul Ballard
Emeritus Professor, School of Religious and Theological Studies,
Cardiff University, UK.
Advent 2008.

Preface

There is a small body of literature about the role and practice of health care chaplaincy in the United Kingdom. Across the years leading into the twenty-first century this literature has grown at an exponential rate, reflecting a new turn of interest in the place of spiritual and religious care in the NHS. In this book I have attempted to add to this growing debate by questioning some of the basic perceptions about the chaplain's historic and contemporary position in the life of the hospital. While this is an approach that developed during my academic research it is a consideration that is informed by my own work as a chaplain and as a manager of chaplains. Chaplains are a small group of staff in the health service who find themselves at the intersection of some of the most important and powerful struggles of our society. In the presence of chaplains we encounter questions of inter-faith relations; health; mortality; public spirituality; human sexuality and secularization. I hope that readers will discover in what follows chaplains who are more complex, rich and interesting than might be assumed at first sight.

Acknowledgements

The heart of this book developed during my research for a PhD with the University of Sheffield which I completed in 2005. I remain grateful for the wise supervision, constructive insight and personal encouragement of my joint supervisors, Nick Fox and Martyn Percy. In the latter stages of my studies, and subsequently, I worked alongside colleagues in the College of Health Care Chaplains and in Unite during what became demanding days for chaplaincy in England. Their contribution to my thinking about the nature and causes of threats to chaplaincies such as occurred in Worcestershire has added important insights to this book. Carol English at Unite and Jayne Shepherd deserve special thanks in this regard. In my day-to-day work in the Leeds Teaching Hospitals I have been supported by line-managers keen to encourage the kind of deeper reflection about the role of the chaplain that I have attempted to set out in this book. They have done so in the conviction that a greater understanding of the chaplain offers the possibility of fostering better care for patients, greater support for chaplains themselves and a better use of the insights of chaplaincy in the organization as a whole. In some small measure I hope that this book rewards their confidence in what a fuller comprehension of the chaplain might accomplish.

The ministry of the chaplain in the NHS is not easy. I am grateful to colleagues in Leeds who have from time-to-time enabled me to take periods of study leave to work on the ideas that have become part of what is offered here. Alongside this our journal group meetings, impromptu reflections on pastoral care and general commitment to research have added to the progress of my thinking about the chaplain. Beyond Leeds I have benefited from the insights into chaplaincy across the public sector through my teaching on the chaplaincy course offered by the University of Cardiff at St Michael's College, Llandaff. I am grateful to both students and academic colleagues for the stimulation that this association has produced.

For several years Mark Cobb has been a valued conversation partner around a range of topics relating to chaplaincy, the NHS and the Church of England. This has been a critical dialogue in getting to grips with events in the world of chaplaincy that have at times been rapid and unanticipated. Mark's clarity of vision and consistent focus is a considerable asset for the world of chaplaincy in England and beyond.

I am grateful to Roger Witts for proof-reading and correcting the text, as well as for his comments at various points about the content and development of my argument. Further comment by Mary Leigh has contributed to the improvement of the chapters, and I wish to record my appreciation for the questions and insights that Mary has offered. Max Shepherd also added helpful observations to aspects of the draft for which I am grateful.

Lastly, I would like to note my thanks for those nearest to me who have tolerated the constraints and demands of deadlines and the space needed for study.

List of Abbreviations

AHPCC	Association of Hospice and Palliative Care Chaplains
CAAB	Chaplaincy Academic and Accreditation Board
CHCC	College of Health Care Chaplains
CofE	Church of England
CPD	Continuing Professional Development
HOSC	Health Overview and Scrutiny Committee
HCC	Hospital Chaplaincies Council
MFGHC	Multi-Faith Group for Healthcare Chaplaincy
NHS	National Health Service
NIHCA	Northern Ireland Healthcare Chaplains' Association
SACH	Scottish Association of Chaplains in Healthcare
TUC	Trades Union Congress
UKBHC	UK Board of Healthcare Chaplaincy

Introduction

> In a crisis, the issues and priorities suddenly become clearer than they were before. We can, if we will, discern what is going on, and in a crisis we are confronted with stark choices. A crisis is a turning point. Things are unlikely ever to be the same again.[1]

This book emerges out of the personal experience of being a chaplain at a time a great change. Like many of my colleagues I have witnessed the shift from chaplaincy as a 'given' in the NHS to a new climate of both uncertainty and opportunity. Uncertainty whether old patterns of ministry will survive and a sense of possibilities in a new world where chaplains must make the case for their contribution to patient care. Chaplains can offer ample illustrations of how change is affecting their role, and this book will discuss these from a number of perspectives. The intensity of change – and its compression into a few years spanning the Millennium – forms what the title terms the crisis of spiritual care. It is a crisis that is multi-faceted, ranging from the effective de-regulation of spiritual experience among the population at large to the managerial demand that chaplains demonstrate 'value for money'. It is the purpose of this book to reveal in some detail the origins of this crisis; its current manifestations; and to set out some tentative suggestions about how chaplaincy might emerge and progress from its present experience. In many respects the book articulates the questions and reflections that have been embodied in my experience of being a chaplain, and my belief that something precious and useful continues to be present in what the chaplain brings to those in hospital.

When I became the head of chaplaincy in a large NHS Trust in 2001, I was soon informed of one of the pressing issues that had been left in abeyance pending my arrival. A new oncology wing, comprising three hundred beds and many outpatient services, was to be built by a private finance initiative. The plans included no provision for a chapel, prayer space or other similar room for spiritual expression. When the chaplains had raised this issue with the planners they were told that – when needed – individuals or groups could book for set periods of time (and depending on availability) one of many psycho-social rooms dotted throughout the new structure. No dedicated space would be made available.

This flat refusal to emulate traditional (or even modern) patterns of hospital provision for public spirituality indicated the shifting assumptions of contemporary Britain. It was surprising not simply because the new wing would be the size of a district hospital, but also because the entire focus of the building would be on

---

[1] Duncan B. Forrester, *Truthful Action: Explorations in Practical Theology* (Edinburgh, 2000): p. 61.

cancer. It is generally understood that oncology patients find support in spiritual care (as later national guidance would set out[2]) and that families and staff might also find the need for such a space. With much of the health service's pronouncements on chaplaincy only amounting to guidance rather than policy the scope for local determination of questions such as this is considerable. As we will go on to see, this in itself has left both chaplains and chapels with little security about their presence or composition. After internal discussions the arguments for some kind of Faith Centre were accepted and the end result is shown in the pictures on pages 54 and 55. This experience in Leeds is far from unique, and the allocation of space – and what that space contains or leaves aside – is indicative of individual and organizational attitudes towards chaplains, chaplaincy and the spiritual needs of wider society. What the NHS puts into concrete offers an effective route into considering less physical shifts in ideology and public expectations.

In using the terms chaplains and chaplaincy it is important to give a brief account of how these words are utilised in this book. It is sufficient to note here that 'chaplaincy' as it is used today is a very modern construction. It means everything pertaining to the work of chaplains, their theology, pastoral practices and professional identity. Yet before the 1960s this is not how the term would have been understood. Chaplains were office holders and their office was the chaplaincy at a particular hospital. There were chaplains, and these chaplains ran the chaplaincies in places such as Leeds, Oxford and Birmingham. Only when books began to be published by chaplains, conferences held and professional associations formed, did 'chaplaincy' as we know it today emerge. Before the end of the twentieth century, academic degrees in chaplaincy were launched, and much more besides, which served to conceptualize the chaplains' work in an abstract sense. As this book addresses the chaplains in various historic contexts I shall endeavour to restrict my use of 'chaplaincy' to reflect this transition from office-holder practice to corporate identity and professionalization.

A Moment of Crisis

A few years after my local experience of conflicting views about the allocation of space for spiritual care the largely ignored and little understood world of the hospital chaplain came to brief national prominence. In August 2006, and seemingly out of the blue, one NHS trust decided to dispense with virtually all its chaplaincy staff. In reaction to the subsequent publicity some people showed surprise that chaplains existed at all – while others appeared shocked that the chaplains' proposed demise might be just the latest evidence of Christian Britain fading away. The experience ignited a debate about the role of the chaplain which had in truth been smouldering for some time, perhaps as long ago as the 1960s.

---

[2]   National Institute for Clinical Excellence, *Improving supportive and palliative care for adults with cancer*, National Institute for Clinical Excellence (March 2004) London.

The unusual degree of attention given to chaplaincy by the media gained momentum because the news of chaplains being sacked related to a range of other stories already embedded in the public imagination. These spanned a general narrative of the decline in religious orthodoxy to NHS under-funding and public uncertainty about the role of religion in public life. On the other hand, for chaplains and those in leadership positions in the Churches and faith communities, the threat to chaplaincy in the NHS raised with new urgency questions about pastoral care and mission; secularization; professionalization and accountability.

While the immediate crisis about chaplaincy in one NHS Trust saw the original decision to cut chaplains eventually reversed, it was clear that the experience highlighted more general problems in the way chaplains were regarded. Outside the public gaze an intimation of this had come in the first results of work to define a new pay structure for the NHS. Based on a rigorous assessment of work undertaken by two chaplains, the initial pay proposals for the profession placed it alongside cleaning staff and hospital secretaries. Perhaps this had merit from a theological perspective, but it risked a recruitment crisis that may well have been the effective end of chaplaincy. Only vigorous representation by the chaplains' union, as well as more careful selection in the individual chaplains to be re-assessed, secured a positive position in the scheme that came into effect in October 2004.

No longer could it be taken for granted that an Episcopal intervention would outweigh managers' determination to meet financial goals. As we shall go on to see, chaplains once seemed impregnable figures of the Establishment in hospitals. Today the changes in society, health care and the professions suggest that this kind of implicit security is rapidly coming to an end (if it has not ended already). I am not suggesting that this is a bad thing. Professional security can lead to the avoidance of key questions about purpose and practice, role and relationships. It is little wonder that in the years following the election of the New Labour in 1997 chaplaincy bodies began to do far more to articulate what chaplains were about and the contribution they brought to health care. Well before the drastic threat to one chaplaincy department in 2006 astute observers were aware of the weaknesses that made chaplains a soft target in times of financial stringency. The report by Helen Orchard in 2000[3] was the first to ask thorough questions about chaplains – and it came to the conclusion that the chaplaincies it examined in London lacked coherence and were often ill-equipped to meet the needs of a modernizing health service.

What Helen Orchard discovered in detail had been emerging in isolated ways for the previous fifty years. As the NHS began to develop modern forms of health provision chaplains found themselves inhabiting physical and organizational structures that belonged to another era. The changes in the physical places associated with the chaplain in English hospitals are given visual representation in two pictures of worship spaces in St James's University Teaching Hospital in

[3]   Helen Orchard, *Hospital Chaplaincy Modern, Dependable?*, Lincoln Theological Institute for the Study of Religion and Society (Sheffield, 2000).

Leeds (see pages 52–5). Built just one hundred and fifty years apart they illustrate the transition from orthodoxy, formality and dominance to postmodernism, accommodation and abstraction. The space allocated for spiritual expression has been transformed from the task of promoting a particular religious story to a new role in permitting and embracing an assortment of spiritual and religious expressions. Whereas the former provided cues and platforms for the place of the chaplain the latter offers no such privilege. A linear progression from door-to-altar has been succeeded by an elliptical structure turned in upon the visitor. While truth was once both beyond and mediated by the presence of a chaplain it has now become immanent, personal and direct. This physical manifestation of change is present in Leeds but missing at many other hospitals simply because the massive Victorian chapels have been demolished. The altered landscape of the hospital reveals a process of social and religious transformation which is still underway, and whose destination is uncertain. Without doubt this 're-housing' of religion in the NHS has impacted on the identity of the chaplain.

The Wider Relevance of the Chaplain

In this book I present the argument that while the chaplain constitutes a very small part of both the faith communities and the NHS, the particular location of the chaplain yields disproportionately significant insights about religion and society. I shall argue that the unique position of the chaplain, authorized by faith bodies, employed by the NHS and ministering at the extremities of human life, offers a fascinating testimony to the nature of spirituality in modern Britain. Telling this story has to some extent become easier because the crisis in one chaplaincy team brought into clearer focus the elements of debate which I shall address. While I have taken as my primary concern the experience of Church of England chaplains and the acute hospitals in England, this is a book that has relevance to anyone concerned with practical theology in the UK. Anglican chaplains comprise the largest single group of whole-time clergy working in the NHS, and the acute sector in England is the biggest employer of chaplains. If whole-time Anglican chaplains in England were taken together they would equate to the seventh largest diocese in terms of funded ordained staff. It is still the case that most chaplaincy departments are headed by an Anglican chaplain and their role therefore has particular significance in how chaplaincy develops. For this reason I would hope that what follows will be of interest to readers of all faiths, and for those working in hospices and mental health units as well as to those ministering outside England. For anyone interested in the role spirituality plays in modern Britain the story of the chaplain will offer both fresh insights and some familiar resonances.

One of the immediate dangers in beginning any kind of analysis of chaplains is to assume that their history has been largely static and their ministry has been unchanging. For those who see political strength in arguing that the chaplains' presence has been permanent and immutable in English hospitals there is considerable attraction in keeping it this way. But if we take the view that practical theology is concerned with discovering more than that which is political convenient, it is essential to enter into a serious engagement with the history of the chaplain. Is the present crisis an unprecedented change to the way hospitals have operated and the role that chaplains have exercised within them: or is this the most recent in a series of changes affecting the chaplain? Understanding something of the history of the chaplain, and the changing nature of hospitals and illness, will lend greater perspective and insight to a consideration of chaplaincy's contemporary crisis.

The Structure of the Book

Aspects of this book are informed by theoretical approaches found in the work of Michel Foucault, the French academic whose books continue to have a profound influence across many disciplines. Foucault is of interest here for three reasons. Firstly, his methods of enquiry made novel connections between the stresses and fractures evident in systems devoted to practices such as medicine and punishment, and historic changes to individual subjectivity, governmentality and power. In particular his references to professional power demonstrate a strong relationship to the way knowledge is constructed and changed at moments of threshold and crisis. Secondly, Foucault's studies suggested the benefit of sustained examination into the absences discernable in practices – the silences and discontinuities – as much as looking at the positive production of statements and professional activities. Lastly, Foucault gave attention to the nature of physical space in society, and his work in this area will inform a discussion in Chapter 7 about the rooms set aside for spiritual expression in the hospital. In these ways I am indebted to Foucault's approach to certain topics which I believe disturb accepted ways of seeing chaplaincy and are successful in generating new questions about the pastoral role and what it brings to the hospital.

In essence what follows takes the chaplain as the primary focus of discussion. It seeks to engage the circumstances of the chaplain, including relationships to the wider-Church, the sick and to political change, in order to make evident the realities and pressures which chaplains face. From an historical perspective I shall be asking how chaplains came to be part of hospital life – what their role was and how it has changed at particular moments. This early part of the book provides a sense of how the world-view of Medieval Christianity privileged the chaplain's presence, and placed issues of faith and spirituality at the heart of the hospital. It was a world that changed dramatically in the sixteenth century and was further modified by the growing political governance of populations evidence by the workhouses and their accompanying infirmaries. In Foucault's writing these changes constitute crises of subjectivity, when individuals undergo radical changes to the way they experience themselves and others. The present crisis of the chaplain can be seen in the light of what may be the most recent re-conception of the person:

the individual-as-consumer.[4] The modern subject is not only the shopper for goods but also for values, beliefs and health care services.

In examining the present experience of chaplains, consideration will be made both of the general influence of the New Labour Government's first decade on the circumstances of chaplaincy and also of the case study offered by the threat to chaplaincy in one particular NHS Trust. In the organizational and political detail of these chapters we see the chaplain related to broader social issues, including secularization (to be discussed more fully in Chapter 6) and the Government's ambiguous engagement with faith communities and the Established Church. While this provides important insights into the connection between chaplains and the overall environment of the NHS, it is important to set alongside it examples of the chaplain's work at the level of day-to-day practice. In preparation for this discussion in Chapter 7, an earlier chapter will draw on some of my own auto-ethnography to explore in detail three episodes of care provided by a chaplain. I shall use these small accounts of chaplaincy work as a kind of 'keyhole theology': a minuscule opening into the practice of chaplaincy which enables broader themes and debates to be observed and discussed. Chaplaincy is fascinating, and in its minute detail it is possible to trace connections to questions about the nature of life; personhood; pastoral power; resistance to medical culture; religious fragmentation and spiritual hope. As will be set out in advance of the material itself, the ethnographic approach does not claim to be representative of chaplains' work in general – or statistically significant in any way. It is not that kind of research. But I shall suggest that sustained attention to detail in the work of the chaplain is essential if we are to understand more deeply what chaplains are about and how their role relates to patients and other NHS staff. For a Church whose liturgical and pastoral focus tends to be parish based, the experiences of chaplains – often in grey areas that lack a standard liturgical provision – might appear both unwelcome and challenging.

To date what little research has been done about chaplains themselves has largely focused on what they do and the way their services are received. In this book I wish to examine *who* chaplains are, and ask whether their identity and concerns are in any way connected to an ambiguous status within both health care *and* their endorsing faith communities. For the theological task I am attempting it is important to move beyond the veneer of the official to engage more deeply with the reality of the chaplains' relationships and priorities. I will offer some reflections on research that lead to the conclusion that many chaplains are in fact 'refugees' from the parish system for a variety of reasons. These include deployment problems experienced by clergy couples, marginalization arising from increasing theological conservatism, and issues of human sexuality. This suggests that both the pastoral practice of chaplains, and aspects of their beliefs or identity, contribute to the sustained disengagement between the experiences of chaplains

---

[4]   Benjamen Barber, *Con$umed: how markets corrupt children, infantilize adults, and swallow citizens whole* (New York, 2007).

and the theology and politics of the Church. This is a great pity because, as the rest of the book contends, chaplains stand in a place of significant intersection between the historic presence of the Church in public spaces; secularization; contemporary spiritual expression and close engagement with the life-changing effects of illness. In short, I shall suggest that the sense of distance between chaplains and the Church arises from a concealed concern about the personal status and pastoral dilemmas of those clergy working in the NHS. The fear that sustains this separation is a barrier to the real learning and growth that would arise from a more honest and integrated engagement with a ministry that is in the forefront of some of the major questions of the twenty-first century. It is my premise in this book that attention to the detail of the chaplain's work in the health service, and especially with the spirituality of those un-churched or post-Church, will reveal something of how God is encountered by people in the turmoil of events that stand out in their lives in ways that lead to permanent change. The crisis of chaplaincy is not only about the chaplain's relationship to the NHS and society at large: it is also about the chaplain's relationship to the Church. Fortunately, as Duncan Forrester suggests, recognizing this crisis offers a moment of fresh understanding and opportunity – an engagement that could generate a deeper knowledge of God and the mystery of love that is hidden in the depths of human experience.

Outcomes

I hope that this book will reveal the chaplain to be a far more interesting and complex figure than has previously been assumed. We shall see the place of the chaplain in the NHS as a site sustained by relationships to historic beliefs, contemporary spiritual needs and greater religious pluralism. The experience of the chaplain is shaped partly by a will to survive as well as by a desire to live with spiritual integrity. In this much the public witness of the chaplain amounts to a wrestling with questions that are pertinent to many other individuals and institutions in society. This is not unique to chaplains but their unusual location betwixt and between the worlds of secular employment, pastoral ministry among the sick and the perceived hardening of religious conservatism, makes their experience a compelling account of ministry in modern Britain. Chaplains work on the cusp of medicine, a parish-focused Church and with a nascent sense of professional identity. The tantalizing challenge for chaplaincy in the twenty-first century may be to resist the pull to move entirely away from the margins. Holding a position between these worlds may offer unique opportunities to patients and staff. There is plenty of evidence to suggest that the construction of an auditor has a major influence on the kind of stories they hear. Compared with the Establishment chaplains of the past the crisis of the contemporary chaplain, and its consequent sense of marginalization, potentially makes the chaplain far more available to the authentic experiences of patients and staff. It lies with chaplains themselves to see whether they can develop this experience into a professional virtue, and draw on the insights of this position to speak more persuasively to both the faith communities and the health service. To achieve this, chaplains will have to move beyond the paralysis arising from crisis and decide that their commitment to the care of the patient exceeds even their own desire for professional survival.

Chapter 1
A History of the Chaplain

Introduction

The practice of assigning clergy to work in hospitals has been a part of life in England for a thousand years. Yet chaplains have been the subject of relatively little historical study, perhaps reflecting the fact that histories are most often written by those whose influence is in the ascendant. An absent history may be a contributory factor in the crisis of contemporary chaplaincy, emphasizing the lack of a clear sense of identity and forward momentum. In this chapter, the history of the chaplain's presence in hospitals will be explored in moments of crisis and critical change. Through this approach, it will be possible to identify the shifting expectations that have surrounded the chaplain as well as the ways in which chaplains have regarded themselves at times of re-definition. It is a necessary and illuminating piece of work in relation to the subsequent examination of the current challenges facing chaplaincy.

Foundation

The moment when hospitals emerged in anything like their modern sense, as free-standing buildings with significant local governance, is difficult to pinpoint. In their study of hospitals in England, Orme and Webster doubt that such hospitals existed before 1066 AD. The diversity of institutions and the variability of evidence for this early period make them reticent about any definite claims. Their research, however, points to a particular expansion in the number of hospitals in the early part of the period between 1066 and 1540 AD. In just 150 years, starting in 1151 AD, 72 per cent of all the hospitals built between the Conquest and the Reformation came into being. While the exactness of this figure is open to question, the disproportionate number of hospitals founded in this short period is beyond serious doubt. It was a time of pastoral reform in the Church as well as a period that saw strengthening interest in the economy of salvation and the role of purgatory. Chantry Chapels (often existing within hospitals) were endowed with funds to guarantee prayers in perpetuity for individuals once they had died. In the view of Faye Getz, 'the main purpose of hospital care was not to save lives but to allow the pious to exercise Christian charity through healing'.[1] To consider hospitals in this period is to enter a world which is at once familiar and strange. Architecturally, many hospitals featured a connection between the church or chapel and the infirmary halls. In all cases, if an altar was present, it was central to the layout of the building. These designs serve to emphasize the reproduction of a public narrative which is distinctive of the Medieval period. In the teachings of the Church, and aided by the Crown, a Christian theology and cosmology was traced into every detail of human experience. Sickness was no exception. In the public spectacle of the York Corpus Christi play, the community was drawn into a narrative which brought together all aspects of city life, and set them under the keystone of temporal and spiritual authority: Jesus Christ. Tradition gave different parts of the play to the various Guilds of the city. In a way which exemplifies the understanding of a society over which the Son of God presides, the Barber Surgeons conclude their rendition of John the Baptist with a prayer that includes the following:

> I loue þe lorde, as souereyne leche,
> That come to salue men of þare sore,
>
> (I love thee Lord, as Sovereign Leech,
> That comes to heal men of their sore.)

It may seem odd to modern readers, but as the perfection of all things – and within the context of a world seen through the prism of the spiritual – Christ is the ultimate leech: the sucker-out of human sin.

Yet if the mystery plays marked out the physical and spiritual unity of the city, the Church itself during this period was doing much to delineate the roles of physicians and clergy. In the Canons of Lateran Council IV, the relationship between the physicians of the body and physicians of the soul is made clear. It is the task of medical doctors to 'to warn and persuade' the sick to see a priest before medical treatment begins, as sickness may sometimes be the result of sin, and if the priest can remove the 'cause' then the person will respond better to the bodily treatment. These instructions of the Council sit under the central truth of the times, that 'the soul is more precious than the body'. In fact the physical exists to provide a visible analogy of the spiritual realm. Commenting on a sermon preached to hospital clergy by the French theologian Jacques de Vitry, Bird[2] argues that the first 'line of treatment for bodily illness was reconciliation with God, and spiritual healing and preparation for death by confession and enjoined penance preceded bed-rest and medical treatment'. This overriding emphasis on the fashioning

---

[1]   Faye Getz, *Medicine in the English Middle Ages* (Chichester, 1998) p. 91.

[2]   J. Bird, 'Medicine for Body and Soul', in P. Biller and J. Zeigler (eds), *Religion and Medicine in the Middle Ages* (York, 2001) p. 109.

of the spirit can be seen in almost every detail of a hospital's organization and operation.

Under Pope Innocent III, the Canons of Lateran Council IV emerge as a major pastoral reform of the Church. Their impetus carried change forward long after his death and may be seen to be a partial explanation of the early explosion in English hospital foundations. The concern for sin and its expiation is more strongly regulated in the Council's requirement for annual confession to a priest by every lay person at least once a year. As places where those close to death were brought, the importance of confession is beyond doubt in the early hospitals. In the years following Lateran IV, a relative explosion of writing occurred about the practice of confession. In a popular manual of confession from the diocese of Exeter – typical of several such works emerging in England after the Council of 1215 AD – the act of confession is described in close comparison to physical healing. In the Summula, confession is an activity in which the clergy are 'performing an operation to repair those earthly desires' that can leave the sinner oblivious to the perilous state of his soul. As the best physician, Christ 'orders therapeutic baths through our outpouring of tears' and the healthful diet of 'fasts'. And the strongest and most effective medicine of all was penance. In the context of the hospital, an institution where the poor begged for assistance and the sick were admitted, the Church found an additional way to enact in public the forms of knowledge it believed to be right. As Koch says in his study of medieval epistemology, 'knowledge of the world is useful only to make the word of God more clear'.[3]

When hospitals began to emerge as separate foundations, they nevertheless retained in full the religious character of the monasteries from which they sprang. As Risse puts it, 'hospital inmates were viewed primarily as members of a new spiritual community, temporarily living in a *locus religiosus*'.[4] This view is supported by an examination of the records pertaining to early hospitals. In the provisions and rules set down by Lord Walter de Langton in 1294 AD for St Leonard's Hospital in York, no mention is made of the sick. Instead the document makes detailed statements about the conduct of the *opus Dei*, and the movement and accountability of the brothers and sisters. For example, at the start of the day the priest on duty is charged to hear 'the accusations of sins and give correction'. Where brothers and sisters should go, how they should associate, which doors are to be locked and when, and what sins only the Master of the hospital can absolve, are all described in detail. It is striking how much provision in the document manifests a concern about a brother or sister being on his or her own, communicating with unknown persons or acquiring knowledge and learning beyond that required for their role. The underlying structure for the day continues to be that of the monastery, with its many offices. Into this world the sick-poor were admitted, re-clothed in a hospital

---

[3] A. Koch, 'Interpreting God's truth: A postmodern interpretation of medieval epistemology', *International Social Science Review*, 57/3 & 4 (2000): 50.

[4] G. Risse, *Mending Bodies, Saving Souls: A History of Hospitals* (New York, 1999) p. 106.

livery (often with a cross motif) and put to bed in the infirmary. The basis on which they were admitted appears to have varied considerably. In some cases those of advancing years, and with modest means, could effectively buy life-long care by purchasing a 'corrodie' in order to enter the hospital. This gave the hospital cash in the short term but created financial liabilities for the future. Even the process for admitting the sick-poor to the receipt of alms each day reflected the overarching religious narrative of the time. Orme and Webster describe the following policy practised in a medieval hospital in Fotheringhay in Northamptonshire:

> ... three were welcomed on Sundays in honour of the Trinity, nine on Mondays to represent the nine orders of angels, five on Fridays for the five wounds of Christ and a similar number on Saturdays for the five joys of the Virgin. Here above all the poor were symbols, not just people.[5]

Within this religious economy of the hospital the chaplain was a key figure. Rawcliffe cites St Leonard's at York, and later papal letters, which stipulate that chaplains should patrol the infirmary to ensure that those 'at the point of death and when death is expected' receive opportunity for confession and absolution.[6] This was a place of religious immersion, an opportunity to demonstrate the faithful life a lay Christian could aspire to under religious direction. The silent presence of many hospital buildings, like the constant appearance of clergy, reminded the sick-poor of the eternity to which this life was simply a preparation. Hospitals also served a valuable purpose for the rich by getting the poor to pray for their endangered souls. They were institutions that extended the influence of the Church out of the monasteries and into the towns and cities alongside parish churches, providing the poor with shelter, food and basic care. Within all these functions and relationships, the chaplain was a central figure, ensuring the regular conduct of worship and usually overseeing the distribution of goods donated or purchased for the hospital. It would have been a demanding task if carried out faithfully, although there is significant evidence that in many instances it was not. Harper-Bell's investigation of the charters for medieval hospitals in Bury St Edmunds found references at the end of the thirteenth century to the hospital's staff 'damnably converting charity into profit'. This theme occurs throughout the medieval period, although it is impossible now to estimate with any accuracy its extent within English hospitals or to ascertain whether such abuses were protracted or occasional.

Both at the time of foundation and in subsequent years, what amounted to the medical care of the time largely took place away from the hospital. While there is evidence that some women caring for the sick had knowledge in the use of herbs, any cutting or puncturing of the body (for bleeding or surgery) either took place away from the hospital or involved someone coming in. Stell, referring

---

[5]   N. Orme and M. Webster, 'The English Hospital 1070–1570', in *Bulletin of the History of Medicine* 71 (1995): 57.

[6]   C. Rawcliffe, *Medicine for the Soul* (Stroud, 1999) p. 105.

specifically to York, identifies barbers, chandlers and brewers as those trades most closely associated with medical care in the early medieval period.

In summary, whilst it is difficult to generalize the nature of hospitals in the four hundred years before the events of the sixteenth century, some conclusions can be drawn with confidence. Whilst hospitals were founded by a number of different means, from ecclesiastical intervention to endowment by an individual, they all shared many characteristics of monastic life. Both in the structure of the buildings and in the division of the day, those living and working within early hospitals were required to relate to one another as occupants of ecclesiastical space. The scale and economic impact of hospitals may have varied from simple shelters to elaborate institutions, but the central activities of care, prayer and good administration remained the declared intention. In practice, the Church demonstrated a practical social endeavour alongside similar enterprises in education and the distribution of alms. But the creation of hospitals also enabled the Church to govern the conduct of some of the sick-poor, and to produce stories that bolstered its public narrative of sin, forgiveness, death and salvation. One example of this can be found in The Book of the Foundation of St Bartholomew's Smithfield in 1174. Adwyn, who came to the hospital severely crippled, is cared for by charitable alms at the hospital until he makes a gradual recovery. At first he becomes fit enough to make some small items but ends up practising carpentry in the hospital church and throughout the City of London. The entry ends by commenting 'blessed be God whose eyes are on them that fear Him and on those who hope in His mercy'. Adwyn is an illustration of the hospital as a place of hope, recovery and eventual utility. Other inmates served to provide the Church with tales of miraculous healings – and of lives brought to completion within the embrace of the sacred. In the medieval hospital, the sick entered a hall of mirrors in which they saw their lives reflected in the narratives of the Church and caught up in the infinitely receding image of eternity. As Christ's poor, they were drawn into the subtle politics of salvation, earning the care they received with the prayers they offered for the imperilled souls of the rich. And over this relationship between the poor and the rich, between sin and salvation, the chaplain presided.

Reformation

The early period of hospital foundations in England to the opening years of the sixteenth century was by no means homogeneous. Changes took place, not least in the way the sick body was both understood and cared for within the hospital. While reticent about the potentially misleading nature of summarizing such change, Louth nevertheless feels able to trace a general movement of 'the body as microcosm reflecting in itself a cosmic story, to seeing the body as interpreter of human inwardness'.[7] The first part of this statement certainly rings true with the descriptions of the earliest hospitals, the fledgling surgeons in the Barbers' Company and the sick-poor in whose bodies physical decay were seen to be written spiritual realities. An examination of the social revolution brought about by religious changes in the sixteenth century will demonstrate that the redefinition of the hospitalized body is much as Louth suggests. In England, this period marks a moment (or a collection of moments) of sudden discontinuity, resistance and enduring change. There is a danger, widely recognized amongst historians of the sixteenth century, in talking about '*The* Reformation', and I concur with Bernard (2005) that at best this term describes a disparate set of events that left the England of 1599 a very different place from the England of 1501. To provide some sense of context for these momentous developments, it will first be helpful to examine the situation of hospitals in the period leading up to the great changes of the sixteenth century.

The Eve of Reformation

In 1414 AD, hospitals had made a rare appearance as the subject of a debate in the House of Commons. Members of the House declared that hospitals were 'now for the most part decayed'. The Black Death, labour shortages and the decline in cases of leprosy all contributed to a stagnation or reversal of the previous growth of hospitals. By the start of the sixteenth century, however, Henry VII had developed ambitious plans, influenced by events on the continent, to found a series of major new hospitals in England. While events precluded the full scale of the developments which he envisaged, the first of his new hospitals was endowed by Henry in 1505 AD.

It is believed that the construction of the Savoy Hospital in London drew heavily on the statutes of the Santa Maria Nuova Hospital in Florence. A copy of these Statutes had been given to Henry VII, and a version of them is in the British Library. Park and Henderson have argued that an analysis of both sets of statutes does attest some connection, although the precise extent of the influence cannot be known. There are also some clear differences between the hospitals, for example:

> Whereas Santa Maria Nuova took the sick-poor as its unique charge, the Savoy
> only gave them preference, admitting also (in order of descending priority) the
> crippled, blind or infirm; 'shamefaced poor beggars'; and 'all others'.[8]

The Savoy offered accommodation to one hundred people per night. Clergy remained in charge of the hospital but a physician and a surgeon were to call

---

[7]   A. Louth, 'The Body in Western Catholic Christianity', in Sarah Coakley (ed.), *Religion and the Body* (Cambridge, 1997) p. 129.

[8]   K. Park and J. Henderson, 'The First Hospital Among Christians', *Medical History* 35/2 (1991): 168.

each day to attend those who were sick.[9] While this was a change when compared with the evidence relating to the hospitals founded between 1151 and 1300 AD, it did not parallel the level of care provided at the Santa Maria Nuova. Park and Henderson describe the hospital in Florence as the first Western European hospital in the modern sense, with ten doctors employed by the sixteenth century. In the statutes of the Nuova, there is even a fascinating account of the more sophisticated organization being used by chaplains in their work with patients:

> We put up a board in a visible place divided by ruled lines into four sections. In one section we write the names of those patients making confession; in the second we record those about to receive the Eucharist; in the third, those commending their souls to God; and in the fourth those receiving extreme unction. This board is looked after by the chaplains and priests responsible for the sick.[10]

It is worth reflecting on whether this categorization of patients in some way mirrored other developments taking place in European patient care. As yet the distancing of the humanities from the sciences had not taken effect, and the approach of the chaplains may have had much in common with the triaging of patients for physical care by the doctors and other staff. At the Savoy, although the letter of the Santa Maria Nuova statutes was not followed, there is evidence of a growing interest in the way a hospital might improve the condition of the poor beyond simply feeding them. Sommerville[11] notes the existence of 'two specially constructed ovens' for the purpose of delousing clothes. At the same time, the Savoy retained a rather *laissez-faire* approach to the sick-poor, turfing out the able bodied each day only to readmit them again the same evening. In the statutes of the Savoy, an orderly process for admitting a poor person is described. At dusk the hospitaller, matron, one of the matron's women and a porter were to stand at the gate to receive the poor. The poor were to be led into the chapel to express their gratitude to the founder in prayer; they were then assessed for their state of cleanliness. Next they were stripped of their own clothing, washed and re-clothed in hospital uniform. Finally, they were allowed to sit near the fire and engage in 'modest conversation'. In the morning two masses were celebrated in sight of the inmates and, apart from those who were unwell, everyone had to vacate the hospital by 8 a.m. The sick were visited by the doctor or surgeon as well as a confessor. Just how much this was put into practice is unclear. In Robert Copland's poem of 1535/6, *The Highway to the Spital-house*, set outside another London hospital (St Bartholomew's), he paints a rather different picture. Here only the porter greets the poor, and Copland enters into dialogue with him about the state of the poor, and particularly a perception that they commit roguery in the country during the warmer months only to seek refuge in the hospitals of the city when it

---

9   Orme and Webster (1995): 150.

10   Park and Henderson (1991): 180.

11   R. Sommerville *The Savoy: Manor; Hospital; Chapel* (London, 1960) p. 30.

is cold. It is no doubt a polemical poem, caught up in the emerging politics of the time. Yet this in itself is not to say it is a less reliable history than official accounts and does far more to capture the character and circumstances of the poor who entered the hospital each night.

At the Savoy, the statutes required the Master (a clergyman) to make a round of the hospital two or three times a week, accompanied by a chaplain. In total there were to be four chaplains in addition to the Master. The master – the 'Rector' – was to be a priest aged over 40; the staff were to live together 'in piety for the salvation of their souls'; typically, they were to receive the sick 'as Christ Himself'; and all 'should wear a simple habit of coarse and inexpensive grey cloth marked with the seal of the hospital'. Everyone living in the hospital was required to make confession three times a year and to receive the sacrament twice a year.[12] As regards the specific work of the chaplains:

> The Rector of the hospital chooses two chaplains to hear the confessions of the sick and to give them the sacraments. One of these chaplains stays in the men's infirmary, alternating day and night duties with the other; the other celebrates mass in the hospital chapel so that the sick can hear it, sometimes in the morning and sometimes in the evening and at vespers. The same priest leads confession in a loud voice, so that all the sick can hear, and commends them to God for the night.[13]

Once again we can have no great certainty about the extent to which these instructions were put into practice. Yet the central intention of holy care, and the technical relationship it sought to establish between the Christ-like sick and the piety of the staff, is pronounced. The Savoy stands as one of a number of Royal initiatives for ambitious public works (others include the conversion of St John's Hospital Cambridge into an academic college) which on the eve of Reformation retain chaplains at the heart of their operation. Modern thinking would be misleading if it saw too great a divide between these kinds of institution. At the Savoy, the chaplains were expected to have academic distinctions ('B.D., or M.A., or B.L.L., or at least a canonry') and later – in 1550 AD – were addressed by the Privy Council as 'master and fellows'.

In the momentous religious and social changes that occurred later in the sixteenth century, the exact extent of official care for the sick is difficult to quantify.[14] What we do know is that the institutions of care, and especially the hospitals, underwent major changes – and within them the role of the chaplain was recast. In effect, the hospitals of the sixteenth century offer a fascinating microcosm of the relationships between religion, government, the sick body and human salvation.

---

[12]   Park and Henderson (1991): 177.

[13]   Ibid., 180.

[14]   S. Brigden, 'Religion and Social Obligation in Early Sixteenth-Century London', *Past and Present*, 103 (1984): 67–112.

Reformation

For Foucault, the Reformation consisted of all those movements in the fifteenth and sixteenth centuries which were expressed as 'a great crisis of the Western experience of subjectivity'.[15] Furthermore, this crisis was a revolt against those forms of moral and religious power that gave form to that subjectivity. Examining this from the perspective of hospitals in England, we can see that the events of the Reformation did mark a major shift in the way both body and soul were seen and acted upon in society.

In the turmoil that arose from changes in political will and the growth of protestant ideas among the people, the hospitals were vulnerable. For example, St Bartholomew's Hospital had grown from the Priory of the same dedication and, although it had established a separate identity by the sixteenth century, its finances and patronage were entwined with the founding institution. Perhaps more than anything else it was these enduring links to monastic life, and the dominance of clergy in the administration, that sealed their fate. For a decade or more from the mid-1530s it is difficult to trace whether any hospitals in England were functioning and, if they were, how effective their care of the sick was in this period. This is the only period for which this can be said in a thousand years of hospital life in the country. Hospitals were suppressed as religious houses, their assets seized and the clergy pensioned off or punished depending on their cooperation or otherwise. In this period of change, the conception of both the chaplain and the patient would be redefined in ways which are still of significance today.

Henry VIII and his administrators were from the outset interested in both the management of the population and the role of medicine. In 1511, the Physicians and Surgeons Act restricted the practice of medicine to those who had been examined. In effect, using the title of either of these forms of clinical care became protected by statute. Apart from the Oxbridge Colleges, the issuing of licences was to follow examination by a Bishop with the assistance of physicians or surgeons. In 1518, Henry granted a charter to found the Royal College of Physicians with authority to oversee the practice of medicine within a seven-mile radius round London. In 1540, the Barber Surgeons and the Fellowship of Surgeons had combined into a new body, after which Henry signed an Act limiting barbers solely to the surgery involved in drawing teeth. These changes represent the first emergence of medical practice in England as a corporate activity with social authority and the power to intervene, regulate and restrict the practice of medicine.

The precise nature of Henry's developing policies for both social and religious life is a matter of continuing debate. Even as late as 1546, just a year before his death, the case for believing that Henry was leaning more strongly towards reformist ideas is doubtful. Bernard (2005) sees Henry as a pragmatic centrist, who changes policy in order to preserve a middle course. Towards the end of

---

[15]   M. Foucault and G. Deleuze, 'Intellectuals and Power', in D.F. Bouchard (ed.), *Michel Foucault. Language, counter-memory, practice* (Ithaca, NY, 1980) pp. 205–17.

his reign, we find some church services being put into English, but Latin is also retained. The abuse of chantries is the subject of legislation, but this is practical and self-interested rather than ideological. The dissolution of London's hospitals was just one of many moves against perceived superstition and the ineffective use of religious resources.

In response to the inevitable dilapidation of London's hospitals during these years (more beggars and sick people on the streets), Henry agreed to a petition to hand sites for four hospitals to the City of London – if the City undertook to run them. While the precise nature of Henry's religious stance by the mid-1540s is debatable, the references in the City's petition give an indication of the arguments perceived to be effective on the sovereign at that time. If the hospitals were handed to the City they would not be for 'priests, canons and monks carnally living'.[16] In making the request, the City leaders are asking for the power to 'have the order, rule, disposition and governance of all the said hospitals'.[17] The petition contrasts the 'small number of canons, priests and monks' using the resources of endowments for their 'profit, lucre and commodity', with a promise of 'common utility' for the Royal realm. If the petition is granted, the City elders will ensure the care of the sick through the employment of surgeons, physicians and apothecaries. Chantry prayers are not promised – but there is reference to the prayers of the poor being offered for the 'health wealth and prosperity of your Highness and the noble prince your son'.

In the indenture signed by Henry, this motivating factor in the need for re-founding is clear:

> ... considering the miserable estate of the poor aged sick sore and impotent people, as well men as women, lying and going about begging in the common streets of the said City of London and the suburbs of the same, to the great pain and sorrow of the same poor aged sick and impotent people, and to the great infection hurt and annoyance of his Grace's loving subjects, which of necessity must daily go and pass by the same poor sick sore and impotent people being infected with divers great and horrible sicknesses and diseases, his Highness, of his bountiful goodness and charitable mind, moved with great pity for and toward the relief aid succour and help of the said poor aged sick sore and impotent people, and for the great danger and infection which daily doth and may ensue to his loving subjects by reason of the great sickness and horrible diseases of the same sick and sore people, and for divers other good and godly purposes and intents, is pleased and content that his Highness by his Grace's letters patents under his great seal of England in due form to be made, will give and grant to the Mayor and Commonality and Citizens of the said City of

---

[16]   The Royal Hospitals, Appendix 1, p. 2.
[17]   Ibid.

London and to their successors for ever ... the late hospital of St Bartholomew
in West Smithfield ....[18]

To appreciate fully the operation of a hospital like St Bartholomew's on re-
founding, it is striking to note the role to be played by a new category of staff, the
beadles:

... the said Mayor and Commonality and Citizens and their successors shall
find eight persons to be beadles to bring to the said late hospital, hereafter to be
called the House for the Poor, such poor sick aged and impotent people as shall
be found going abroad in the City of London and the suburbs of the same not
having wherewith to be sustained, and to expulse and avoid such valiant and
sturdy vagabonds and beggars as they shall find daily within the said City ....[19]

This is fascinating. Rather than the picture painted by the Savoy statutes and
Copland's poem of a party at the gate benignly receiving the sick-poor, we now find
a hospital equipped to seek out and retrieve them from the streets. Furthermore, note
the new title. 'Hospital', a word perhaps too closely associated with the dissolved
monasteries is gone, and 'House for the Poor' becomes the new phrase. In keeping
with a number of other ecclesiastical and college foundations made by Henry, the
new title also refers to the role of the King as the creator of the new institution.[20]
The indenture for Bart's – and the similar one for St Thomas's – reveals a new
attitude to both the accommodation of the sick-poor and the responsibilities of
civil government. In all, five institutions were re-founded around London during
this period. They show a new sophistication by establishing institutions having
specific functions relating to the poor: a workhouse (Bridewell), a place for orphans
(Christ's Hospital), a hospital for the mad (Bedlam) as well as the two 'general'
hospitals already mentioned. Each of these was commissioned to play its part in
managing the growing population of London, and the rootless nature of many
municipal beggars. In other places, basic relief was addressed by Henry's Poor
Law Act of 1535, which required local and regional civil authorities to care for all
persons in need who were either born there or had three years of residency. In all
these instances, the precise translation of law into practice is a matter for debate.

Once again it is important not to impose our present understanding of hospitals
on these re-formed institutions. While the sick were cared for at Bart's and
St Thomas's, there were also links between the hospitals in terms of local policing,
education and the control of vagrancy. In a changing social order, the relationships
of the sick and poor are carefully constructed with the 'deserving poor' sitting

[18]   Crown, *Indenture for the Re-Founding of St Bartholemew's Hospital* (St
Bartholomew's Historical Archives), 1546.

[19]   Ibid.

[20]   R. Rex and C.D.C. Armstrong, 'Henry VIII's Ecclesiastical and Collegiate
Foundations', *Historical Research*, 75/190 (2002): 401.

perilously close to the 'criminal poor'. With the exception of the Bridewell, the London hospitals served as a mechanism for categorizing the poor and sick. They admitted those capable of physical recovery and moral improvement. Those unwilling or unable to improve became a matter for the attention of the hospital-based beadles, moving people on – expelling them from the city and thereby cleansing the streets of individuals who failed to fit in with the narratives of the new governance. And how, within all of this, is the role of the chaplain reformed?

The Reformation of the Chaplain

Inside hospitals during the period of the reformation, the poor found both familiarity and difference. This was still a religious space, as the presence of a chaplain (hospitaller[21]) and daily prayers suggest. But the hospitalized body was no longer surrounded by the artefacts of faith, or subject to the daily sacrifice of the mass. Ornaments had been disposed of, and altar linen from a number of London churches served as bed sheets at St Thomas's.[22]

Within a few years of the founding of both Bart's and St Thomas's, detailed descriptions of the organization and staff of the hospitals were produced in response to popular criticism. The *Book of the Government of the Hospital*, produced by St Thomas's during Mary's reign in 1556, gives a full description of the Office of Hospitaller. The opening sentence of the description of his work in the Book of Government comments on why the term 'hospitaller' is used in preference to any other chaplain's role prior to the re-founding (for example, sacrist):

> The name of your office doth in manner put you in remembrance of your charge and duty. Ye are called an Hospitaller, for that ye have the oversight and order of the hospitality kept in this hospital or house of God.[23]

The re-founded hospital used the pre-reformation title for the chaplain most involved in the practical running of a hospital – and the one perhaps least identified with chantries, confession or the saying of mass. Unlike the almoners or treasurer who serve freely in the house, the hospitaller is paid 'a large salary' (£10 a year

---

[21] As we are concerned with the both the commonality of chaplains across history as well as the diversity of ways in which they have worked it is necessary to ask whether the term 'hospitaller' properly qualifies? There can be no doubt from the list of duties that the hospitallers of the mid-sixteenth century were performing spiritual (as well as administrative) functions in a similar way to the chaplain-hospitaller of the Savoy and earlier institutions. What is of interest is the selection of *this* chaplaincy title in preference to the other models that were available. It was the most practical and least mysterious.

[22] Archivist, *St Thomas' Hospital: Historical Notes* (London: London Metropolitan Archives, (1957).

[23] Ibid.

plus allowances). The duty of the hospitaller is 'both to God and to the Governors of this house'. There are two parts to the hospitaller's work – both clearly defined. As 'an ecclesiastical person and minister of the church', he should be 'a light burning and shining in virtuous life' set before 'the great number of lewd and naughty people harboured in this house'. Furthermore, these people have been 'touched with the finger and hand of Almighty God' because of their conduct, and the evidence for this is seen by 'their sundry plagues'. The hospitaller is to comfort the sick by the example of his own 'good life'; in frequent visiting, by administering the sacraments of the church, and by having 'in readiness the most wholesome sentences of Holy Scripture, that may comfort a desperate person'.

As part of the motivation for his work, the hospitaller is reminded that if any in the house 'perish for lack of counsel and help and die in their sin, their blood shall be required at your hand'. In other words, come the day of judgement, for anyone who had failed to gain salvation because of his neglect, the hospitaller will have to make answer. Such a loss 'shall be laid to your charge', says the *Book of Government.*

The second part of the hospitaller's duties relates directly to the ordering and smooth running of the hospital. He is to be next in seniority after the 'president and almoners', sharing with them in the 'oversight and governance' of the house like a 'good father' walking 'virtuously among the poor'. The hospitaller is to ensure that there is no 'drunkenness disorder or blasphemy' and, if there is, to rebuke and reprove it. He is required to be present when the residents of the hospital go to bed, ensuring that they do so 'in quiet, rest, peace and prayer, rendering thanks to Almighty God for the great charity that is extended unto them by the good citizens of this City of London'. The hospitaller is to keep records of those who enter and leave the hospital as well as accounts and a record of any property the poor bring in with them. He is to receive and ensure that 'victuals' are safely delivered to the cook and shared out fairly at meal times. It is only through his direct negotiation with the surgeon that a diet may be altered.

In the Minutes of the Court of Governors for 26 June 1564, the hospitaller William Wight is given further instructions. Unless prevented by illness he is to 'every day, daily … rede and teach unto the poor lame sick and diseased within the said hospital, the Common Service and administration … and minister the Sacraments'. The prayers to be recited in hospital each day are also laid down in the various 'Order' books and statutes of the 1550s. At Bart's, the prayers were to be said twice a day, and participation was not optional. All patients were charged to make the responses in the liturgy 'upon pain to be dismissed out of this house'.[24] Furthermore, it is the living who are exclusively prayed for and not the deceased. And just as authority in London was becoming more concerned with the ordering of society, so we find a number of prayers addressed to 'O Lord our governor – and in one short prayer:

---

[24]   St Bartholomew's Hospital, The Ordre of the Hofpital of S. Bartholomewes in Weft'fmythfielde in London (Orpington, 1997).

> We beseech thee O Lord to prosper and keep the governors of this house, and according to thy most holy promise to bless and increase all such as tend and heal hungry and sick bodies, not only with the increase of goods in this world, but also with life everlasting, which of thy great mercy thou hast promised them, through Jesus Christ our Lord Amen.[25]

Just as the sick-poor were at one time the humble supplicants of prayer for the dead founders of hospitals, now they are constrained to pray for the living staff and governors. The hospitalized body is the passive surface upon which notions of physical and moral improvement are being inscribed. At no time was this more clearly seen than at the point of discharge. Here the recovered inmate appeared in the Hall before the hospitaller and 'two Masters' (on his knees!) and recited a passage which he had previously been taught by the hospitaller. It included the following:

> … grant us now O Lord, thy most holy and working spirit, that setting aside all our vice and idleness, we may in thy fear walk, and go forward in all vertue and godliness. And for thou art moved O Lord, the hearts of godly men, and the Governours of this house, to shew their exceeding charity towards us, in curing of our maladies and diseases, we yeeld most humble and hearty thanks to the Majesty … .[26]

These litanies of wretchedness attempted to subdue and locate the patient in a posture of deference and gratitude both to God and to God's agents of care. The fact that this passage was set out to be recited from memory powerfully illustrates the attempts by authority to inculcate the values they advocated for the patient. The poor are not worthy of what they receive – so they had better be grateful, and they had better behave.

This approach to the poor was not confined to the governors and hospitaller. In the Order, it is also stated that the surgeons should play their part. Significantly, they are charged to admit only those who can be cured – a judgement that entirely rests with them. But the surgeons should:

> Also at all such times as ye shall go to the dressing of any infected person in this house, as much as in you is, ye shall give unto him or her, faithful and good counsel, willing them to mind to sin no more, and to be thankful to Almighty God, for whose sake they are here comforted by men.[27]

This revision of the relationship between surgeon and patient replaces that stipulated in Lateran Council IV. There the physician was charged to 'warn and persuade' the

---

[25]   *The ordre of the hospital of S. Bartholomewes* (London: Richard Grafton, 1552); see also a reprint of the 1552 edition in *The ordre of the Hospital of S. Bartholomowes in West-Smythfielde in London* (London: The Hospital, 1997).

[26]   Ibid.

[27]   St Bartholomew's Hospital (1997) p. 63.

sick to call in a 'physician of the soul' before receiving physical care. Now the physician of the body is directed to annex these responsibilities, uniting the tasks of moral and physical inscription. This marks a significant reconfiguration of roles for staff in the re-founded hospitals. Hospitals under Catholic control in Europe had the instruction of Lateran IV restated in a papal bull of 1566: the moral state of the sick required the intervention of a chaplain before anyone else.

The whole hospital is orientated towards this new duty of gratitude to God as the provider of those who govern in his name. The dead are not mentioned and neither is the patron saint of the foundation, to whom so much used to be attributed (for example, as was the case with Rahere at St Bartholemew's Hospital). The simple transaction which seems to underlie this approach to hospital care is that the hospitalized body accepts the virtue of what is being done and is moved to aspire to a more virtuous life. It is also clear that those admitted are assisted in that process by both those primarily concerned with the body and those having care of the soul. In the Order, Indenture and Statutes of the Royal Hospitals, we see the intention for a unity of purpose and co-ordination for the social improvement of the sick not previously seen in England. It may well be that the key to this approach lay in the common answerability of all these institutions to the Lord Mayor and City.

In the sixteenth century, London's population began to increase significantly. There was a perception of increased begging – although it is unclear how real this was.[28] It appears that for roughly a decade London had no functioning hospitals. These factors may help to explain the rapid re-founding and new objectives of London's hospitals, and the experience of civil administration, which may have contributed to a more penal attitude to the sick-poor. Certainly the cost of caring for the poor was being made evident: it is quoted in 1552 as £500 a year at St Bartholomew's, paid by 'the citizens'.[29] It was also becoming clear that provision for the poor was the mutual responsibility of sovereign and citizen.

However, a question needs to be addressed as to whether these actions met real needs, or utilized the perception of need in order to legitimize the creation of a range of disciplinary institutions. The passage cited earlier from Henry VIII's Indenture for Bart's clearly indicates that it was the geography of the poor, and their visibility to persons of consequence, which was an ostensible reason for founding the new hospitals. Whatever the motivation for their founding, the Royal Hospitals of the capital shared an unprecedented amount of financial and statistical information about the poor – and related to each other through complementary functions. In petitioning the King to give the house at Bridewell to the City, the leaders of London showed their own reflection on the causes and remedy of vagrancy:

---

[28]   Ibid., p. 19; Manzione cites the work of a committee formed in 1552 to estimate a possible figure of 6 per cent for the total proportion in the population of deserving and undeserving poor in the city.

[29]   R.H. Tawney and E.E. Power, *Tudor economic documents* (London, 1924) p. 309.

> ... we evidently perceived that the cause of all this misery and beggary was idleness: and the mean and remedy to cure the same must be by its contrary, which is labour.[30]

Furthermore, in establishing the new hospitals, the citizens of London had first classified the poor in need of assistance into three categories:

> ... we espied three sundry sorts which were diversly to be provided for; the succourless poor child, the sick and impotent, the sturdy vagabond, or idle person.[31]

To enter a Tudor hospital was to accept forms of classification which reflected on moral and physical conditions – a judgement made by the surgeons and the hospitaller. Once inside the hospital, forms of prayer were used to locate the patient in a position of submission and gratitude. No longer was the emphasis on exposure to the central celebration of the mass, now the role of religious authority was to instruct the poor. Once physically recovered, any further evidence of begging classified the ex-patient as a criminal.

The one notable exception to this general approach to the sick-poor adult was found at Bedlam, the hospital for the mentally ill. This too shared aspects of public discipline alongside any curative work it effected on the mind. The classification of madness has been a particular concern of Foucault, and evidence from Bedlam well illustrates the relative nature of such decisions. People were sent here for 'sedicious wordes' or apparent madness.[32] It appears the case that at least 'since the reformation, Bethlem's patients had traditionally received no formal pastoral care'.[33] In other words, following the dissolution and handing over to City authority, no chaplain had any part in the running of the hospital. Not until 1677 did the issue arise for further debate, and then the reason given for only offering limited resources may well have echoed the reason for the absence of chaplaincy provision a hundred years earlier, namely:

> ... that If any of the Lunaticks kept in the said hospital be capable to receive Instruccion they are not soe fit to be kept there.[34]

With the transition of spiritual care from the passive benefits of exposure to the sacrament to the verbal inculcation of ideology, insanity became a bar to the exercise of faith. In fact, religion could be seen as the cause of madness when a weak mind had been exposed to immoderate doctrines.

---

[30]   Ibid., p. 307.

[31]   Ibid.

[32]   J. Andrews, A. Briggs and others, *The History of Bethlem* (London, 1997) p. 117.

[33]   Ibid., p. 336.

[34]   Ibid., p. 337.

The provision of chaplains in the general hospitals and workhouse, and their exclusion from Bethlem, indicate the instrumental role of religious instruction for the poor. The tasks assigned to medical and other personnel show how the work of physical and moral improvement was the *raison d'être* of these re-founded institutions. The absence of the 'old ways', of ornaments, masses and chantry prayer, further illustrate the re-casting of the hospitalized body as a surface for the active inscription of normative civic values – and not the passive immersion in sacred atmosphere. The hospitaller/chaplain is charged with giving religious instruction, with fitting religious texts to appropriate situations, and with paternal responsibility for the sick. His *presence* is one of the key strategies for the governance and policing of the re-founded hospitals. A 'light burning and shining' – no doubt offered as a benign image – nevertheless sees into every crevice, allows little room in which to be hidden, and thereby moderates and conforms behaviour.

The preoccupation of the new hospitals is with *government*. It is a word that is constantly reproduced in the statutes, prayers and information books about the re-founded institutions. Emerging so strongly in the sixteenth century, it models the hospitals on the central principle of governing people and behaviour according to the united sovereignty of God and King.

Without the tool of confession, the new regime of hospitals like Bart's and St Thomas's sets out a strategy intended to generate outward compliance. After all, if the poor are biddable and placid in their social actions why is inner surveillance required? It has been observed that these events marked a new departure in which the body would be framed by the narratives of self, and judged against sanctions and prohibitions of Scripture.[35] Moderate conversation, an absence of blasphemy and drunkenness, and gratitude to God and the citizens of London is the ambition of these institutions. It is only later, when aspects of government re-form to 'repair desire' in the care of the self, that the inner truth becomes once again the site and focus for new strategies of domination.

Conclusion

The period commonly titled 'the Reformation' reveals a moment of profound dislocation both for hospitals and also for their chaplains. The emphasis on clerical staff, and the religious immersion of the sick-poor, is still demonstrated on the eve of Reformation by the statutes and accounts of the Savoy Hospital. Following the dissolution of the hospitals, their re-founding marks a shift towards civil control and accountability. The chaplain's obligations are no longer unified but separated, described in terms of duty to both God through the King and governors as representatives of the City. This defines a moment of fraction in the construction

---

[35] P.A. Mellor and C. Shilling, *Re-forming the body: religion, community and modernity* (London and California, 1997) p. 44.

of the chaplain that is enshrined in state policy. At the same time, the overall purpose of hospitals is changing, demonstrated by an intention to admit only the curable. Within the City of London, there is also an attempt to co-ordinate the Royal Hospitals to provide differentiated institutions for the management of the poor. There is further evidence for this in the role of hospital beadles and other measures by which the policing of the poor became intimately connected to the functioning of the Royal Hospitals.

Perhaps most significantly, there is a political move to change the language of both institution and staff. The St Bartholomew's indenture speaks of 'house for the poor' rather than 'hospital', and of all the available titles the one chosen for the chaplain is 'hospitaller'. As we saw at both St Thomas's and St Bartholomew's, this was just one role for a chaplain prior to the Reformation – and the function that incorporated the most practical aspects of the hospital, such as responsibility for victuals. Although there is within a space of months evidence that popular language retained the forms of 'hospital' and 'chaplain', the formal statements remained in use in the legal agreements of these hospitals as late as 1972.

Analysis of the prayers prescribed for use by the chaplain demonstrates the use of language and metaphysical beliefs to locate the sick-poor in a posture of both gratitude and obedience. The discharged patients became vehicles to demonstrate the value of the hospital's work through the parish system, and therefore protect the livelihoods of those employed by the institutions. We have seen the evidence of the popular criticism that led to the publication of 'ordre' books by two London hospitals within a short time of their re-founding. This seems to suggest that since they had been reformed once, a precedent had been set that left these institutions with a diminished sense of security. They had to make their case and demonstrate efficacy to civil, as well as ecclesiastical, authority.

Prior to the sixteenth century, hospitals had not voiced any kind of corporate defence against popular criticism. Occasionally, in the report of a visitation, we might hear a member of staff defending his actions. The two London 'Order Books' therefore mark a departure, and a political will to defend the institution not on ecclesiastical power but on the written word (in English) that contains the right order of duty. It is the age, according to Foucault, when the word attains a fundamental place in the West. It 'harbours the truth'[36] and requires everything to 'speak'. The patient, passive and silent in the medieval period, is now compelled to articulate the power of the institution – to bear verbal witness to its value. In this new episteme, the chaplain undoubtedly has a role, and we see time and again the imperative for him to use language; to teach, instruct and have a ready supply of 'comfortable words'. The chaplain has been changed to fit this new world of knowledge, and his non-verbal acts are significantly diminished. The sacraments seem to have moved into the semi-private world of the bedside, while the recitation of prayer and scripture has become central.

---

[36]   M. Foucault, *The Order of Things: An Archaeology of the Human Sciences* (London, 2000) p. 39.

At the same time, the chaplain now finds himself with a new role in the government of the patient, in the production of a new subjectivity. We have seen that this revolves round the opposition of work and idleness; virtue and vice. The hospital admits the curable and expects the well who are discharged to be morally improved and therefore useful. We can identify here a discrimination that determines the difference of the sick-poor, rather than their similitude. In Foucauldian terms, it is an example of the new episteme – the shift from the work to draw things together to the task of establishing an identity within a series.[37] The Royal Hospitals distinguish the poor and also relate them within an order.

The patient receives the chaplain as part of the new religion of the state, in which sovereignty unites temporal and spiritual power. The chaplain is charged with making the patient compliant to authority, a willing worker who contributes to the commonwealth. The surgeons are also expected to share in the task of ensuring the patient's moral improvement. In part, this is achieved through the coercion of the patient into public statements – prayers/thanksgivings – that accept the narrative which the hospital tells of itself. 'Salvation' is the verbal rendering of the moral purpose the patient is required to bear.

With the priority of establishing similitude dislodged, the repetitious rites of the chaplain – his part in the power of re-telling the order of the cosmos – no longer find the potency they were once accorded. When, in 1592, St Bartholomew's 'hospitaller' demanded extra payment from the governors because of his pains in 'setting the bones and joints of xii persons',[38] we may be seeing a manifestation of the chaplain's desire to gain a recognition that religious duties alone could not accord him. The episteme had changed and, as religious ritual was no longer the keystone of the social order, the chaplain's centrality to the hospital had been removed.

---

[37] Ibid., p. 55.

[38] N. Moore, *The History of St. Bartholomew's Hospital* (London, 1918) p. 446.

Chapter 2
The Chaplains' Professionalization

Introduction

In the previous chapter, the scene was set for some explanation of the relative decline in the influence of hospital chaplains with regard to the moral and physical improvement of the sick. The violent shifts in the organization of society during the era of Reformation led to a much stronger sense of government in the lives of both individuals and the nation. Where once there had been a close interest in the inner workings of those in hospital, now there was a desire to engender outward compliance and evidence of moral conduct. Through the hospitaller's instruction of the prayers to be said on discharge, patients assumed responsibility for their future behaviour. Kneeling in the presence of two representatives of the City and the hospitaller, the former patients petitioned God for a 'working spirit' which set aside 'all our vice and idleness'. In effect, the discharged patients were placed in the position of breaking their word if they did not mend their ways and prove to be useful.

While the sixteenth century marks a unique moment of threshold between alternative narratives of the sick, the City and the role of religion, there are other points of change worthy of note. Before examining the effects of nationalization, and the emerging concept of chaplains as a professional group, I shall first examine two particular forms of change that serve to increase our understanding of the position of chaplains before 1948. These two developments appear under the general headings of voluntary hospitals and workhouses. Although stretching over a long period of time, these voluntary and civic initiatives for the sick-poor both came to a conclusion with nationalization. Given that both kinds of institution had objectives couched in religious language, and both appointed chaplains, they warrant some brief consideration before moving on to examine the founding of the NHS.

Voluntary Hospitals

The re-founding and creation of the institutions which made up London's five Royal Hospitals remained the sole provision of hospitals until the beginning of the eighteenth century. A growing tide of interest in hospitals – their perceived lack in England and profusion in Europe – was the start of what became known as the voluntary hospital movement.[1] There is ample evidence regarding these, particularly for Westminster Hospital which stands out as the first such venture. Woodward's work remains a significant text on the voluntary movement, although it is now rather dated and lacks the insights generated by the renewed interest in the study of hospitals during the last twenty years.

A small group convened to initiate a 'Charitable Proposal' to launch the Westminster, arising out of concerns listed in 1716:

> Notwithstanding the provision settled by our laws and the collections made by the charity of well disposed Christians for the relief of the poor, it is obvious to anyone that walks the street that the same is not sufficient to preserve great numbers of them from beggary, to the great grief of all good men and the no small reproach of our religion and country.[2]

This statement demonstrates an awareness of the Henrician hospital provision enshrined in statute, and most evident in the operation of Bart's and St Thomas's. In addition, it alludes to the various poor laws and the perceived philanthropic activity of some Christians. Yet, with clear sixteenth-century resonance, it focuses attention onto the streets, and the poor and sick who turn to beggary. It is this public manifestation of poverty and illness which is utilized as the key argument for new acts of policy or public charity. It can be argued that it is this overriding concern with the appearance of order in the public eye that enables a rationality for institutional development to be made. Once again, we are reminded of the significant part played by geography in the State's activities in relation to poverty. Appealing to civic pride, it is the location and quantity of the poor that are seen to reflect on the extent of religious and national success.

The five aims of the 'Charitable Proposal' can be summarized as:

- The provision for sick poor people of food and physic, as well as the attendance of physicians, surgeons, nursing and charitable care. (This includes a note that if a person in receipt of care has a parish pension then the parish should be charged for his or her care in hospital – a clear link between a voluntary hospital and an element of the local system of financial responsibility);
- The care of pregnant women who have been turned out because of their condition. A nurse assists them only if they do not have a friend or relative;
- The visiting of the sick in prison and the provision of food and other facilities for them;
- The care of strangers so that they can return to their native country; and

---

[1] J. Woodward, *To do the sick no harm: a study of the British voluntary hospital system to 1875* (London and Boston, 1974).

[2] J. Humble and P. Hansell, *Westminster Hospital 1716–1974* (London, 1974) p. 6.

- 'The Society designs to reclaim the souls of the sick.' This last aim was supported by the promise to ensure daily visits by clergy.

The foundation of a voluntary hospital was intended to relieve the sick-poor while at the same time using the opportunity to try and improve their moral and spiritual state. There is evidence that those admitted were expected to conform their behaviour to a certain standard, and expulsions of those breaking the rules were not uncommon. On 17 September 1720, a patient appeared before the Board charged with 'behaving in a very rude and scandalous manner and cursing and swearing and complaining of the food'.[3] Such behaviour was not in keeping with the aim of reclaiming the souls of the sick, and lack of compliance led to exclusion.

Admission to voluntary hospitals was by recommendation of a Trustee, who was entitled to have one inpatient and one outpatient at any one time. Given that this structure gave a considerable power to the Trustees, it is easy to imagine that the sick admitted in this way were inclined to be grateful. And as any disagreeable behaviour could lead to expulsion, it is likely that this system inspired some fear. In the 1720–1724 'Orders for Inpatients', it is noted that 'Every One Discharged Cured from this Infirmary be enjoined by the Chairman to give Publick Thanks in their Parish Churches.'[4] This expectation of public gratitude served as a way both to control the poor and to dissuade excessive use of the new voluntary hospitals.

There is some evidence that the creation of voluntary hospitals provided a place for medical 'experiment' on those already subdued into gratitude. Adrian Wilson notes that the voluntary hospitals 'constructed a new political space for the practice of medicine' and that 'in the voluntary hospitals the possibility was opened of far greater medical authority over the patient'.[5] Wilson goes on to argue that this change in hospital organization effectively created a *medico–charitable* space, where the most powerful interests were those of the medical staff and the subscribers.

Unlike the rigid – and perhaps rather revered – founding regulations of the Royal Hospitals, the voluntary hospitals were far less stable. The Westminster itself suffered dissension, and in 1733 many subscribers and all the medical staff left to found St George's Hospital. The fact that the Westminster was the first, and gave rise to other London institutions as well as inspiring replication in other parts of the country, marks it out as a significant development in hospital practice. Although the founding principles (outlined above) do not specify physical *improvement*, it is implied in the stipulation for the provision of *physic*.

The political context for the founding of the Westminster is very important, and is explored in some detail by Adrian Wilson. At a time of Tory/Whig rivalry, the

---

[3] Ibid., p. 17.

[4] Ibid., p. 22.

[5] Adrian Wilson, 'The politics of medical improvement in early Hanoverian London', in A. Cunningham and R. French (eds), *The Medical Enlightenment of the Eighteenth Century* (Cambridge, 1990) p. 10.

perception of rising Whig dominance led many Tory citizens and clergy to consider other avenues for acting in society; the creation of hospitals under their control appeared attractive. Of the group which met in 1719 to found the Westminster, seven of the twelve were clergy – reflecting a split within the Church between Whig and Tory supporters. In this atmosphere, an apparently innocuous aspiration (the aim to 'take care of the souls' of the sick) takes on a political dimension. Those financing hospitals effectively bought the right to deploy whichever brand of Christian ministry the subscribers favoured. The grateful patients who were obliged to return to their parish churches to give testimony to their healing through the agency of a voluntary hospital were effectively making a political, as much as a religious, point.

The London, founded in 1740, had rules in which a cured (or 'relieved') patient was made to give thanks before the house committee. Such patients were then strongly encouraged to give thanks in their own parish church:

> A patient who refused to return thanks was never to be treated again. (A black list of these offenders was kept.) But those who conformed to this rule were given a certificate entitling them to further relief at the hospital, should they ever want it.[6]

In time, when the chapel was built, the patient would have to give thanks there at 9 a.m. before going to see the committee at 11 a.m. This follows the pattern of the Royal Hospitals, which had similar provision for thanksgiving both within the hospitals and then within the patient's parish. In the case of The London, the duties of the chaplain indicate some modelling on earlier practice. The first Chaplain, the Revd M. Audley, appears to have had a similar working pattern to those indicated at Bart's and St Thomas's in the sixteenth century. This is described in an inquiry into 'The Practice in management and Conduct of all the officers and Servants of the Hospital', and quoted by Clark-Kennedy:

> As to the Reverent Mr Audley, your Chaplain, we find that he constantly reads Prayers at the Hospital every Tuesday and Saturday; that he always visits and prays by Such of the Patients, in their respective Wards, as desire it, and administers the Sacraments to Such of them, as upon enquiry into their Lives and Conversations, he thinks fitly Qualified to Receive it; That he Generally goes through the House on Thursdays to give the Patients an Opportunity of Asking him his advice and assistance in the way of His Profession; and that besides his assistance, they have the Bishop of Sodor and Man's Christian Instructions fixed up in every Ward for their Perusal.[7]

---

[6]   A. Clark-Kennedy, *The London: A Study in the Voluntary Hospital System* (London, 1962) p. 34.

[7]   Ibid., pp. 101–2.

This short summary of the chaplain's work illustrates the degree of change since the pre-Reformation hospitals were at their height. Holy Communion, or Mass, is not the focal point of the hospital – or of the chaplain's activity. Now prayer and instruction are central, but only in a corporate sense twice a week. It may well be that other staff performed this function on other days. Now, communion is solely an individual activity carried out at the bedside. Although not hearing confession, the chaplain is nevertheless charged to assess the fitness of patients to receive communion: this involves enquiry and evaluation of their conversation in order to see if they 'qualify'. Thursdays offer an opportunity for the patients to speak with him and gain advice and help within the parameters of 'His Profession'. And in case this was not sufficient, in lieu of religious imagery, there are now texts of Christian instruction permanently fixed to the walls. In its moral purposes, and the desire to reclaim the souls of the sick, the hospital building spoke to the poor at every turn.

Audley had begun as a voluntary chaplain, offering his services when the hospital was first envisaged. He had been made a life governor and was subsequently given an annual gift of thirty guineas. Eventually, and due in part to the frequent complaints by the Bishop of Oxford that services were not read in the Chapel on Sundays, Audley was appointed as full-time chaplain on £100 a year. When, in 1758, the hospital gained a royal charter and became incorporated, it was only the serving chaplain and physicians who were entitled from the staff to sit as governors. Both as a governor and as chaplain, the Revd M. Audley had other relevant duties in the development of the hospital. When The London moved to a new site, it needed its own burial ground, and Audley, with other governors, was charged with inspecting and adapting some suitable land.

Research into the precise nature of the 'texts by the Bishop of Sodor and Man' indicates that they would have been extracts of works written by the Rt Revd Thomas Wilson (1663–1755). Wilson was Bishop of Sodor and Man during the founding of the hospital and was a prolific writer, not least concerning the instruction of the poor. It may well be that the instructions kept on the wards of The London were taken from his comprehensively titled book:

> The knowledge and practice of Christianity made easy to the meanest capacities, or, An essay towards an instruction for the Indians: which will likewise be of use to all such Christians as have not well considered the meaning of the religion they profess; or, who profess to know God, but in works do deny Him; in nineteen dialogues, together with directions and prayers.[8]

Some insight into the approach of Bishop Wilson can be found in his comments 'Concerning the Poor'. Here he writes of the need for the poor to have patience in their adversity and remember that the rich have their share of troubles. Wilson

---

8   Thomas Wilson, *The works of the Right Reverend Thomas Wilson, D.D. Lord Bishop of Sodor and Man* (Bath, 1779).

adds that God has made poverty 'the lot of his dearest servants' and that they should put up with temporal difficulties in the light of their eternal inheritance.[9] He cites a small number of Bible passages that he believes can comfort the poor. Furthermore, Wilson has advice for 'Persons in Affliction' – which comes immediately after his comments concerning the poor. Here it is the role of the pastor 'to *guide* and *support* the spirits of the afflicted', and to 'teach such as are in trouble to seek comfort in God and in the aids of religion'.

The attraction of Wilson's work might have been its dialogical structure, so that he describes the complaint of the afflicted before giving an apologia. These 'Christian Instructions' would have been a permanent argument set before those liable to complain about their lot. No doubt, if they could not read, it provided opportunity for the chaplain or other staff to read them and to discuss them with patients.

There can be little doubt that the chaplain's role within the hospital was one of both comforting the genuinely miserable and also guiding and instructing those judged able to amend their life into more conventional living. The fact that the chaplain preached at the annual festival for the hospital in 1744 indicates that he could be expected to play an important part in affirming the moral purpose of an organization that relied (at least in part) on charitable funds.

Compared to the ancient foundations which had emerged in the sixteenth century, these new hospitals made no assumption that their life would be indefinite. The Royal gift to the City of Bart's and St Thomas's was in perpetuity – it tied the hospitals to the State in a way which gave some security but encouraged conservatism. With the backing of subscribers, the voluntary hospitals were self-financing and potentially vulnerable to scandal or to difficult economic circumstances. However, their autonomy from the establishment opened up new opportunities for medical staff – some of whom would have been effectively excluded from other hospitals by their religious and political beliefs.

In the texts which survive from the founding of the Westminster, it is clear that this new hospital venture was on a modest scale. It initially involved the rental of a house to serve as the hospital – not the creation of a new building. From the listed purposes of the Westminster, both physical care and spiritual improvement feature strongly. As in the provision of education for the children of the poor, the new hospital was linked into the system of parish relief; it supplemented and extended it. Although it is possible to see the growth of medical power in these new institutions, the overall project of care for the poor was constructed in terms of Christian charity. The failure of the traditional hospitals to resolve the problems of the sick-poor was part of the context in which voluntary hospitals gained both financial support and social relevance. Coupled to this, the exclusion of some clergy and medical men from other hospitals and places of education meant that a steady supply of financial, spiritual and medical support was readily available.

[9] Ibid., pp. 418–19.

Ostensibly the object of this new philanthropy, the patient remained impotent. Regulated by the regimes of the leading subscribers, the sick had little option but to use whatever free medical services were available to them. The patients were to be well-behaved, to be grateful, and to offer a public testimony of the usefulness of the hospital. Clergy came into the hospital to visit – but they were not resident. It is quite possible that this marks the first time that the role of chaplains becomes in some measure external to the power systems of the hospital. In such limited space there is no 'chapel' – no dedicated focal point for the religious work of the hospital.

Workhouses

The combined efforts of the Royal and voluntary hospitals were not sufficient to deal with the numbers of poor, destitute and sick people generated during the industrial revolution. Poor Law legislation created new ways to process the poor – particularly those displaced from traditional communities. From 1834, workhouses and their infirmaries enjoyed vigorous growth, fuelled by a belief that institutions 'were now seen as the only desirable place for the treatment of certain social and medical conditions – the distinction between the two was not always clearly made'.[10]

If there was little difference between the functions of the workhouses and their infirmaries, there was also little distinction between the architecture used to house Victorian prisoners, paupers and the sick. In a variety of ways, the design of these social spaces promoted observation and the detailed management of the daily life of the destitute. In the 'Orders and Regulations to be Observed in Workhouses' (1835), it is stated that all needing assistance should first report to the workhouse medical officer who would then allocate them to either the infirmary, the workhouse or the wards for lunatics and imbeciles. In other words, the poor could not simply turn up to a hospital – they had to face the prospect that medical examination might judge them well enough to go onto an adult workhouse ward instead.[11]

No single plan was dictated by central government, but there was inevitably a great deal of conformity between designs. Cost was always a significant factor, and the initial hope that the sick-poor might have been deterred by fear of the workhouse led to inadequate and modest infirmaries. In an example of the growing influence of professional medical corporate action, *The Lancet* appointed a commission to assess the state of workhouse infirmaries in 1866. The report of the commission highlighted the significance of the infirmaries which – in London – contained nearly four times as many patients as all the capital's voluntary hospitals.

---

[10]   Anne Crowther, *The workhouse system, 1834–1929: the history of an English social institution* (London, 1981) p. 56.

[11]   Royal Commission on the Historic Medieval Hospital, *English Hospitals 1660– 1948* (London, 1998).

The report in *The Lancet*, and other investigations by the Poor Law Board, called for greater ventilation, improved sanitation and the segregation of patients according to their illnesses. It demonstrated the capacity of the medical profession to use scientific findings in order to gain greater resources and wider public recognition of its role.

By contrast, chaplains appointed to large institutions did little to advance their claims to either resources or recognition. In many cases, they rested on the institutional rules that required compulsory attendance at Sunday worship. In fact the 'philanthropic' motives of those who contributed to the building of large chapels need to be explored alongside their desire to keep the destitute away from middle-class worship. Victorian Christianity could hardly say that the poor did not need to go to church – but it could certainly define where that worship was to take place. Famously, Anne Crowther described the chaplain as 'the Sunday gaoler'.[12]

The most detailed study of any workhouse/infirmary chaplain comes in research published in *The London Journal*.[13] Here the career of one chaplain, employed by England's largest workhouse, is explored in depth. Tanner notes the bishops' support for the 1834 Poor Law Amendment Act, in part because they saw new opportunities for clergy employment – as chaplains were required to be appointed to all the new institutions. Indeed, she describes the role of such institutions in advocating the 'norm' of Anglican practice:

> All mobile inmates were expected to attend services, those who were not Anglicans were discouraged from pursuing their own faith, and their own pastors gained admission to the workhouse only with the greatest difficulty.[14]

Tanner draws attention to the staggering absence of literature about – or by – these key staff in the operation of the Poor Law. Chaplains are conspicuous by their absence. Her conclusion is that:

> The chaplains were already part of an ancient profession, and were protected by their ultimate accountability to their bishops, therefore they had no need to form themselves into a separate organisation, or meet in conference and petition for professional safeguards, as was the case with the Medical Officers. To a greater extent than even the workhouse masters, they represented the establishment within the workhouses, and, as such, had little to gain by forming themselves into a single, identifiable, body.[15]

---

[12]   Crowther (London, 1981).

[13]   A. Tanner, 'A Troublesome Priest: A Victorian Workhouse Chaplain in the City of London', *London Journal* 23 (London, 1998): 15–31.

[14]   Ibid., p. 18.

[15]   Ibid., p. 23.

In Tanner's study of the Reverend Frederick Pocock, this lack of group consciousness is clear. Pocock is portrayed as a maverick, unable to be controlled by the Board of Governors and finding uncritical support from his Diocesan Bishop. A detailed analysis of his work revealed that, although his was a full-time post, Pocock managed to run a private school from his home and had a 'highly individual working routine'. Tanner summarizes the expectation about the differing roles of master and chaplain as:

> The master, as father of the house, was expected to instil order and discipline, and it was the role of the chaplain to apply the tempering influence of Christianity to make the institution a place of harmony, peace and regulation.[16]

The perception of the chaplain as the 'friend of the poor' nevertheless sits uneasily with the inevitable disparities of education, economic position and social status. The quotation given above could be seen as the basis for viewing the chaplain in a role of making acceptable the Master's discipline. In Tanner's words, the guardians who governed the workhouse saw that the role of the chaplain was to 'bring solace and comfort to the aged, and encourage the young towards a life of purity, and towards self-reliance when they left the workhouse'. Yet in Pocock even the most critical aspects of his role – such as the baptizing of babies born in the workhouse – were neglected. Not only did the poor fail to find a friend, they even found him failing in the most basic things they could expect from a priest. Pocock delegated morning and evening prayer in the workhouse to a lay officer. The Poor Law Board saw the inappropriateness of this, because the lay officer had a disciplinary function as well – and that mixing the two was unhelpful.

Tanner's exploration of a particular – and not necessarily typical – workhouse chaplain illustrates something of what was expected from religious leadership in such institutions. Chapels and chaplaincies continued to be created in workhouses right up to the founding of the NHS. In 1922, the Bishop of St Albans dedicated the St Alban Chapel at Barnet in North London. The Barnet Union Institution had appointed its first chaplain in 1910, and it was the same chaplain who had led the work to create a chapel. In his sermon at the dedication, the Bishop spoke highly of the chaplain and a summary of his words carried in the local press included the following:

> He hoped the chapel would be the centre of the life of the Institution. *(To the staff)* There must be no suggestion of condescension, of superiority, but they must remember that those whom they were helping were of their own flesh and blood. *(To the inmates)* They could do a great deal and make a big difference to the people around them by just keeping cheery … Some people were always

---

[16]   Ibid.

ready and willing to share their troubles, but he asked them to share their good things and keep their troubles to themselves.[17]

This is an extract from a sermon in which moderation as a means to unity is demonstrated as an Anglican ideology. It is significant, when compared with earlier episcopal statements, that the relational virtue of staff and inmates lies in their common humanity (flesh and blood) – rather than the concept of the poor as those favoured by God or icons of Christ. This is not to say that the idea of common humanity is an irreligious idea, simply that its theology is less explicit. The Bishop is a paternal figure employing rational argument in an attempt to curb excesses of behaviour and thereby temper conduct. Although it is a rare visit, and he has no direct means of turning these words into action, it nevertheless illustrates the kind of approach taken by an establishment figure – of whom the chaplain is a direct representative within the institution. Nor is it out of keeping with the comments made by the governors of the London Workhouse about their expectations of a chaplain.

In Leeds, the foundation in 1861 of a new workhouse brought with it an attendant chaplain. The chaplain had his own report book, and was required to complete a section headed: 'Account of the Moral and Religious State of the Inmates Generally'. There were also sections for stating the day and time of his visiting, the duty the chaplain performed, and the catechizing and progress of children. In January 1870, the chaplain fills in the book to report where he has visited and the duties undertaken, including pastoral visits to the workhouse infirmary.[18] In the section concerning the moral and religious state of the inmates (which is generally left blank) he comments that it is 'as good as can be expected'. A similar Report Book is later supplied in 1927 and contains an extract from the Leeds Union (Infirmaries Order) under the heading 'Duties of the Chaplain':

> The Chaplain of the Infirmary shall: – Record in a journal, to be laid before the appropriate Infirmary Committee at each meeting, his attendances, and any services conducted by him, and any matters touching his office which he may think it desirable to report for their consideration.[19]

This would seem to indicate a stronger attempt to make the work of the chaplain accountable within the workings of the Union. It is quite clear, however, that there is still enormous scope for independent action and only the most basic requirement to record activities and the division of his time.

On the eve of nationalization, there are some poignant and instructive comments in the half-year report of the Leeds chaplain, the Revd Matthews. Dated 31 December 1947, his typed comments quote in full the BMA statement 'Medicine and the Church'. He puts the case for an internal segregation of the Chapel to give

---

[17]   Staff Reporter, 'Chapel Opened', (Barnet, 1922).
[18]   Chaplain, *Chaplain's Report Book* (Leeds, 1870).
[19]   Ibid.

space for Roman Catholic and Free Church worship; he recommends books and a suggestion for increased staffing to assist his work before adding:

> You will see from various aspects of the report that a change is developing throughout the country regarding the Chaplains position in the Hospitals. For a period, far too long, the Chaplains department has been in the background of the Medical profession …[20]

Not yet chaplain*cy*, but nevertheless a sense that what chaplains do is beginning to have some collegiate and corporate sense of identity. Part of that perception seems to be drawn from a recognition that chaplains have been displaced by the medical profession in holding a recognized authority over the sick. Not only displaced, but there is even the hint that the 'gap' between them might be widening. It is no wonder that Matthews was keen to set out the BMA statement in full and to recommend books that demonstrate a literary and academic turn by some chaplains. He was presenting the Board with a new perception of the chaplain, a chaplain who could strive to sit alongside the dominant hospital profession.

Although this is a brief consideration of what is at most a minor threshold in the history of the chaplains, I believe that it demonstrates a number of important points. First, the chaplain appointed to workhouses and their infirmaries could work (or not work) with considerable independence from the governors. Second, that this position was supported by his connection to the establishment in the form of the bishop. Last, that for much of the century in which workhouses flourished, chaplains relied on their church connections more than on any sense of specialist ministry or corporate identity as chaplains. In practice, the chaplain had a broad and ill-defined job description: to be a friend to the sick and poor, to offer structured rites and comfortable words, and to moderate the excesses of institutional life. In the conduct of his duties, the chaplain was wedded to the *status quo*, required to use his position to ensure conformity to social expectation through a particular form of biblical and theological understanding. Namely, that God had determined the social order and that faithfulness required acceptance of one's circumstances with equanimity. In such a position, the chaplain was effectively being asked to reconcile the sick to the power of the workhouse within Victorian society. This is a conclusion borne out by the role of chaplains in providing 'entertainments' for the sick – particularly mental health patients, to relieve the boredom and oppression of the workhouse regime.[21]

In such a context, spiritual care amounted to ensuring the outward religious conformity of those destined to use workhouses throughout the nineteenth and early twentieth centuries. This was a task the chaplain fulfilled in relation to

---

[20]   Ibid.

[21]   In Leeds the chaplain in 1931 was petitioning the Board for the 'installation of Wireless unit Loud Speakers, to Mental Wards' (Chaplains, 1927). This would have enabled services to be broadcast directly to the wards.

staff and patients, reminding both of the inter-related duties of providing care and exhibiting gratitude. Attendance at religious services, ward prayers, godly conversation and quiescence all marked the intended power and effect generated by the chaplain's presence. The chaplain was in no sense the equal of the sick or poor – indeed, as we have seen, he might even see himself as the social superior of every other member of staff. Pocock's work was perhaps an extreme case, but it nevertheless illustrates the *capacity* for individual action. The Governor's intention that the chaplain would form a point of unity and harmony within the house – and acceptance by the poor of his authority – was unrealized. This was not due to any dispute about the right to expect this, but rather to the distraction caused by Pocock's wide interests external to the workhouse. It would seem that, at least for one chaplain, the work represented little other than an inconvenient sinecure.

In a comment that speaks volumes about the entwined nature of religious presence and civil policy towards the sick, Matthews adds, at the end of his 1947 report:

> For instance, the Chalice, (Communion Cup) and Paten, (Salver) of the Hospital is of Nickel Plate tarnished instead of silver, and is stamped LEEDS WORK HOUSE. I suggest that the Hospital property of Chalice and Paten be passed on to the Museum as an entertaining relic of a bye gone age.[22]

Even in their compulsory religious observance, the sick-poor could not escape the ownership implied by the rate-payers' maintenance of the workhouse. The vessels of religious practice were stamped with that ownership, and were a reminder that chaplains were representatives of the state religion – just as workhouses were a manifestation of state policy towards the poor. Perhaps the real challenge for chaplains at the time of nationalization was to ensure that it was just the chalice and paten – and not they themselves – who were to become an entertaining relic.

The Founding of the NHS

It is not easy now to appreciate fully the world into which the NHS was born. After sixty years, the socialist ideals that sought to harness the state's war-time direction of resources for national peace and prosperity seem very distant indeed. Even in terms of religious practice and popular support for the Church, 1948 seems light-years distant from the present. For example, 1948 was a Lambeth year – the first post-war gathering of Anglican bishops from around the world. As still happens today, the visiting bishops were accommodated before the conference around the dioceses of the Church of England. On a Friday evening in June 1948 three of these bishops – and their three episcopal hosts – led a service at Leeds Parish Church. The local paper tells us that almost 5,000 people came to hear them.

---

[22]   Chaplains (Leeds, 1927).

In an age of declining interest in almost all membership organizations, it is hard to imagine that a similar service for a Lambeth Conference in the twenty-first century would attract anything more than a fraction of the attendance raised in 1948.

It is well-documented that the National Health Service came into being amid considerable controversy. Both medical doctors and dental associations prevaricated about their level of involvement with the new organization up to (and beyond) the 5 July starting date. There is some evidence, however, that the view of medical staff was not uniform, and that more junior staff saw it as a way of breaking up aspects of nepotism present within the profession.

For chaplains, the early years of the new organization appear to show little evidence of impact upon the work that was being done. Chaplains were small in number, with only the larger hospitals having whole-time members of staff. It is estimated that in 1948 there would have been about 28 chaplains in post, and the expectation was that these clergy would return to parish ministry after a short period (five or seven years). This had the effect of keeping chaplains closely connected to the Church, as few would have retired from chaplaincy work in those days. With the advent of nationalization, the Church appointed a commission to examine the future status of hospital chaplains. In its final report in 1951, the commission stated that it had received firm assurances from government ministers that the future both of chaplains and of hospital chapels would be met financially by the NHS.[23] There is evidence that Aneurin Bevan as Minister of Health went out of his way to assure the Church that he believed every hospital should have a chaplain working in it.[24] There followed a spate of government circulars which confirmed this view and emphasized the need for both a chapel and a chaplain.[25] In the light of these developments, in 1951 the Church Assembly of the Church of England created the Hospital Chaplaincies Council, and this body has continued to resource and co-ordinate the Church's approach to chaplaincy. Overall, the view of the Church at this time was that it constituted an area of specialist – but temporary – ministry which should be encouraged, supported but carefully controlled. When the Tunbridge Report of 1974 reflected on the early days of the NHS, it clearly saw the chief change to lie in the direct *employment* of the chaplain by the service. This removed the somewhat patchy nature of past provision and had the potential to provide education and training for those ministering in a common structure with shared expectations. Gradually, this understanding enabled the Hospital Chaplaincies Council to 'sell' training to the NHS for its chaplaincy workforce, allowing the appointment of a training officer and growth of administrative support.

---

[23]   Church of England, *Church Assembly, Hospital Chaplaincies Commission, Final Report* CA 1003, August 1951, p. 3.

[24]   J.W. Woodward, *A Study of the Role of the Acute Health Care Chaplain in England* (1998).

[25]   National Health Service. *Appointment of chaplains.* HMC (48) 62 (1948).

Most recent writers on the work of chaplains allude to the history of chaplaincy only after 1948. Woodward researched the correspondence between the Ministry of Health and the Archbishop of Canterbury between 1946 and 1948 and concludes that 'there was some considerable anxiety on the part of the Church of England about the effects on the provision of spiritual ministrations to hospital patients of the advent of the NHS'.[26] In the end, the role of chaplain was safeguarded, and the Church of England received assurances that both the chaplain and any chapels would be funded out of a hospital's main budget. At this time, within all the structural changes taking place, the question arose as to what a chaplain should be paid – and to which other group of staff he should be compared. Woodward cites evidence that an initial suggestion that a chaplain should be paid at the same level as a consultant was resisted by the Church. The link with the consultant grade was not simply a question of pay, but an evaluation of status (probably reflecting the fact that many hospital chaplains had a university education). According to Woodward, this suggestion was resisted by the Archbishop of Canterbury out of fear that highly-paid career chaplaincies might draw clergy away from parish ministry. This view gains further support from a Hospital Chaplaincies Commission report to the Church Assembly in 1948 which stated:

> In the development of a structure for terms and conditions for chaplains, care must be taken to ensure that clergy do not opt for hospital service as an alternative to mainstream work in the parishes.[27]

Ministry of Health circulars in 1948 stipulated that chaplains should be employed and chapels provided. The calculation of chaplaincy requirement was one whole-time post per 750 in-patients. This level of patient-to-chaplain ratio favoured Church of England chaplains and perpetuated the marginal status of ministers from other denominations.

The period from 1958 to 1968 saw the most intense growth in the consideration of professional identity for chaplains working in the NHS. Chaplains themselves began to write and disseminate their views about the nature of their work and its differences from what other clergy were doing in parishes. In 1955, Cox's book appeared and, in 1968, Autton produced *Pastoral Care in Hospitals*. The intervening period saw a report from the King's Fund into chaplaincy, a pamphlet by Autton for the Church of England's ministry advisory committee and the appearance in Britain of works from the USA such as Young and Meiburg's *Spiritual Therapy*. By 1971, there was another significant overseas reflection with Hugo de Wall's translation of Heije Faber's 1968 Dutch work *Pastoral Care in the Modern Hospital*.

---

[26]   Woodward (1998) p. 87.

[27]   Hospital Chaplaincies Commission, *Hospital Chaplaincies Interim Report (CA 871)* (1948).

Cox's work forms an Anglican manual for the use of both parish clergy and hospital chaplains. Illustrated with photographs of clergy working in hospitals, it is an effective attempt to describe the work of a chaplain in detail, and makes extensive reference to both theological texts and NHS policy. Writing within the first decade of the NHS, Cox makes a point of noting the impact of such major change for the chaplain:

> Since the hospitals were nationalized, the direction that every hospital must have its officially appointed chaplain has underlined this point *(distinction between chaplain and vicar)*. Any priest may visit his own people in hospital; but the officially appointed chaplain is in a different position; he is "on the strength", and the staff is not complete without him.[28]

Cox dedicated the book to the 'Church of England Hospital Chaplains' Fellowship', which suggests that his approach is mainstream within chaplaincy. The language he uses at various points in the book is of particular interest, including reference to 'clinical Baptism' and 'clinical communions'.

The book contains a fold-out sheet setting out an organizational chart that shows the position of the chaplains directly answerable to the Hospital Secretary (the equivalent at that time of the Chief Executive). In this way, the chaplain is shown on a par with the consultants, matron, head porter and the lead staff for medical auxiliaries and clerical staff. Overall it is an optimistic and confident book that demonstrates what the author believes to be an effective way to be a chaplain within the new NHS. As Cox states in his introduction:

> The modern hospital service with its aims and ideals is undoubtedly the product of many centuries of Christian belief and practice.[29]

In terms of how pastoral power had shaped the modern clinic, Foucault may well have agreed with such a statement – although perhaps not in the way Cox intended the remark to be taken. Yet Cox is opening his book with a claim that the chaplain's work has a foundational link to the primary purpose, ethics and moral outlook of the modern hospital. And at the end of his book he also seeks to demonstrate the compatibility of Christianity with the ongoing story of medicine. In Appendix A, he sets out in full the 1947 publication *Medicine and the Church*, a statement approved by the Council of the BMA. The statement describes a process of consultation between the Central Ethical Committee of the BMA and the Churches' Council of Healing. In somewhat mysterious words the Statement says:

---

[28] J.G. Cox, *A Priest's Work in Hospital* (London, 1955) p. 48.

[29] Ibid., p. ix.

Inquiries have been received on the subject at the B.M.A. Headquarters, particularly on the propriety of the association of doctors with clergy as unqualified persons who might be concerned with the treatment of patients.[30]

It becomes apparent later in the Statement that these concerns pertain in particular to 'faith healers', where much 'harm has been done to individuals by unreasonable appeals to the emotions and by mass hysteria'. In order to safeguard the patients – a stated aim of the Churches' Council of Healing – it is even suggested that co-operation between the BMA and the Churches' Council could extend to:

> ... the appointment of and co-operation with hospital chaplains and their deputies, education of the public, and informal discussions between doctors and the clergy.[31]

The Statement concludes:

> Medicine and the Church working together should encourage a dynamic philosophy of health which would enable every citizen to find a way of life based on moral principle and on a sound knowledge of the factors which promote health and well-being. Health is more than a physical problem, and the patient's attitude both to illness and to other problems is an important factor in his recovery and adjustment to life. Negative forces such as fear, resentment, jealousy, indulgence and carelessness play no small part in the level of both personal and national health. For these reasons we welcome opportunities for discussion and co-operation in the future between qualified medical practitioners and all who have a concern for the religious needs of their patients.[32]

Here it appears to be medicine that is setting the agenda – creating a vision in which the clergy can assist by moulding patient attitudes. The chaplains could placate and diminish what the BMA Statement calls the 'negative forces' by planting and nurturing in each potential patient (that is, everyone) 'moral principle'. Attitudes would be engineered and intemperate emotions quelled – all for the benefit of our health. Nor is this simply an individual exercise for the specific patient: it is for the good of our *national* health. The most significant element in the Statement in respect of the clergy–doctor relationship, however, comes in its closing sentence: this is a partnership between the 'qualified' and the 'concerned'. In such a compact, the qualified will always have an elevated position because their knowledge privileges their discourse. Those who have a 'concern' are useful – perhaps even helpful – allies, but ultimately they are the ancillaries of the science by which the truth of the patient is known.

---

[30]   Ibid., p. 183.
[31]   Ibid., p. 184.
[32]   Ibid.

Autton, referred to by Orchard as 'the father of chaplaincy' (or, I would suggest, modern chaplaincy) offers considerable insight into the self-perception and work of chaplains. In a pamphlet,[33] he produces a text on chaplaincy that, in the context of being a Church of England publication, can be read as an official view. There can be no doubt that Autton is confident about the chaplain's role:

> ... the chaplain comes with no mechanical tools, but rather with spiritual instruments to instil faith, implant courage and create meaningful relationships and opens the way for restoration of the body.[34]

Autton's pamphlet is full of energy and zeal, revealing a chaplain with few doubts about his place in an NHS hospital. He is a technologist of the soul, able to effect positive psycho-spiritual changes in patients and thereby remove obstacles to physical recovery. No wonder he saw the chaplain's place to be alongside other health professionals. Prayer is recommended at the start of a visit as it will 'help *him* to assess their needs and prompt *them* to open their hearts'(Autton's emphases). And through the chaplain's effective care, Autton sees the potential to re-define the patient's view of God: 'God now becomes for many no longer a fearsome image but a real and loving person.' For those inclined to depression, the chaplain 'will lead them out of themselves', and for others 'He will try to bring insight to those who are blind to the real causes of their trouble.' Finally, in his role as an evangelist, the chaplain comes 'to interpret or articulate to his patients what God is like':

> When the consultant talks he knows what he has to say to be effective. The chaplain whose ways are vague, uncertain and misdirected, whose speech is trivial, and whose prayers are meaningless and irrelevant will not be effective.[35]

In many ways, Autton is re-stating the doctrine of the chaplain set out in the twelfth century, namely of the two physicians: 'training is as necessary for the chaplain, dealing as he is with the cure of souls, as for the doctor given the care of the body'.[36] In his lengthier book two years later, Autton writes further of those chaplains vague or doubtful about their role, and advocates sustained reflection: 'What does his chaplaincy involve and what does it mean, not only to staff and patients, but also to himself?' Autton asks:

> Does he come to dispense 'religion' in the same way as the psychiatrist uses his psychiatry and the psychologist applies his psychology? ... His role as chaplain must be as meaningful as medicine itself. His position must not be less

33   N. Autton, *The Hospital Ministry* (London, 1966).
34   Ibid., p. 6.
35   Ibid., p. 9.
36   Ibid., p. 27.

professional than that of other members of staff, and his science and skill not less marked than those of the surgeon.[37]

Yet Autton's introduction indicates that the priest in hospital is 'chaplain rather than clinician and he works not to compete but to complement'. His work is built on considerable experience, gained both as a chaplain and as the Director of Training at the Hospital Chaplaincies Council, and Autton sets out in detail the various areas of a chaplain's work including a number of drawings. *Pastoral Care in Hospital* identifies the need to train chaplains so that there is something more substantial than a mere 'switch-over' from parish to hospital. In fact Autton advocates 'a clinical training programme' in the hospital, where the trainee is led to examine 'The exact goals of his ministry, the effectiveness of his work, the meaning of his relationships, to the patients, to the staff and to himself'.[38]

Autton's work, although still with something to say to chaplains, is of its era. It is a confident portrayal of what he sees to be an 'effective' chaplaincy that re-shapes the patient's view of God and encourages reflection on the underlying causes of illness. Autton's concept of chaplaincy is both moral and disciplinary, and only a little removed from the Victorian chaplain's obligation to comment on the moral state of inmates. It is unchallenged by the greater faith diversity already developing in Britain, or the emerging role of women in ministry. As with Cox's approach, Autton draws on his experience as the raw material for his writing. It was not until 1971 that opinion-based writing about chaplaincy was replaced by something more akin to the mainstream of research and professional development.

'The Hospital – A Place of Truth'

'The general aim has been to study the role, selection and training of hospital chaplains in varied situations.'[39]

Wilson's study arose in rather unusual circumstances. In 1966, plans were put forward for a new chapel at the Queen Elizabeth Medical Centre in Birmingham. However, rather than survey other such plans – or fall back on past models – it was suggested that the provision of a new facility should follow a study of the role of the hospital chaplain. The idea being that an understanding of that role would help to define precisely what kind of architectural requirements were needed. A working party was formed to direct the research consisting of senior medical staff, a matron, chaplain and a lecturer in pastoral studies.

---

[37] N. Autton, *Pastoral Care in Hospital* (London, 1968) p. 1.

[38] Ibid., p. 115.

[39] M. Wilson, *The Hospital – A Place of Truth* (Birmingham, 1971) p. iii.

Pilot questionnaires led to the development of a number of surveys designed to acquire data on the role of chaplains. In addition to insights gained at national and international conferences, Wilson used semi-structured interviews and questionnaires to gather views from house officers, nursing staff, ward sisters, ward clerks patients and, of course, chaplains. The nature of the questions, perhaps reflecting the breadth of the working group directing the study, are extensive and pertinent. We find questions on the source of the chaplain's sense of authority, differences in visiting styles, variations in the emphases within a chaplain's work, and analysis of the patients' views about what a chaplain is for.

Wilson's study was unprecedented in its carefully focused and multi-angled examination of the chaplain's role. In his introduction, Wilson noted that the study as a whole was chiefly confined to hospitals in the large conurbations of the Midlands. But the most important thing to consider in evaluating Wilson's work is the theological and ecclesiastical framework through which he views the chaplain. This is made clear right at the start of the study:

> Before the role of the hospital chaplain can be discussed, the work of the Church as a community must be explored to find its rightful place in the whole task. And before the specific task of the Church in the hospital can be discussed some attempt must be made to understand the primary task of the hospital in society.[40]

In other words, this is far from an inductive enquiry. Theories of both Church and hospital are established *before* the data is discussed in any depth. In a series of essays (such as 'The Meaning of Health'), key ideological frames are considered with little reference to the material gathered from interviews and questionnaires. At the same time, these essays are interwoven with biblical references and theological assumptions without prior consideration of the hermeneutical techniques being applied. This inevitably leaves the feeling that no rationale has been given to why some texts are more relevant than others, or what theological ideas lie below the surface of what is emerging. This is the main point of criticism for a project that asked serious questions about chaplains for the first time in their history.

As with the writings of Autton, Wilson articulates the chaplain's role as biblically based and sacramentally expressed.[41] It is argued that hospitals are communities being weakened by all kinds of change and medical advances, and that the chaplain can play a key part if he is 'himself'. For this reason, time and again, the significance of the chaplain is seen to rest in his personal qualities and how he relates to both patients and staff in the hospital.[42]

---

[40]   Ibid.
[41]   Ibid., p. 55.
[42]   Ibid., p. 62.

Wilson's work concludes with eighteen proposals about the future shape and support for hospital chaplains.[43] In these proposals, he makes a notable distinction between a community-based chaplaincy to wards (local clergy and laity visiting an agreed area) and a whole-time chaplain or chaplains serving the institution. The latter would become more involved in teaching, training, research and staff support than had traditionally been expected from the chaplain. Such a role would also open up all posts to applications from across the Christian denominations, rather than limiting them by the demographics of in-patient religion.

The report as a whole makes an invaluable contribution to the debate about chaplains and their function in a way not previously attempted. It reveals that patients evaluate chaplains 'by non-professional criteria, meaning non-clerical and non-hospital criteria'.[44] At the same time, this has the effect of making the chaplain's work (apart from its sacramental aspects) 'common property'. The chaplain is distinct from other hospital staff because he 'has no manipulative skills' but rather:

> ... helping people to find purpose, meaning and value in their lives and relationships ... . He must know how to work with people and elicit their response in the realms of wonder, trust, forgiveness, love, justice and human dignity.[45]

The study demonstrates time and again Wilson's central preoccupation that the chaplain is effective only when he properly grasps his role as 'a man of faith in God'. When this is understood, the chaplain can play his part in the hospital's purpose as a community of carers and cared-for: the 'realisation of their humanity in unity'.[46] Wilson locates the work of chaplaincy within an incarnational understanding of the mission of the Church (chiefly the Church of England) underpinned by concepts of wholeness and restoration. It is this theological outlook that informs his research.

In conclusion, Wilson's work does much to describe the place of the chaplain at the beginning of the 1970s. It bears the unspoken assumptions of its period, with a lack of consideration for gender and faith diversity. Although he notes that the first appointment of a part-time Muslim chaplain occurred in 1970, there is no conception of how this small beginning might grow to impact on chaplaincy as a whole. The world of chaplains in this study is still white, male and Christian. Indeed, going back to the earlier quotation, the chaplain's role is inextricably attached to the 'specific task of the Church in the hospital'. Today there is surprisingly little discussion of the chaplain in these terms. Despite these limitations, the following aspects of his study are of particular relevance:

---

[43]   Ibid., pp. 150–51.
[44]   Ibid., p. 102.
[45]   Ibid., p. 104.
[46]   Ibid., p. 103.

- the tensions identified around the chaplain's sense of authorization have, if anything, become more acute and pressing in recent years;
- Wilson's strong emphasis on the chaplain's non-professional characteristics, supported by his research, is of note in the debate about professionalization;
- the significance of the chaplain's personality and personal qualities, over and against technical skills, demonstrated the degree to which his ability to act within the hospital was more akin to a vicar than a health professional;
- following on from the above, the references to the chaplain's missionary purpose – 'helping people' and eliciting their 'response' – indicate a set of behaviours and priorities embedded in the chaplain's innocent 'presence';
- out of eight images offered of a chaplain whom they had met, over 92 per cent of patients stated that they saw him as 'a friend'. This was the highest score across all four categories of patients interviewed.

These five points will be referred to later and helpfully begin to lift into view deeply inscribed patterns of behaviour and activity that can bear various kinds of interpretation. The purpose now is to note that Wilson's work was in many respects soundly structured and well directed, and provides the earliest attempt to define in detail the role of a hospital chaplain. Indeed, the most recent review of research about chaplains describes Wilson's work as a 'seminal text' that raised 'crucial and abiding questions about hospital chaplaincy'.[47]

Towards the end of the NHS's first 50 years, a further study of note was published, dealing with the Church of England's relationship to other faiths. Part of this is worthy of consideration here because it raises concerns that became of increasing importance once New Labour came into power.

> There were clear signs in chaplaincies that rapid changes had already taken place and/or that they might be imminent … . The idea that a turning-point or crisis had been reached was common in prison chaplaincies … . Health care chaplains and representatives of other faiths seemed to be more excited than dismayed by the pace of events which had certainly caused difficulties throughout the NHS but which had also opened up fresh opportunities for religious and pastoral care.[48]

This report arises from research carried out by Beckford and Gilliat at the University of Warwick into the Church of England and its relation with other faiths in prisons, universities, hospitals and civic life. It was a major project that resulted in a number of books – although the health care chaplaincy section in Volume II

---

[47] H. Mowat, *The potential for efficacy of healthcare chaplaincy and spiritual care provision in the NHS (UK)* (Aberdeen, 2008) p. 12.

[48] J.A. Beckford and S. Gilliat, *The Church of England and Other Faiths in a Multi-Faith Society* (Warwick, 1996) p. 512.

remains unpublished. The data for the research came both from 109 completed questionnaires and a smaller number of site visits by the researchers.

Beckford and Gilliat's perspective is carefully focused: they are interested in Church of England chaplains and their relationship to other faiths. Their questions are therefore about multi-faith aspects of chaplaincy training, experience of multi-faith working, attitudes to the inclusion of a broad range of faiths in chaplaincy, and facilities for 'other faiths'. A brief history of multi-faith publications and legislation concerning health care chaplaincy is also included.[49] Although limited in scope, the report is a valuable insight into the state of religious diversification in the NHS in 1996.

The key findings of this study can be identified as follows:

- Unlike civil religion, the NHS and other statutory providers constitute a major *incentive* to achieve change and greater inclusivity. However, there was still found to be a strong element of *paternalism* in the application of this,[50] with a distinction between inclusion *by right* and inclusion *by concession*;
- The researchers discovered a *wide range of practices* for both Christian chaplains facilitating multi-faith working and the attitude of Trusts in employing a broader range of chaplains;[51]
- Systems of allocating chaplaincy work by *proportionality* were seen to militate against local faith minorities – and the researchers argue for alternative criteria to be used to achieve the more effective meeting of religious needs;
- Beckford and Gilliat note the lack of central management bodies for some faiths – but also observe that faiths sometimes find it 'undesirable' to be represented by such a standardized (or standardizing) structure.

The issue of movement away from an almost wholly Christian chaplaincy to a new multi-faith philosophy of service is intimately connected with concepts of power. It also extends the range of staff involved in the spiritual governmentality of patients and reflects the operation through state institutions of political ideologies about the role of religion. In identifying the role of paternalism, Beckford and Gilliat have touched on the attempts by a dominant denomination to accommodate change while retaining status.

In any event, from the mid-1970s Orchard (2001) can identify only brief papers and articles (with the exception of Woodward's unpublished doctoral thesis) dealing directly with acute hospital chaplaincy. By and large, this was the position relating to published material about chaplains (whether written by individuals, the NHS or churches) until 1997. For what was to follow, the first fifty years of the

49 Ibid., pp. 225–30.
50 Ibid., p. 508.
51 Ibid., p. 332.

health service provided a valuable formative experience for chaplains. In these five decades, there is evidence for the first time of individuals grasping for the notion of a distinctive 'chaplaincy profession'. Sporadic writings, the merging of professional associations and early signs of collaborative research (King and Speck, 1995) are all evidence of a professionalization occurring on a number of levels but lacking the co-ordination needed to bring them into clearer focus.

Conclusion

This chapter has reminded us of the relationship between the political aspirations of health provision and the role of the chaplain. While the voluntary hospitals often began without the inclusion of a whole-time chaplain, most gradually moved over to this – not least because of the role of the chaplain in fundraising for these precarious institutions. In the workhouse, the chaplain was required to tend the sick and also instil a sense of moral purpose for both staff and inmates. In the organizations destined to become general hospitals, the chaplain was required to comment on the morality of those he encountered and provide some brief account of his activities. However, as we saw in the case of Pocock, the power of the religious establishment was capable of defending even the most indigent of its clergy from being disciplined by the secular authorities of the institution.

From an unassailable position of the chaplain as the bishop's 'man' in the hospital, the creation of the NHS marked the beginning of a steady shift in accountability. Perhaps the single most significant change brought about by the creation of the NHS was the huge decline in the influence of the Church in health provision. Without the need to raise funds, the boards of the infirmaries, workhouses and teaching hospitals quickly shed the number of clerical members sitting on their governing committees. At the same time the office-holder status and mentality of the chaplains was gradually eroded by a deeper inclusion in the pay structures and professional expectations of the health service. Nationalization slowly changed chaplains and the way in which they regarded themselves. The behaviour of an institutional chaplain like Pocock in the Victorian period became increasingly unacceptable in the new world where public money collectively funded chaplains across the UK. As we have seen, several chaplains took up the challenge and opportunities of the new service to write about their work as figures combining theological convictions with health care professionalism. In effect, the fact of the NHS became the single greatest influence in the development of chaplaincy – the idea that individual chaplains related to a shared body of knowledge, practice and professional standards. These developments in the provision of health care in the UK up to 1997 laid the foundations for the relative explosion in activity which was set to follow.

The Chapel at St James's Hospital in Leeds (with clock tower showing) was begun in 1858. A building readily identified within the city it is often the first image shown on local news reports from the site. Its tower formed the outline of the Trust logo prior to organizational change in 1998. It is built in the Byzantine style, seats 150 and may be unique in the NHS as a workhouse chapel that is still in use. Photographs by John Sherbourne.

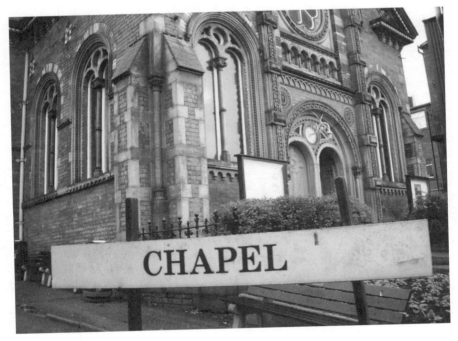

The Faith Centre in the Bexley Wing at St James's was opened 150 years after the main Chapel was begun. The main prayer room (pictured) sits alongside a quiet room; office; interview room, toilet for the disabled and a room with ablution facilities. The glass artwork is by Keiko Mukaide (see page 160). Photographs by John Sherbourne

Chapter 3
Chaplaincy under New Labour

Introduction

It would be misleading to suggest that the incoming Labour Government of 1997 had any specific plans relating to the development of health care chaplaincy. However, it has been noted that the new administration 'placed much greater emphasis than any predecessor Government in the modern era on religion, widely defined, as a form of social capital and on the role of faith communities'.[1] In the case of chaplaincy this requires a careful analysis to establish whether, and to what extent, the advent of New Labour stimulated change in chaplaincy. It is more likely that as the paymaster for chaplaincy, New Labour's Department of Health had an implicit influence on both the content and the form of appeals for funding and development. In this chapter attention will be given to the exponential growth in activity which characterized chaplaincy under the first ten years of New Labour. Contrasted with a history in which the Department of Health seemed largely oblivious to the existence of chaplains, the years crossing the Millennium offer a fascinating testimony to a belief in the power of the centre to engineer change even at the peripheries of the health service. New Labour's mantra of modernization – backed by the unprecedented election mandate of 1997 – ensured that change was swift and deep. Utilizing greater patient involvement as a moral counterbalance to the power of the professions New Labour opted for a pragmatic use of public and private capacity in order to provide 'a tax-funded, universal service offering comprehensive care in the pursuit of equity and social solidarity'.[2] The Government defined the framework for the regulated market that would deliver reform and improvement. If nothing else, this process of change witnessed 'wave after wave of policy documents and guidance' in the process of which 'new NHS agencies were born and died'.[3]

Impact on Chaplaincy

A running theme throughout the period in question concerns data protection. In 1998 the Data Protection Act came into force throughout the UK. Acting on an

---

[1] C.D. Field, 'Rendering unto Caesar', *Journal of Anglican Studies* 5/1(2007): 81–109.

[2] R. Klein, 'The new model NHS: performance, perceptions and expectations', *British Medical Bulletin* 81–2/39–50 (2007).

[3] Ibid., p. 42.

advice letter issued by the Chief Executive of the Hospital Chaplaincies Council many NHS Trusts ended the practice of routinely providing patients' religious information to chaplains. This impacted on chaplains in an uneven way, with Roman Catholic chaplains and smaller faith groups being most affected by the change due to their historic practice of visiting on the basis of a patient's declaration of religion. The Church of England was less affected as the large number of patients stating their religion as 'C of E' meant that the practice of Anglican chaplains had become largely referral led rather than list directed. Nevertheless, even for Anglican chaplains the change had the effect of distancing them from other health workers – and multi-disciplinary meetings – and the Church of England supported a small group of MPs who challenged the interpretation of the Data Commissioner. In an adjournment debate in 2002 the Parliamentary Secretary, Yvette Cooper MP, re-affirmed the restrictive interpretation of the Act and commented:

> Much wider questions about the definition of health professionals and the way in which they are classified arise. They cannot be answered purely in the context of data protection. In the first instance, they would have to be raised with the Department of Health and the Health Professions Council in terms of the nature of health professionals and the way in which hospital chaplains want to be regarded.[4]

The most prominent characteristic of chaplaincy under New Labour has been a wrestling with the question of just how much chaplains are, or ought to be, classed as health professionals. For some it is a pragmatic question about access to information and resources: for others it is a question about theological identity and ecclesiological belonging. Either way, the changing context in which chaplains work – which includes the legal framework of the NHS – has fed a vigorous debate about what it means to be a chaplain in the twenty-first century.

It should be acknowledged here that there are inherent problems with any study of a past which is so recent. It is difficult to discern at present what the lasting legacies of New Labour will be. At the same time I have been an actor in some of the events I shall be analysing. As President of the College of Health Care Chaplains from 2004–2007, I was involved in making decisions and contributed to debate directly. This is both an advantage and a limitation in writing this chapter, and I shall make every effort to encompass views that are different from my own.

The present chapter will set out a broad consideration of strategic changes to chaplaincy between 1997 and 2007 to be followed by a more detailed examination of the protracted 'critical incident' at Worcester (Chapter 4) and an ethnographic exploration of chaplaincy work (Chapter 5). Although the decision in Worcestershire to effectively end its chaplaincy arrangements began as a local decision it would come to be addressed by the Prime Minister and across a wide range of national media. Together it is intended that the three chapters will provide a comprehensive

---

[4]   Hansard, 25 Jun 2002: Column 220WH.

exploration of where chaplaincy has come to in the last ten years. Building on this analysis greater attention will be given to theological concerns in Chapter 7.

Earlier chapters have noted the tiny amount of research, debate and publication that has characterized – and conceivably maintained – chaplaincy's marginal status in both Church and NHS. By contrast, the years after 1997 have witnessed a steady growth in published material about chaplaincy. The origins of this work are diverse, but notable among the literature are a study by the King's Fund; Department of Health guidance documents; a revised Code of Conduct; and a number of books and journal articles. In what follows the key documents are summarized, and consideration is given to their strategic contribution and impact on professionalization.

Increasing Debate

A Study of the Role of the Acute Health Care Chaplain in England (1998)

Woodward's unpublished PhD thesis comes usefully at the beginning of the period covered by this chapter – and in the year that marked the fiftieth anniversary of the founding of the NHS. His research was designed to 'explore the world view and work of the acute health care chaplain'.[5]

At its centre is data gained through semi-structured interviews with fifteen whole-time acute hospital chaplains, all but two of whom were team leaders. These interviews are used to identify how chaplains themselves 'understand and manage their roles in health care'. His methods draw on the sociology of the professions and elements of qualitative research related to interviews and questionnaires.

The thesis builds on Wilson's work (1971) but is written in a very different context, and one in which Woodward sees growing tension. This is primarily experienced as an anxiety caused by the rapidly-increasing complexity of health care delivery as well as the clearer definition of roles allocated to other staff. In the midst of this, Woodward claims that 'chaplaincy is still in search of itself'. The faith communities to which the chaplain belongs may not grasp what is happening in health care – and the hospital itself can be puzzled about the exact nature of the chaplain's role. All this is drawn on in order to support Woodward's central thesis; that chaplains occupy a difficult but potentially fruitful 'in-betweenness'.[6] However, the thesis does not set out with any clarity how this largely metaphysical vision might be turned into some form of practical virtue or altered practice.

While Woodward senses the inevitability of greater professionalism in chaplaincy he does so with a degree of reluctance. The reader is told that there are 'dangers' in the professional approach, and that chaplains are largely reluctant

---

[5]   J. Woodward, *A Study of the Role of the Acute Health Care Chaplain in England* (1998), p. 13.

[6]   Ibid., p. 229.

to take on 'the role of saboteur, mole or whistle-blower' because they are in the pay of the institution. The final sentence in the thesis – 'Hospitals may well be poorer places without them *(chaplains)*' – is hardly a ringing endorsement of the profession or a strong indicator of occupational security.

Although the doctorate was awarded in 1998, it is fair to say that its insights and conclusions are drawn from the early 1990s. This was the era immediately before New Labour, and Woodward's work draws energy from the position of chaplaincy under late Thatcherite Conservatism. Included in the thesis is an analysis of a sermon delivered to the BMA by the Bishop of Birmingham in 1994. Here we find a strong critique of market forces in the NHS, and the call for a restoration of a 'service' ethos in health care. In a Britain polarized by opposing political convictions the Bishop calls for a 'shared understanding of purpose and culture' as the basis for policy development.

In the light of Labour's 1997 landslide, it would be reasonable to suggest that a significant majority of people responded to a new political vision. This gave Labour both an electoral and a moral mandate to direct change within British society. It was soon clear to chaplains and the rest of the population that the new government intended to use its authority to implement a radical agenda.

Hospital Chaplaincy: Modern, Dependable? (2000)

The title of Orchard's work draws on the Department of Health's publication in December 1997 of 'The new NHS: modern, dependable'. Among other topics the new White Paper stated that: 'Patients will be guaranteed national standards of excellence so that they can have confidence in the quality of the services they receive.' Orchard, who has a background in both NHS management and theology, was supported by investment from the King's Fund to research the performance of chaplaincies in London in the light of new Government expectations. Orchard's findings were effective and blunt. The chaplaincies she studied demonstrated that care was collectively capricious, revealing a lack of agreed operating standards and a bewildering range of service models. The ways in which the capital's chaplaincies differed from each other was not wholly accounted for by the nature of hospitals or – entirely – by denominational variety.

Helen Orchard's study into hospital chaplaincy in London is by far the most thorough and analytical enquiry into the chaplain's role and structure. As the title of the report suggests, the framework for the research was constructed with the latest NHS policy documents in mind. In addition to the main research question (above), the underlying thesis of the report might be summarized as: 'if chaplains are part of the NHS, and the NHS has standards and competencies, where do chaplains fit in?'

Although limited to London, the combination of questionnaires and case studies produces a picture of chaplaincy that can be recognized more widely. With a response rate from acute Trusts of over 80 per cent, the research has significant credibility. Well-established methods of randomization for the case studies were employed, enabling a representative sample of London Trusts to be selected. These studies focused on the views of chaplains as well as a range of other staff in a Trust. In all, 91 interviews were carried out in the case study sites.

Orchard describes a situation in which chaplaincy is 'poorly understood', 'vulnerable', and experiences 'marginalization'.[7] There is considerable doubt expressed in the research about the seriousness with which chaplaincy has taken the needs of minority faith groups. The study notes that there appears to have been a move in the focus of chaplaincy away from patients to other aspects of hospital activity. Perhaps what stands out most clearly in Orchard's work – and caused most uneasiness when the findings were published – is the *vagueness* of operation and disparity of practice between individual chaplaincy teams. This is set in stark contrast to the modernization of the NHS that aims at a consistent and dependable service throughout the UK.

The following points, made in Chapter 10 of Orchard's report, provide a useful summary of her main findings:

- Orchard identifies that the *focus* of chaplaincy has moved away from patients in part because the patient experience has changed (shorter stays).
- The report is effective in drawing attention to the inherent inequities arrived at by the quota system of appointing chaplains in relation to patient numbers.
- The evidence suggests that chaplains have been unreflective in prioritizing their work, with an over-emphasis in technical areas like intensive care.
- In the course of her work Orchard discerns a lack of serious management commitment to chaplaincy, with the result that it can appear to be peripheral.
- The question of professional development is raised in the report, including the need to demonstrate a role that is 'therapeutically effective, rather than simply edifying'.[8]

The distinctive flavour of the Orchard report lies in the author's own background in NHS management. The only other writers to take this approach either come to it *via* management as a senior chaplain or as someone with management experience who has left chaplaincy practice at some point in the past (e.g. Pattison). From this perspective, the report offers a view of chaplaincy measured against mainstream expectations for the provision of health care in London between April 1999 and October 2000.

---

[7]   Helen Orchard, *Hospital Chaplaincy Modern, Dependable?* (Sheffield, 2000) p. 9.
[8]   Ibid., p. 151.

NHS and Department of Health Guidance (2003)

On 5 November 2003, two employer documents were launched at an event in St Bartholomew's Hospital in London. The first was longest in gestation, and was the conclusion of the work begun at a multi-faith event, attended by the Secretary of State for Health, in 1998. It was unprecedented for such a senior Government figure to give a public face to chaplaincy in the NHS. Here we see evidence of the interest shown in the early days of New Labour in reaching out to the smaller faith communities present in the UK. The long tradition of Christian domination in chaplaincy appeared to be giving way to a broader and more inclusive stage of development. Frank Dobson had come to lend his support to the founding of a Department of Health working party to draft new chaplaincy guidance for the NHS. It was clear from the outset that a more inclusive and representative chaplaincy was at the heart of the ministerial involvement.

The second document launched in November 2003 was more recent in origin. *Caring for the Spirit* is a workforce strategy pioneered by one of the newly-created English NHS workforce development corporations (WDC). While WDCs were regional entities a number of them adopted national leads for specific areas of work. The chaplaincy brief was chosen by the South Yorkshire Workforce Confederation, and developed rapidly as a strategy for chaplains in the English health service. Whether as its instigator or enthusiastic promoter, Tim Battle, the Training Officer for the Hospital Chaplaincies Council, soon emerged as the strategy's Project Officer. There was strong support for the work from the Chief Executive of the WDC. Using his past experience as a senior manager in the NHS, Battle's capabilities soon had the project up and running. In what follows the key points from both documents will be summarized and evaluated in terms of explicit and implicit models of chaplaincy.

NHS Chaplaincy: Meeting the Spiritual Needs of Staff and Patients (2003)

This Department of Health guidance was the fruit of work begin in 1998 in the presence of the Secretary of State for Health. It represents a 'meeting of minds' between a government committed to greater social inclusion and chaplaincy bodies keen to harness political support for the security and development of chaplaincy as a whole. Writing the Foreword, the Chief Nurse for England described the context of the document as follows:

> The cornerstone of the modern NHS is the ability to respond sensitively to the diverse nature of the communities it serves; all services, including spiritual ones, should be delivered appropriately to service users and NHS staff. One of the key aims of this guidance is to enable chaplaincy services to meet the needs of today's multi-cultural and spiritually diverse society.

Perhaps what is most striking about the document is its title. In the past the Department of Health had spoken – if it spoke at all – about chaplains and chaplaincy 'in' the NHS.[9] There had persisted a sense of the semi-detached nature of chaplaincy, as something provided by the churches to the heath service. The new guidance broke that mould as it proclaimed itself to be concerned not with Catholic, Anglican or Jewish chaplaincy: but with 'NHS Chaplaincy'. The guidance effectively engineered a new framework for chaplaincy, and stated that the greatest element of identity was its common location in the health service – not any creedal or theological allegiance. In creating this new entity the Department of Health was effecting a change that had considerable benefits for management. The Chief Nurse concluded her introductory comments with the statement that the document would ensure that 'these services develop to their full potential and maximise their utility for all'.

The new guidance reflected shifts in the Government's approach to the NHS and the delivery of health services. There were to be fewer targets, greater local decision making and an altogether less 'hands-on' approach. Nevertheless, the way in which the document describes the work of chaplains both reflects and consolidates a governmental approach to spirituality in the public sector. Although it claims to make no 'theological or doctrinal definitions' this reflects a narrow understanding of both doctrine and theology. In fact the document implicitly makes what is perhaps one of the boldest State claims about the nature of spirituality in modern Britain. Chaplains are to 'deliver services' which meet needs, and where the service as a whole is for the 'utility of all'. In other words, chaplaincy is to be managed and applied within the same concept of personhood and society used by the State wherever it has authority over institutions. Those who seek the service are consumers of faith-based products, and chaplaincy must therefore be branded and graded according to a centrally determined set of standards.

Caring for the Spirit (2003)

Issued on the same day as *NHS Chaplaincy*, *Caring for the Spirit* describes a ten-year development plan for the chaplaincy and spiritual care workforce. This document is not only aimed at chaplains, but at all those who – at least in part – have duties falling under the broad heading of spiritual care. More than any other previous NHS publication *Caring for the Spirit* locates spiritual care and chaplaincy in a developed management model.

This is most clearly seen in the outline for a 'practice model' to be used in guiding the way chaplains work. Here the action of sharing Holy Communion with a patient is divided into the elements of assessment, care planning, care delivery and review. It would be simplistic to suggest that this is only the re-packaging of religious activity into the language of management. There are important and

---

9   This can also be seen in J.G. Cox's (*A Priest's Work in Hospital* (London, 1955)) way of discussing the chaplain's work.

largely implicit values in the process of meeting spiritual needs as described by *Caring for the Spirit*. In another example cited in the guidance, a pastoral encounter is described concerning an elderly patient who is 'struggling to accept that she will need to live in a nursing home'. The chaplain assesses the situation, identifying issues of 'loss and social dislocation'. This then leads to the chaplain creating a plan to facilitate the patient's faith practices, working with other staff the achieve this, and finally referring her to the local minister when she is discharged to the home.

There is a strong implication in *Caring for the Spirit* that the chaplain should develop a role as the expert who possesses unique goods which can be delivered to those in need. In this scenario spirituality is like any other aspect of the health care environment, where qualified experts manage the patient's acceptance of the skills they offer. This is a very particular, and by no means universal, understanding of religion. It does not lay strong emphasis on the idea that the patient is an equal in the world of spirituality, and that the primary need for a chaplain for either communion or pastoral support is to be the 'other' necessary in order to constitute a community in which the patient can express their faith. That faith may include convictions about the nature of health, life, sin and love which are not accommodated in other aspects of health care. At various points in their history chaplains have noted concern when spiritual acts have come to be overly expressed in therapeutic terms.[10] Without their sacrificial and eschatological significance the whole purpose of the Christian sacraments become obscured. They concern the purposes of individual and corporate life, and express commitments that are not bounded solely by the extent of physical mortality.

The general assumptions of this approach may be described as follows:

• The chaplain is an expert applying knowledge and skill to deliver actions that a patient is incapable of doing alone or with the aid of other staff
• Like any other procedure the service is time-tabled and 'administered'
• Needs continue to be monitored; and changing needs are to be met.

The reader is introduced to five levels of chaplain, from 'trainee' to 'consultant'. The grading of chaplains is done with reference to knowledge, skills and behaviours. Without doubt a medical rather than theological criteria is being applied to chaplaincy structures, and the document envisages a spiritual care 'expert', the consultant, who will have demonstrably advanced skills and knowledge in patient care. It is a model that is strikingly different from the way in which progress and development have been modelled in the ecclesiastical world.

Without doubt, *Caring for the Spirit* provided a focus and energy for the employer-led professional development of chaplaincy. Numerous papers have been spawned by the strategy, including advice on a 'minimum data set for spiritual healthcare' and guidance for establishing local chaplaincy collaboratives. Much of the underpinning work involved in these activities has come from

---

10   Cox (London, 1955) p. 23.

the appointment of four lead chaplains in England. Recruited from existing chaplaincy posts, what the *Health Service Journal* described as the four 'super chaplains' were attached around the country to local Strategic Health Authorities. Together they supported the work outlined in the strategy for the completion of twenty milestones between 2003 and 2007. However, these developments have not always enjoyed the support of chaplaincy bodies, none of which were invited to join the original group designing the strategy. As a result the *Caring for the Spirit* process has sometimes been perceived to be a coercive force operating upon chaplains rather than with them.

Caring for the Spirit raises questions about the identity of chaplains, the nature of spiritual care and its purpose within health care. The strategy describes its production as a response to the fact that the 'chaplaincy and spiritual healthcare workforce needs support in modernizing to match the changes in healthcare and in spirituality within the UK'. In a single sentence, and without further elaboration, the ideology of modernization and the subject of changes in national spirituality are cited as the motivation for the project. Affirming the distinctive beliefs of individual chaplains the strategy argues that a main plank of modernization must be an increased pace in faith diversification within chaplaincies. Yet the document fails to include, or to reference, any significant body of work that supports its beliefs about change or its conceptualization of spiritual health care. A brief section quotes one theoretical model of spiritual care by David Lyall, but the only indication of a systematic study of available literature is in a 'milestone' set for work that will follow the publication of the strategy.

Academic and Health Care Titles

In the same year as Woodward's PhD thesis was submitted. Cobb and Robshaw published *The Spiritual Challenge of Health Care.*[11] Between 1998 and 2007, six significant chaplaincy/spiritual care titles appeared, marking a new pulse in professional debate. Some titles were produced jointly by chaplains and other health care staff, and this in itself suggests an appetite for inter-disciplinary engagement that was not widely evident before the late 1990s. The one notable exception was the collaboration between Peter Speck and King. Speck's work enjoys a 'classic' status in chaplaincy literature, but it has been criticized for too strongly favouring medical models of illness and healing.

The trajectory of literature in this period suggests a path away from theology and towards 'spirituality'. Nurses in particular, perhaps identifying a need to re-emphasize their caring role alongside a rising technical status, developed a stronger interest in spiritual care. Much of this work recognizes the chaplain as a valuable colleague, while at the same time tending to associate the chaplain with more specific religious functions. A few chaplains have engaged with the issues

---

[11] M. Cobb and V. Robshaw, *The spiritual challenge of health care* (Edinburgh and New York, 1998).

of spiritual care within health care publications,[12] but the work is tiny compared with that authored by nurses and midwives. The general perspective of the nursing literature has been the contribution that spirituality makes to patient well-being. However, research supports the view that most nurses are ill equipped to assess spiritual needs, or to act in support of needs when they are identified.[13] The aspects of spirituality with which nursing literature is most clearly concerned include holistic therapy and personal dignity, with the nurse seen as the member of staff best placed to provide spiritual care.[14] The work of nurses in this area is inevitably tempered by the context of health care literature. Spirituality is addressed in a manner akin to other health care practices, and philosophical considerations are limited. A notable exception is a paper by Neil Henery.[15] Henery uses discourse analysis to examine the construction of spirituality as an attribute of the patient. This leads to a critique of the nursing literature in which 'spirituality' is shown to lie in an uncertain territory between scientific and religious discourse. There is concern that a pseudo-scientific approach to spirituality is 'smuggling in' various unacknowledged value statements in the guise of a non-judgemental universalism. This rare approach within nursing literature is more strongly argued elsewhere in the work of Carrette and King,[16] and Stephen Pattison.[17] In all these works there is the suggestion that spirituality within health care is becoming a form of sanitized religious discourse where prophetic and institutional critiques have been discarded.

If nothing else, the papers demonstrate one of the central tensions in the location of spiritual care in the health service. It is predicated on the idea that all manner of activity, encounter and exchange in health care can be analysed effectively in a clinical manner. And with this goes the implicit threat that anything incapable of being subject to such an approach is ultimately irrelevant. If it isn't health care why fund it: if it is health care then it must generate evidence in the discipline of

[12] C.P. Johnson, 'Assessment tools: are they an effective approach to implementing spiritual health care within the NHS?', *Accident & Emergency Nursing* 9/3 (2001): 177–86.

[13] L. Ross, 'The nurse's role in assessing and responding to patients' spiritual needs', *International Journal of Palliative Nursing* 3/1 (1997): 37–42. W. McSherry and L. Ross, 'Dilemmas of spiritual assessment: considerations for nursing practice', *Journal of Advanced Nursing* 38/5 (2002): 479–88.

[14] W. McSherry, 'Spiritual crisis? Call a nurse', in H. Orchard (ed.), *Spirituality in Health Care Contexts* (London, 2001).

[15] N. Henery, 'Constructions of spirituality in contemporary nursing theory', *Journal of Advanced Nursing* 42/6 (2003): 550–57.

[16] J.R. Carrette and R. King, *Selling spirituality: the silent takeover of religion* (London, 2004).

[17] S. Pattison, 'Dumbing down the spirit', in H. Orchard (ed.), *Spirituality in Health Care Contexts* (London, 2001).

science or, at the very least, in the discourse of scientifically-related disciplines such as psychology.

Nurse researchers have understandably developed their interest in spirituality in the language and practices of science. It is science and the increasingly technical aspects of care that have helped advance nurses' professional claims ever since 1948. It follows that while much of the published research can be both interesting and helpful it is at best a very partial account of spirituality and spiritual care. There may even be a fear amongst nurse academics that metaphysical language is dangerous because it potentially links 'professional people' to ideas that by their nature appear unscientific. The papers produced under the decade of New Labour are conspicuously silent about God – except as a facet of an individual's spiritual expression. Readers are in no doubt that faith is a cultural artefact, a personal matter to be respected and managed for the betterment of health. By and large this approach minimizes or leaves to silence issues of faith that stretch beyond the individual, and are to some extent embedded in the framework of the NHS (such as the aspiration to care for all equally). For this reason the nursing literature is symptomatic of broader views about spiritual care that have become increasingly influential in recent years. As the volume of literature has grown so too have the voices of caution and criticism. For John Paley:

> nurses and chaplains have a shared agenda: to stretch the definition of 'spirituality' well beyond its anchorage in formal religion, to vindicate the claim that 'spiritual needs' are universal.[18]

We shall return to this issue in detail in Chapter 6, but it is important to note here that spiritual care may well constitute an aspirant discipline: just another post-Enlightenment construction designed to protect or extend professional boundaries.

Professional Associations

Just a year before New Labour came to power, the College of Health Care Chaplains had voted for a transfer of instruments to the trade union MSF. This had been a contentious issue for some chaplains but arose from an awareness that an independent body with just 1,000 members (albeit affiliated to the TUC) simply could not provide the professional employment support its members required. Chaplains in England and Wales are employed directly by the NHS which means that issues of pay and representation occur outside the faith communities. While membership has fluctuated in the past decade it has remained around the one thousand mark, with a significant minority of members working in the mental

---

[18] J. Paley, 'Spirituality and secularization: nursing and the sociology of religion', *Journal of Clinical Nursing* 17/2 (2008): 175–86.

health sector. In addition to union representation College members receive a journal twice a year, have a website, and gain professional updates either through newsletters or in correspondence from the CHCC President.

While CHCC represents chaplains across the UK and Northern Ireland its decision to become part of MSF had some ramifications in Scotland. In Scotland the health service paid the Church of Scotland in order to run a chaplaincy service throughout the country. Largely for this reason, linked with trends in Scotland towards greater independence, the decision by the College to go into MSF sparked the creation of the Scottish Association of Chaplains in Healthcare (SACH). This new association shared many of the aims of the College (collegial support; conferences; a journal) but lacked employer recognition as a negotiating body. In effect this meant that the College in MSF – which retained a small number of members in Scotland – was the only body able to negotiate with the health service north of the border on matters of pay as well as terms and conditions of employment. However, with all the impetus of secession and a stronger local identity SACH focused closely on issues of professional development and the improvement of competences.

A similar approach to that of SACH was taken by the Association of Hospice and Palliative Care Chaplains (AHPCC). This body represents chaplains who work chiefly in the charitable sector in independent hospices. Like the other two bodies AHPCC runs training events and conferences in order to promote the contribution of chaplains working in palliative care. While small in numbers AHPCC benefits from the collegiality of scale and runs an annual conference that is attended by a significant proportion of its membership.

Lastly, chaplains in Northern Ireland have their own body – which is probably the smallest in terms of numbers of all the UK associations. The Northern Ireland Healthcare Chaplains Association exists to support its members and advance the cause of health-care chaplaincy within Northern Ireland.

Between 1997 and 2007, these various associations have moved steadily closer together in developing shared goals and mechanisms for achieving a stronger professional identity. In 2004, the then president of CHCC instituted an annual meeting for the heads of SACH, AHPCC and the College. In 2007 the invitation was extended to include the NIHCA. At the same time an independent initiative to create a *Chaplaincy Academic and Accreditation Board* (CAAB) for the UK found support in all the UK professional associations. Set up as a body distinct from the associations CAAB nevertheless reported to the bodies and had a separate reference panel for its work. The membership of CAAB was drawn from across the UK and this has been one of its greatest strengths since its inception. Perhaps the most concrete sign of this new spirit of joint working came in the publication of a UK Code of Conduct for chaplains in 2005 (there had previously been separate codes for CHCC, AHPCC and SACH members). This was followed in 2007 by the production and distribution of over a thousand folders for recording continuing professional development to all the associations' members. The latter was an initiative by CAAB which had produced guidelines for CPD that had been accepted by all the professional bodies in the UK.

While the professional bodies have worked more closely together since 1997 it is important to note that this has in part been a response to the position of the Hospital Chaplaincies Council in England. For many years the HCC has represented the concerns of the Church of England (including the General Synod and Archbishops' Council) in all matters to do with hospital chaplaincy. The nexus of influence empowering the activities of the HCC relate to its position in the Established Church; its role in advising the Department of Health; the Chief Officer's commanding knowledge of personnel movement (through his management of an unpublished list of assessors for appointment interviews); extensive contact with entry level chaplains through training events; and the facilitation of the Multi-Faith Group for Healthcare Chaplaincy (the HCC Chief Executive is the MFGHC Chief Officer). In essence, prior to the growing capabilities of the professional bodies, the HCC officers orchestrated the activities of the various denominations and professional bodies in order to manage the provision and development of chaplaincy in England and, to a certain extent, in Wales. During the first decade of New Labour the HCC was able to marshal the new mood in Government to extend its influence in chaplaincy through a close association with the activities of the South Yorkshire Workforce Development Confederation. Early in the new millennium, as the professional associations sought to pursue the agenda of their members more fully, there was an inevitable clash of priorities between the HCC and – in particular – the College of Health Care Chaplains. As the HCC continued to provide a number of functions which in other areas of health care would be done by professional associations, differences arose which concerned the very nature of what it meant to be a health care chaplain. While the College and its partner organizations worked to establish a voluntary professional register in conjunction with a revised Code of Conduct,[19] this was clearly seen by the HCC as an encroachment into its jurisdiction. There emerged a fundamental disagreement about the identity of the chaplain as either a) a faith-mandated representative figure solely accountable (barring employer requirements) for their professional practice to the faith community (HCC etc.) or b) a health professional working within collegially defined professional standards for all faiths while holding a valid mandate from their own faith community (AHPCC/CHCC/SACH). If a) was the prevailing view of everyone concerned there would be little point in the professional associations existing in any other form other than as 'fellowship' bodies and as organizers of occasional training. However, on various occasions the CHCC has tested the views of its members through questionnaire surveys

---

[19] The joint Code of Conduct emerged from a review of the codes previously held separately by each professional body. The Revd Mark Cobb edited the new Code, and members of all the chaplaincy organizations were consulted on the document. While making some special considerations of the chaplain's role the format is similar to that of other health professions.

and, each time, the members showed an overwhelming desire to achieve stronger recognition as a health profession. In 1999, just 52 per cent of members wished to see professional registration for chaplains but in 2004 the figure had risen to 95 per cent.[20] Not surprisingly, these ontological disagreements about the nature of the chaplain have bemused the NHS, which has largely opted to work with the HCC without looking too deeply into what interests are being served or how chaplaincy is best developed for the future.

Recent research may help in understanding some of the deep and often hidden dynamics that operate in the Church of England in its relationship to chaplains. The findings of a survey conducted in 2007[21] revealed significance evidence that many Church of England chaplains are alienated from the Church as an institution. Over 20 per cent of male respondents stated that they were in a same-sex relationship and 27 per cent of the whole group were clergy married or in partnership with another ordained person. Overwhelmingly liberal, and decidedly high church, the chaplains shared a common experience of being 'refugees' from the institutional (and hierarchical) Church. Many had enjoyed good experiences in parishes, but they found the tone and direction of the Church to be at odds with their theological convictions and pastoral priorities. While only 25 per cent had felt valued and supported when employed in the Church this figure rose to 75 per cent when it was asked about their health care employers. Perhaps it is not surprising that a group of clergy which sees itself as largely disadvantaged by the churches' exemption from employment law (regarding equality) should be doubtful about the wisdom of leaving the fate of chaplaincy in the hands of the institution about which they feel so ambivalent.

Multi-Faith Development

In 1998, as the Hospital Chaplaincies Council of the Church of England worked to meet the agenda brought in by New Labour, a multi-faith conference was convened at London Colney in Hertfordshire and attended by the then Secretary of State for Health, Frank Dobson. This set in train work towards the production of the 2003 guidance *NHS Chaplaincy: Meeting the Spiritual Needs of Staff and Patients* discussed above. A multi-faith working party emerged from the meeting at London Colney and this became – following the production of the guidance – the Multi-Faith Group for Healthcare Chaplaincy. The purpose of the group was to develop multi-faith working and, in particular, co-ordinate those activities required to ensure smaller UK faith communities had the training and opportunity to become involved in chaplaincy. Given the lack of funding for the Group itself the HCC continues to provide its administrative support. Furthermore, as the

---

[20]   College of Health Care Chaplains, *Questionnaire Newsletter* (London, 2005).
[21]   G. Hancocks, J. Sherbourne and C. Swift, 'Are they Refugees? Why Church of England male clergy enter health care chaplaincy', *Practical Theology* 1/2 (2008): 163–79.

Chief Officer for the Group is at the same time the Chief Executive of the HCC, there is a very close identification between the agenda of the two organizations. Given that the Chair of the Group changes every two years while the Chief Officer appears to be in post for an indefinite period, the focus of influence and experience appears to reside at the executive level rather than with those who chair it. While wholly understandable in terms of fledgling organizations and finite resources the facilitation of the Group by the HCC inevitably relates to the politics of chaplaincy in England. This is a sensitive subject, as I discovered when the following was published:

> While professional associations for chaplains were once welcomed and promoted by churches as fellowship organisations, they were only permitted a strategic role in the development of chaplaincy by patronage and invitation. It was only a matter of time before the political identity of these organisations would strengthen to such an extent that continued influence on development in the NHS by church bodies would be challenged. The inception of the Multi-Faith Group can in this light be seen as an attempt to retain authority for chaplaincy through faith leadership, and re-assert the model of chaplain involvement via patronage. There is ample evidence that the English Multi-Faith Group is built to a significant degree on Anglican foundations – and this inevitably gives a certain shape to what is being constructed.[22]

The HCC characterizes its role in the creation of the Group as one of facilitation, assistance and a living out of its social mandate as the Established Church. This kind of public discourse has been questioned in research undertaken Beckford and Gilliat who note that the NHS and other statutory providers constitute a major incentive to achieve change and greater inclusivity within society. However, they still found a strong element of *paternalism* in the way the Church of England assisted these developments in public bodies,[23] and noted the significant distinction between inclusion *by right* and inclusion *by concession*. So long as the HCC underpins the Multi-Faith Group it is likely that the progress of the Group to develop an independent agenda will be severely curtailed. In her analysis of inclusion within the planning of the faith zone in the Millennium Dome, Gilliat-Ray[24] identifies a particular dynamic linking New Labour, established religion and the exclusion of informal spiritualities and small faith groups. What began as the 'Spirit Level' evolved into the *faith zone* as the Lambeth Group consolidated its

---

[22]   C. Swift, 'The Political Awakening of Contemporary Chaplaincy', *Journal of Health Care Chaplaincy* 7/1 (2006): 57–62.

[23]   J.A. Beckford and S. Gilliat, *The Church of England and Other Faiths in a Multi-Faith Society* (Warwick, 1996) p. 508.

[24]   S. Gilliat-Ray, '"Sacralising" Sacred Space in Public Institutions: A Case Study of the Prayer Space at the Millennium Dome', *Journal of Contemporary Religion* 20/3 (2005): 357–72.

advisory role and ensured that the group's membership was restricted to 'the likely lads'.[25] This meant a certain conformity to the government's implicit views about inclusion, such as faiths having a representative structure – even if that structure was in many ways exclusive e.g., the experience of women being largely ignored. If religious groups follow the carrot of funding and influence then they do so at the price of accepting the government's view of their place and role in society. In effect religions are encouraged to conceal their messiness, complexity and inner diversities in order to gain resources and status. Just as university students have become more biddable under the burden of loans so too many faith groups have readily adopted the language of inclusion, partnership, cohesion and social capital in order to access grants. This approach is achieved at the price of ignoring private, individual and unofficial expressions of spirituality. Gilliat-Ray's field work in the Dome revealed that many members of the public felt estranged from the faith zone where 'at least some didn't see content which reflected themselves and their own paths. They saw other people's certainties and convictions.' As we shall see later, the utilization of rhetoric that conforms with government ideology has been a strategic tool for the Hospital Chaplaincies Council. However, the reality beneath the surface of this discourse has preserved the influence of Anglican religious provision and views in the NHS.

Research published in 2004 found the majority of chaplaincy and worship space to be overwhelmingly Christian in character. Following a survey of 72 health care providers Sheikh and others[26] headed their article 'The myth of multifaith chaplaincy'. The researchers found the number of posts held by chaplains of faiths other than Christian to be severely limited – the one exception being in Muslim chaplaincy. At the same time they conducted a study of patient and staff experience of the quality of care measured by ten-point Lickert scales. This found a lower standard of experience for those of faiths other than Islam and Christianity. These findings raise a number of issues, not least whether (and to what extent) Christian chaplains are simply ministering to Christian patients or are in fact spending much of their time ministering to those without any definitive religious affiliation. This makes the use of census data and other statistics highly problematic in this discussion. In part the researchers acknowledge this by calling for future research to 'explore issues to do with the care of denominations within these faith groups, because there may be particular needs that are overlooked using a broad-brush approach to canvassing religious affiliation'.[27] Yet this still focuses research onto religion without a proper appreciation of contemporary secularity and the complex reality of spiritual identification for many people.

---

[25]   Ibid., p. 466.

[26]   A. Sheikh and others, 'The myth of multifaith chaplaincy: a national survey of hospital chaplaincy departments in England and Wales', *Diversity in Health and Social Care* 1/2 (2004): 93–8.

[27]   Ibid., p. 95.

The reality within NHS Trusts is that scant resources can often only be stretched to accommodate faith diversification in chaplaincy if existing provision is changed. In other words, resources to finance a Sikh or Hindu chaplain would need to come from resources previously allocated for Christian chaplains. In the language of the NHS this would come about through a review of the 'skill mix' to see whether the current arrangements made best use of the resources, or if needs had changed in such a way that alterations were required in either staff composition or staff working patterns. However, this process does not take place in a vacuum and may create significant difficulty partly because it can be resisted within the local faith communities, and the community more widely, as a 'de-Christianizing' of what is provided.[28] As many chaplaincies are already operating below their per capita staffing level for Christian chaplains it can make the suggestion of cuts operationally difficult. For example, most chaplains in the acute sector will carry out funerals on behalf of the hospital in circumstances where there is either no next-of-kin or where such relatives are unable to afford the funeral costs. Many of these will be identified as having a connection with the Christian faith, and a Christian chaplain will conduct the ceremony at no additional cost to the hospital. In some trusts this will be well in excess of 100 services each year. The number of requests for hospital funerals from other faiths has not been systematically studied although, from conversations with chaplains, the figures are believed to be very small. This is not an argument that where provision is high demand follows suit because chaplains seldom conduct the funerals of those who have clear church affiliations. In other words, chaplains are by and large conducting funerals for members of the general population whose religious identification may be very nominal in terms of practice and where there is no association with a given church. The relationship of Christian chaplains with those whose faith is of a fragmentary nature will be discussed in Chapter 6 when the whole issue of secularization will be raised.

Multi-Faith chaplaincy has been a slogan for change in spiritual care under New Labour but its impact on the ground has been limited. Orchard[29] notes the disadvantage caused to smaller faith groups by the calculation of chaplaincy provision based on absolute numbers of patients by faith in each hospital. In effect this means that in isolation many Trusts will not achieve the mass to warrant an appointment even if, regionally and nationally, the faith community is numerically significant. It must remain a matter of concern and future monitoring that the group which steered the production of the 2003 guidance (and became the Multi-Faith Group) is facilitated by the denomination with most to gain from the quota system that the guidance advocates: the Church of England.

---

28   H.T. Engelhardt Jr, 'The Dechristianization of Christian Hospital Chaplaincy: Some Bioethics Reflections on Professionalization, Ecumenization, and Secularization', *Christian Bioethics* 9/1(2003): 139–60.

29   Orchard (Sheffield, 2000).

Chaplains & Theologians

Not many chaplains have published work over this ten-year period. In the UK the flagship publication has been the *Scottish Journal of Health Care Chaplaincy*, launched in 1997, closely followed by the College of Health Care Chaplains' older *Journal of Health Care Chaplaincy*. To some extent, both of these journals have worked to foster a culture of research and writing more sympathetic to the ethos of those whose academic training is chiefly drawn from the humanities. While other journals may have struggled to accommodate papers that so openly expressed basic questions about the role and nature of the chaplain, the professions' own journals reflect a wide spectrum of opinion and research. The decision by the CHCC *Journal of Health Care Chaplaincy* to include poetry that has emerged from, or is pertinent to, spiritual care illustrates a desire to embrace the breadth of experience and approaches shared among chaplains. It is important to note that a minority of contributions have come from disciplines outside chaplaincy. Some have been from other health care professions and some from academic theologians. This eclecticism makes for a stimulating range of material in relation to spirituality and care, but is indicative of a subject that resists the application of focused definitions. The submission of papers with titles along the lines of, 'what is spirituality?', has waned as the discussion became increasingly repetitive – and the outcomes remained stubbornly inconclusive. On the whole this has been taken as an indication of a professional impasse that must ultimately be overcome. An equally valid reflection would be that the ambiguity arises from the nature of spirituality, and that academic and professional reductionism will never be able to convey very much about the experience of what people define as spiritual.

Perhaps the most significant current writer, able to draw on the experience of having been a chaplain, is Stephen Pattison. In Orchard's edited volume, Pattison makes a cogent critique of spiritual 'drift', and the dangers of 'dumbing down the spirit'.[30] In addressing the specific role of the chaplain, Pattison issues a call for a more considered engagement with theological roots and resources. An NHS whose birth was influenced by Christian values continues to be open to traditions that share some of its basic ideals. It is right that Christian chaplains are cautious about making reactionary claims to influence in health care, but this should not lead them to disown their heritage. There is an implicit agreement here with Henery, who draws on Touraine[31] to argue that a critique of modernism's failings should not be used as an excuse to return to the kind of pre-modern religious authority we saw exercised in the hospital in Chapter 1.

Although as yet unpublished, the Leeds-based theologian Jacqui Stewart has made a useful contribution to the debate about spiritual care. A professional theological, Stewart analyses the current climate in chaplaincy, and the influences

---

[30]   Stephen Pattison, 'Dumbing down the Spirit', in H. Orchard (ed.), *Spirituality in Health Care Contexts* (London, 2001), pp. 33–46.

[31]   A. Touraine and D. Macey, *Critique of Modernity* (Oxford, 1995).

that appear to have produced the new NHS guidance, by bringing it into critical relationship with Christian protestant theology. Reflecting on much of the nursing literature Stewart takes to task the very idea that spiritual care can be 'delivered':

> I shall argue that the majority of this new literature is seriously flawed. It concentrates on an understanding of spirituality as personal, not communal; as static rather than dynamic and as objectifiable commodity rather than unmanipulated free gift. I will contend that it is subject to serious philosophical and theological critiques.[32]

It is possible to find in Stewart's work a form of analysis that has an affinity with the postmodern rebuttal of modernity. Profoundly different in other respects, Stewart nevertheless shares the conviction that epistemological claims are implicitly provisional because of the Christian conviction that the human ability to truly 'know' and appraise all aspects of a situation is affected by our fallen nature. Most alarmingly Stewart argues that spirituality 'is being wheeled out by the health service as an agent for manipulation of people, although it is perceived to be in their interests'. Following the writings of Bonhoeffer, Stewart states that the role of chaplaincy should be to affirm and support what *cannot* be said, rather than attempt to manufacture and manage various kinds of therapeutic intervention.

While there are a number of writers who raise concerns about the ability to fashion spirituality into another health care activity, others have embraced the notion and lent it their support. Robinson, Kendrick and Brown[33] combined their nursing and theological experience to produce a title firmly angled at a health-care audience. Here we find an approach similar to many of the articles to be found in nursing journals, where spirituality is seen as part of – or the epitome of – holistic care. The book addresses the role of the chaplain and rejects Pattison's concerns about 'dumbing down the spirit'. However, the authors have not fully grasped the extent of the grounds for concern about spiritual care. They write of the chaplain's 'enabling role' without any discussion of the potentially manipulative effects of some enablement.

Overall, the academic and professional contributions in this period reflect fundamental debates about the nature and role of spiritual care within the twenty-first-century health service. This will be addressed further in Chapter 7. It is sufficient to say here that the changes witnessed in chaplaincy under New Labour generated theological responses – albeit that the critiques have been reticent (or unable) to suggest in any detail what the alternative visions of a viable contemporary chaplaincy might be.

---

[32]   J. Stewart, *Theological Considerations in Chaplaincy Development: Humanity. Modernity and Postmodernity*, conference paper (Leeds, 2003).

[33]   S. Robinson, K. Kendrick and A. Brown, *Spirituality and the practice of healthcare* (Basingstoke, 2003).

Continuing Professional Development

In 1998, for the first time, a British university offered an MA course in healthcare chaplaincy. The most striking thing about this course was its location, not in theology, but in a department of health care studies. Until the course folded in 2005, it produced over fifty graduates. A range of factors influenced the decision to end the course, including a declining number of applicants and staff changes. However, other master's level courses were becoming available, some in chaplaincy specific areas and others in practical theology. Most notable among these is the MTh offered at the University of Wales in Cardiff, which in 2008 came to constitute part of the newly launched Chaplaincy Studies Centre at the Anglican theological college in Llandaff. Without doubt a growing number of chaplains were accessing academic courses in areas relevant to their work, and the fruit of some of these studies is finding its way into the professional journals.

One of the chief goals of the professional associations has been to encourage and regulate chaplains' continuing professional development. While a number of bodies have long provided training events and courses few if any of these enjoyed academic status, and there has been no review of the relative value of the various courses on offer. In working to develop a proper system of continuing professional development (CPD) the professional bodies were responding to much clearer CPD requirements in the NHS as a whole. The introduction of the Knowledge and Skills Framework (KSF) in 2004 was linked to a development review process intended for all NHS staff. Not only were chaplains required to demonstrate basic competencies, but they were also expected to engage in continuous professional development. In an attempt to establish the culture of reflection and appraisal more effectively the professional bodies were successful in gaining Unite funding for the printing and distribution of nearly 2,000 continuing professional development portfolios in 2006. Each pack included copies of the agreed advice about how to collate and use the portfolios for the purposes of annual appraisal and performance review. The work done to reach this stage was largely carried out by a new group spearheaded by the Revd Dr Derek Fraser.

In 2003, Fraser's vision of a joint accreditation body saw the three professional associations endorse a proposal to establish the Chaplaincy Academic and Accreditation Board (CAAB). Since then CAAB has grown in status and independence, generating funds though charges levied on its accreditation activities. CAAB has produced guidance papers on continuing professional development, supervision, and a 'body of knowledge' for UK chaplaincy. The strength of the new group lay in its tightly focused remit for accreditation and the areas of development linked to it. This focus has been sustained by a small group of dedicated members and a wider accountability to the three main UK professional bodies. By 2008 CAAB had enlarged its vision to the extent that it was succeeded by a broader professional group covering not only accreditation but also advisers for appointments and structures to carry out disciplinary procedures in relation to the voluntary register. Furthermore, the launch of the new body, the *UK Board of Healthcare Chaplaincy*, witnessed the addition of the Northern Ireland Association of Chaplains in Healthcare (NIACH) alongside the existing sponsoring organizations.

Conclusions

Following its victory in 1997, New Labour took a positive view of the role that religion could play in public life, so long as religious activities supported wider community virtues. This qualified support was noted by Rowan Williams who highlighted the potential pitfalls of a relationship between Government and faith communities in which the latter failed to comprehend the full nature of religious belonging.[34] It has appeared at times that New Labour has wanted the popular outcomes of religion (cohesion; education; identity) without recognizing the complexity which is an intrinsic part of these qualities. So, while officers at the HCC were able to capture something of the energy and direction of the new Government to gain resources for the strategic planning and development of chaplaincy, change on the ground has been stubbornly difficult to identify. The 'myth' of multi-faith chaplaincy might be seen as one example of rhetoric triumphing over practice. One of the general criticisms of New Labour reform in health care has been that the scale of new funding has not been matched by the scale of change and improvement at the coalface. While no official figures have been issued it has been estimated that *Caring for the Spirit* may have involved spending an additional £2 million on chaplaincy in England between 2003 and 2008. Leaving aside developments already in train when *Caring for the Spirit* began, many chaplains question whether £2 million pounds of progress in chaplaincy is discernable. In Scotland systematic and lasting development has been made off the back of less generous resources, and achieved in a happier and more collaborative atmosphere. Within the English NHS under New Labour the depth of change to chaplaincy remains highly questionable. The continuing appearance of job adverts specified by a denomination leads to a 'closed shop' that hampers the more open market that would undoubtedly raise the general quality of applicants. For example, there is no evidence that Church of England patients are less satisfied with care from a Methodist minister when compared with that provided by an Anglican. The continued restrictions on appointments, to serve a population ever less denominationally defined, effectively limits Free Church career opportunities and becomes a disincentive to professional development.

In England, the developments harnessing Government funds for central work enjoyed a mixed response among chaplains themselves. There was a perception

---

[34] Williams commented during his speech at Birmingham University on 11 June 2003: 'What matters is to recognise that the religious person or group starts from a perspective which on some questions will deliver conclusions similar to those of the secular progressive and on some questions definitely will not.'

that chaplains were being 'done to' rather than 'worked with'. A striking example of this was the decision not to involve any of the professional bodies in the initial planning of the workforce plan contained within *Caring for the Spirit*. In effect a church-led strategy for change harnessed NHS resources but left the elected representatives of chaplains outside the equation. New Labour's modernizing Department of Health was encouraged to talk about 'NHS chaplaincy' and a multi-faith service whilst being offered a very traditional and restrictive interpretation of ministry in hospital. The pivotal role of staff at Church House Westminster should not be underestimated. For several years HCC officers held multiple posts within chaplaincy leadership, spanning the HCC itself, the *Caring for the Spirit* strategy, the Department of Health (until 2004) and the Multi-Faith Group for Healthcare Chaplaincy (to name but a few). In effect the HCC's role in managing assessors for appointments and facilitating initial and on-going training gave its officers an opportunity to orchestrate the development of chaplaincy in England.

The Church House hegemony that dominated English chaplaincy at the start of New Labour's first decade had a number of implications. While more funds than ever before were allocated by the Department of Health for strategic planning the impetus of this began to dissipate after 2006 as financial priorities came into sharper focus. As the HCC has typically looked for central solutions to chaplaincy issues the new move to local autonomy raised the prospect of a different operating environment. As we shall see later in the next chapter, this was a central issue in the debacle of the Worcestershire NHS Trust's decision to axe chaplains.

Perhaps the greatest single change for chaplaincy in England between 1997 and 2007 lay in the growing assertiveness of the chaplains' professional bodies. The HCC's overarching role was brought into question by the CHCC when it began to advocate the formal recognition of chaplains as a health profession. Whereas once officers at HCC had known in advance of each initiative and public statement relating to chaplaincy the new environment led them to encounter a more surprising and less certain terrain. The careful testing of members' views carried out by CHCC fed a more organized drive towards the creation of a voluntary professional register; greater co-operation between the four UK professional bodies; and saw the emergence of a focused view about the future of chaplaincy in the NHS which challenged former conventions. While these changes were not inspired by New Labour they arose in response to a growing availability of funds for projects relating to evidence, patient safety and the wider inclusion of minorities. As we shall see later, the public discourse of chaplaincy which rooted it in orthodox religious representatives became increasingly distant from the actual spiritual expression of a growing number of patients.

In the latter years of New Labour's first decade, the Government's reputation for micro-management via targets came to live alongside strategies designed to weaken the power of command and control held by such bodies as the Department of Health.[35] While preserving the ethos of a national service, New Labour looked increasingly to devolve decision making to the local (or regional) community. This had the simultaneous benefits of cutting central budgets and avoiding blame for decisions made at the local level. Yet if the NHS as a whole became more successful, credit could be absorbed by a Government that set the general parameters within which local progress was achieved. This shift in emphasis came at a time of tighter financial regulation of the NHS with a determination by central government to see the service achieve and maintain financial balance. In this new world the provision of chaplaincy could no longer be guaranteed by central edict.

---

[35]   A. Alvarez-Rosete and N. Mays, 'Reconciling Two Conflicting Tales of the English Health Policy Process Since 1997', *British Politics* 3/2 (2008): 183–203.

Chapter 4
The Battle of Worcester

Introduction

In any consideration of the place of chaplaincy in the twenty-first century, the events surrounding the activities of the Worcestershire Acute Hospitals NHS Trust warrant close scrutiny. In August 2006, the Trust Board decided to dispense with its chaplaincy department, cutting it by two-thirds in the first instance. The ensuing debate came to national prominence, and even featured in a response from Tony Blair during Prime Minister's Questions in the House of Commons. For several months in 2006, and at the beginning of 2007, those concerned with chaplaincy watched to see how the situation in Worcestershire would unfold. It is no exaggeration to say that these events constituted a struggle over the fundamental location and professional identity of chaplains, and this made an inevitable impact on the morale of this very small group of NHS staff across England. The decisions taken by the Worcestershire Acute Hospitals NHS Trust constitute a significant case study in the circumstances of chaplaincy.

Although events in Worcestershire placed a great strain on the chaplains employed within that particular Trust, what happened there was seen by some as a potentially constructive opportunity. In general across the UK, when vacant posts were abandoned, part-time chaplains cut or retiring staff un-replaced, there was little traction to be gained in terms of a media debate. The spectacular decision of the Worcestershire Trust to (in effect) put whole-time chaplains on the street was an entirely different story. If some observers feared that an NHS Trust without chaplains would signal the beginning of the end of direct employment, others saw Worcestershire as a potentially revealing episode in which a lack of provision would bring into public view the underlying need for professional spiritual care. A Trust without a chaplaincy team could disclose what had been so elusive to identify – 'hard data' about the extent of patient and staff need for the service in a context where no on-site help was available. The emerging crisis in Worcestershire therefore had the potential to enable an evaluation in a way that had not been possible or attempted in England for the last 450 years.

Setting the Scene

It is clear from every attempt to establish the background and context for the decision by the Worcestershire Trust that almost certainly the proposal was developed without reference to the chaplains themselves. This suggests that the managers involved were aware that the proposal could not be presented with an element of spin which would enable it to be passed off as a process of constructive change, but would effectively mean the end of the service. In the minutes of the public section of the Trust Board meeting of 3 August 2006, no direct mention of the chaplaincy team was made. In later correspondence, the Chief Executive stated that, due to the perceived sensitivity of the subject, it was dealt with by the Board in a private session for which no published minutes exist. The Trust was in grave financial difficulty, and the minutes record the receipt of notification by the Strategic Health Authority that Worcestershire had formally been categorized as a 'turnaround trust'. In other words, the Trust was in special measures due to its financial performance. On 1 August, the Trust's Chief Executive, John Rostill, met with the Bishop of Worcester to advise him of the deep cuts that were planned for the chaplaincy. While the overall cut was around 66 per cent of the budget for chaplaincy services, the Trust's decision actually meant the redundancy of six of the seven part- and whole-time chaplains who made up the team. The one surviving chaplain was the Chaplaincy Team Leader, and this in itself led to questions about the viability of a job which incorporated the responsibility of leading something that would no longer exist.

August is never the best month to mobilize support, but during its course the disquiet over the Trust's decision began to build. The President of the CHCC wrote to the Chief Executive of the Trust on 10 August bringing a wide range of arguments to bear on the need to retain the current chaplaincy. From oncology guidance to the facilitation of human rights, the case was made that the Trust's action was ill-advised. But even in the making of these points the political weakness of chaplaincy was plain to see. It was not being argued that a certain percentage of patients would die, legislation fail to be followed or NHS staff be put at greater personal risk. No one could demonstrate that the decision would lower the Trust's income or make it impossible for the Trust to work effectively with the local population. Ultimately, the case to preserve chaplaincy lacked a 'silver bullet'. The evidence just was not there to land a single argument that would resolve the matter. The lead chaplain in Worcestershire was a very experienced chaplain but had only been appointed by the Trust a year earlier, and the work to develop the chaplaincy in line with the latest national guidance had not yet borne fruit. The situation looked bleak.

Efforts were made to lessen the degree of reduction that had been proposed by the Trust's Executive Team and endorsed by the Board on 3 August. The Bishop of Worcester spoke with the Trust's Chairman; the Chairman and the Chief Executive met with the lead chaplain and the Bishop of Worcester's health adviser; and the lead chaplain was allowed to present his case to the Trust's Finance and Performance Committee on 7 September. Following these interventions and discussions, the Chief Executive wrote to concerned individuals that 'my purpose in going into some detail is to confirm that the decision to reduce chaplaincy services will remain but that every opportunity has been given for the Board to re-consider or modify its decision'.[1]

In arriving at its decision in early August, however, the Trust had made some procedural errors. There had been no period of consultation. The County Council's Health Overview and Scrutiny Committee (HOSC) had not been advised of the proposed change in service, and discussions with the Trust's own staff had been patchy at best. To external observers, it appeared that the Trust had decided to grasp a nettle, anticipating a brief period of pain and publicity which would quickly subside. In fact, the Trust appears to have felt that this cut in funding might not even lead to a cut in service, as there was an expectation that local church leaders would pick up the work at no cost to the Trust. On 5 September, the HOSC included the issue of chaplaincy on its agenda, with emphasis that hospital chaplaincy 'was only undertaken by very carefully selected and trained ordained clergy'.[2] In the debate that followed, the ambiguous status of chaplaincy was evident:

> The Trust's view was that the proposed changes to the chaplaincy service did not equate to a service change and therefore consultation was not required. However, it was suggested that the public and Councillors perceived the proposals to be a service variation. It was therefore agreed that both the Trust and the HOSC would investigate further whether this issue constituted a service change.[3]

While there is no direct evidence to prove a link, it is striking that on 5 September – in the hours prior to the HOSC meeting – the Archbishop of Birmingham and the Bishop of Worcester made concerted efforts to engage with the media about the issue. From the *Today Programme* on BBC Radio 4, to *The Jeremy Vine Show* on BBC Radio 2 and the BBC News 24 television channel, the role of chaplaincy was debated from various angles throughout the day. However, the media did not set the Department of Health or the Trust against the work of chaplaincy – instead they sought the involvement of the National Secular Society. In a situation all too familiar for chaplains, bishops with no direct experience of current chaplaincy ended up arguing the case for chaplaincy within a framework that was almost exclusively religious. Although attempts were made to discuss the existence of non-religious spiritual needs, the polarity of a debate between bishops and secularists inevitably made it an argument about the place of religion in modern society. The most powerful voices on this day of media debate came from patients, relatives and NHS staff. On *The Jeremy Vine Show*, a phone-in elicited some stories about the difference that a chaplain's involvement had made. This discussion about chaplaincy began by hearing the Archbishop of Birmingham and the Bishop of Worcester followed by the Director of the National Secular Society, Keith Porteous

---

[1] John Rostill, letter dated 15 September 2006.

[2] Health Overview and Scrutiny Committee, Worcestershire County Council, Minutes 5 September 2006.

[3] Ibid., pp. 4–5.

Wood. The Church representatives made an effective presentation of the case to retain chaplains, citing in particular the care provided to non-religious patients and those who suddenly found they needed someone to help them consider unexpected questions raised by their illness.

Keith Porteous Wood focused on the decline of religious observance as one reason why NHS funds should not be expended on the provision of chaplains. Although Jeremy Vine countered this by noting the bishops' comments about the needs of those without any clear religious affiliation, Porteous Wood went on to argue:

> *KPW* Well I do agree that peoples' psychological health is important whether they're religious or not. But I don't actually think that in many cases the, er ... the local, chaplain is actually going to provide that. I've heard quite a depressing number of people say that, that they find the chaplains really rather unpleasant and a bit ... unpr ... well 'unpleasant', I mean intrusive, and people feel uncomfortable when they come there, I don't think that's the right answer, and let's ...
>
> *JV*   'intrusive'? You mean forcing themselves upon somebody when they're ill?
> *KPW* Yes, yes, indeed.
> *JV*   Saying, 'Look, can I pray with you' and the person is too weak to say no?
> *KPW* Well yes, they just feel uncomfortable and, erm, don't like to say ... they don't like to say, 'could you just go away I don't want you', but very often that's what people feel. And we're not prohibiting chaplains for coming into hospitals, I mean, there are thousands of chaplains and imams around the country, um, and they can go into these hospitals and I don't think it's asking very much ... the Church is even trying to invoke the Human Rights Act and saying that Worcester and ... are going against their responsibilities under the Human Rights Act. The Human Rights Act doesn't require any public authority to pay for religion, what it does do is say that they should allow freedom of religion and I think that's much more appropriate.

The case against chaplaincy is seldom made, and the views of Porteous Wood are significant in representing an alternative view of the situation. However, the weakness of the opposition debate is identical to the weaknesses of the supporting arguments: they lack data. The National Secular Society does not have systematic evidence of people finding the visit of a chaplain to be 'intrusive'. Given the argument that many non-religious people access chaplaincy, the link between declining religious practice and the needs of patients is not compelling. However, this did reveal – but not address – a logical consequence of the views expressed by the bishops. If chaplains spend a great deal of their time with those who do not identify with formal religious practice, why do chaplains have to be religious in order to do this work? Could a humanist provide the same kind of care equally – if not more – effectively than the religious practitioner? While recognizing the need for psychological support, and playing down the effectiveness of chaplains in doing this, the Director of the National Secular Society did not go on to discuss the potential extra costs for non-religious provision to meet the needs he recognized as existing. After all, counsellors and psychologists do not work for nothing.

The following are some example of views given during the programme by either phone or text:

> *Caller* Yes, I'm over it now, it was 21 years ago, but I lost a little girl – my first baby – there, and all the staff were absolutely wonderful but the chaplains were fantastic. Picking up on what a previous caller said, when I was in my darkest depths those nurses couldn't always be with me – they tried – but they couldn't always be there because they were *nursing*, but the chaplains were. And the following year when I had my little boy who is now 20, he (the chaplain) came back to me. He remembered me, came back and congratulated me. I'm not deeply religious but support ... yeah, their love and support, that was second to none and they provide a really, really valuable service, and it would be a pity to lose that.

> *JV* Paul texted us and said 'I spent three months in intensive care with a 2 per cent chance of survival; Idris, the chaplain, gave tremendous help and support to my family, at such a difficult time. So much so that our children were subsequently christened by him. Our two miracle sons, Will and James. We need all the faith possible in our hospitals. Just what has happened to the taxes that we paid and the promises made by the government?

Another caller said, 'This is now a secular country, virtually, so if something like 43 per cent of people don't believe – so with that amount of decline in religion, surely NHS money should all be spent on nursing staff?'

Responses also included the following from a serving paramedic:

> *JV* Martin Eaton is a paramedic from Dudley, and you're writing in praise of your chaplain?
> *ME* Yes, that's right Jeremy, from my experience as a ground-floor emergency department sort of view. Our chaplain's there, he's got a good understanding of how the department works. He provides a lot of support to the staff, er, he's provided a lot of support to my own staff, he's always available, he does de-briefings, he's also filled in a bit of our training on bereavement sort of counselling and how to approach relatives. Really his support's been invaluable.
> *JV* So what do you say to our last caller, Tony, who says, 'Fine, have them, but the church should pay'?
> *ME* 'I'd say for what he does, in today's world where people sort of require counselling, debriefing and stuff like that, they probably save the NHS money. In terms of doing it sort of locally rather than people sort of going off and having to have it elsewhere.

This sample is by no means scientific, but it was significant during this period of intense public interest because it focused on the recipients of care rather than the professional advocates. While some members of the public were critical of the NHS funding chaplains, no negative comments were made by those who had received care from a chaplain. For some people, the involvement of a chaplain appeared to have been decisive in providing support at a time of great personal trauma.

Among the many avenues that were explored in gaining support for the chaplains' position the Bishop of Worcester made an appeal to the Healthcare Commission. The Bishop attempted to build a case for the provision of chaplaincy on the basis of the Department for Health's *Standards for Better Health*[4] development standard D2, which obliges trusts to provide patients with care that meets their needs and preferences for spiritual care. While this is a development standard it is significant that the document states that health providers can be expected to either meet or aspire to each standard (whether core or developmental). It is difficult to see how the Worcestershire Trust fulfilled this expectation. However, the Commission did not make a response that added any pressure to alter the Trust's decision.

In August, the CHCC mounted a campaign to draw the widest possible attention to the events in Worcestershire. Letters were sent by the President to all Church of England bishops in the House of Lords, as well as to many organizations which would value the chaplain's role, such as Cruse and the Miscarriage Association. On 3 October, the Archbishop of Canterbury, in an unprecedented move, wrote to all NHS chaplains offering encouragement and support. He noted that the crisis in Worcestershire had featured in his planned meeting with Lord Warner, health minister in the House of Lords, on 18 September. On 31 October, six MPs put down an early-day motion calling on the Trust to reconsider its actions, and welcoming the contribution of the Worcestershire division of the BMA in deploring the decision. The county BMA division had called upon the Trust to 'restore the traditional chaplaincy services as a priority in the forthcoming reorganization of clinical services'. However, a stock response was emerging to these approaches – and not one that did much to cheer the chaplains and their supporters. The epitome of this approach came when Peter Luff, MP for Worcester, tackled the Prime Minister during oral questions in the House of Commons. Tony Blair responded:

> I do of course recall the correspondence, and I have corresponded with the priest who has been leading the campaign. I entirely understand the concerns that people have, but I think that such decisions must be taken at local level. As the hon. Gentleman will know, over the past few years there has been a major expansion in the number of people working in the national health service in Worcestershire. Nevertheless, when trusts balance their books and make changes for the future, they must also make those decisions. I hope that they make them

---

[4]   Department of Health, *Standards for Better Health*, (6495) (London, The Crown, 2004).

sensitively, recognising the tremendous pastoral care that is given and its value to local patients; but I do not think it would be right for me to interfere directly in that process.[5]

The government's approach was to devolve decisions down to the local provider. This enabled New Labour to affirm the guidance issued by the Department of Health but avoid the public criticism which emerged when local services were withdrawn. If these responses were not what chaplains wanted, they were not altogether encouraging for the Worcestershire Trust either. If egg was going to land on anyone's face over these decisions, it was not going to be the face of government. The Prime Minister's comments effectively told the Trust 'you're on your own'.

It is not clear whether the Worcestershire County Council's HOSC ever resolved the question as to whether the effective ending of chaplaincy constituted a 'substantial' change of service. But, in October 2006, the Trust did produce a far more detailed *Proposal for Reducing the Chaplaincy Service*, signed by the Chief Executive. For the first time in the history of the NHS, this set out a hostile management rationale for ending the professional provision of spiritual care. Against a background of a 'challenging financial situation', the Trust argued that all areas of work were being re-examined in order to assess their effectiveness. The paper stated that 'had the chaplain not visited the ward a formal referral would probably not have been made as patients rarely ask to see a chaplain'. Overall, the image was created of the chaplains generating work through their presence – without which little real need would be expressed. The paper also resisted the suggestion that the Trust's proposal constituted a substantial service change, and claimed that it did not therefore require public consultation. The HOSC discussed the paper on 30 October and was scathing:

... there was concern that the Trust's paper had been written by someone with no understanding of spiritual support:[6]

... it is stated that most patient–chaplain contacts being made are as a result of ward visits and that formal referrals would not normally have been made. Members would contend that in fact this could suggest that patients are asking for visits once they become aware of the service, possibly indicating that there is a problem with advising patients of the service on admission;[7]

---

[5]   Tony Blair, Hansard, 1 November 2006, Column 296.

[6]   Health Overview and Scrutiny Committee, Worcestershire County Council, 30 October 2006, p. 7.

[7]   Ibid.

... Members were concerned about broad statements in the paper which do not appear to be evidence-based, for example, 'society is changing and becoming increasingly secular and diverse';[8]

... there was concern about contradictory statements within the paper, for example, 'there is no performance or activity data available', yet 'information available does indicate that there are in the region of 30–40 patient contacts per week by a hospital chaplain'.[9]

Committees such as the HOSC do not have great powers. They are able to call leaders in the local health community to appear and to be accountable, but the most they can do in addition to this is refer a change to the Secretary of State for Health for consideration. The members of the HOSC indicated in the meeting of 30 October that they would do this, in part because they were very concerned at the Trust's lack of public and patient involvement in arriving at its decision.

It would be fair to say that, by this point, the Trust was not in a very happy position. It had attempted a quick and clean cut to generate £94,000 of savings during August, when many of those who might oppose the reduction would be away from the office. The Trust Board had taken the decision, and it had taken it without notifying the HOSC or providing a proper local consultation. In a circular letter from the Trust's CEO dated 15 September, sent to all those who had written to the Trust expressing concerns, John Rostill set out in detail the strength of the decision which the Trust had taken. He referred to an additional opportunity given to the Lead Chaplain to make his case to Board members on 7 September as 'an unprecedented situation to date'. Having heard the case, Rostill wrote that 'my purpose in going into some detail is to confirm that the decision to reduce chaplaincy services will remain'. There was no sign that the matter would go away, and the CHCC had notified Worcestershire's Strategic Health Authority that if the cuts went through it would begin a local advertising campaign to elicit evidence about the effects on patients and staff of the reduced or absent provision.

At the November meeting of the HOSC, comments by the Trust's representatives suggested that its resolution was beginning to wane. Pre-empting further discussion of the topic, the Trust announced that 'a possible way forward had been identified' but that it was not at liberty to go into precise details while the plan was in formation. An assurance was given that during this time no redundancies would be made. Despite some unhappiness about the apparent secrecy of the plan, this move effectively took the heat out of the public debate.

---

[8]   Ibid.
[9]   Ibid.

A way forward?

The detail of the Trust's new proposals did not emerge until the final days of 2006. On 13 December, the Trust issued a press release announcing the agreement it had reached with local church leaders and the charitable League of Friends branches at Kidderminster, Redditch and Worcester. In effect, the charities were to fund most of the original saving for the financial years 2006/2007 and 2007/2008. While the short term was secured, there was no guarantee that a return to full establishment would occur at the end of the agreed period. The Trust was buoyant in claiming that this three-way agreement meant the continuation of the chaplaincy without any back-down over their financial cuts. Local church leaders reported that the Trust had said it would return the chaplaincy to funding from the main budget in the future: the Trust itself said only that it intended to do so depending on the financial situation at the time.

Compared with the Trust's previous statements supporting the cuts, the tone of the press release is strikingly different. The paper given to the HOSC concluded with the 'clinical view that chaplaincy services are not accessed formally frequently enough to warrant the ongoing employment of 3 WTE (whole time equivalents)'. In the press release, the Chairman of the Trust now said, 'We never doubted the enormous value of the service.' Politically, the Trust had avoided an embarrassing climb-down, and potentially postponed the return to full budget to a time when media attention would be lessened. It is likely that in terms of local NHS resources, comprising senior staff time, public relations expenditure and the weakening of local support, the 'value' of the whole affair had cost the Trust well in excess of £100,000. Even at this point, the Trust was not out of the woods.

While the churches and the Trust appeared to have called a truce with this announcement, others were less sanguine. The detail of the proposal suggested that in effect local churches were being asked to finance the injection of cash through the various Leagues of Friends. In securing the agreement, church leaders had apparently made a commitment to 'launch a fundraising appeal which, it is hoped, will generate significant extra money for hospital chaplaincy services'. The trade union AMICUS issued an immediate response arguing that this created the alarming precedent for core NHS activities being funded by 'jumble sales'. At the same time, the Worcester MP Peter Luff issued a statement saying:

> It is not good enough to rely on charity for an essential part of the service offered by our hospitals. It is not good enough to leave the future of the service in doubt after 2008. I sympathise with local hospital managers as they wrestle with a financial problem that is made in Whitehall, not Worcestershire, but this is not an acceptable way to deal with it. This 'resolution' raises more questions

than it answers and puts the Trust in breach of its obligations, clearly set out in government guidance.[10]

For the College of Health Care Chaplains, the wider concerns raised by this announcement related to the precedent being set for other trust chaplaincies. It appeared to weaken the place of chaplaincies within the core services of acute hospitals and to encourage the idea of the churches paying for chaplaincy work in the NHS (albeit indirectly). At about this time, at least one other NHS Trust began to look at how it could dispense with the financial responsibility for chaplaincy. The CHCC wrote to the Charity Commissioners to query the use of the League funds in order to finance an NHS saving. The Commissioners could not establish a legal requirement for the chaplaincy and, for this reason, found no cause to intervene. However, the story once again created national publicity about the outcome of the Worcestershire chaplaincy dispute – and served to remind the Trust that its actions would continue to be monitored very closely.

Finally, in October 2007, the Trust announced that chaplaincy services in the Worcestershire Acute Hospitals NHS Trust would be reinstated in the main budget. The news came during a planned visit to the Trust by the Chair of the Hospital Chaplaincies Council, the Rt Revd Michael Perham, who used the occasion to state: 'what I want to do now is stop Worcester being used as a by-word for cuts'.[11] Evidently the Worcestershire Trust had been in the chaplaincy limelight long enough, and wanted the news of a return to budget to put an end to a year of bad publicity. In welcoming the outcome, the acting Bishop of Worcester, David Walker, commented that the decision 'sends a very positive signal to Churches and to Health trusts across the country'.

Analysis

The events that unfolded in Worcestershire in 2006 are notable for a number of reasons. First, the Trust's original plans included the redundancy of two members of chaplaincy staff. This is within a professional group very unlikely to be able to find similar work without relocating. Second, the Trust appears to have assumed that the local churches would in effect pick up the work done by the chaplains once the redundancies were made. And third, the debate quickly became connected to both the status of religion in public life *and* the emerging voice of chaplaincy as a profession.

During the Worcestershire debacle, evidence about the scale and extent of cuts across the NHS in England was scant. The College of Health Care Chaplains sought information from its members about reductions in chaplaincy at a local

---

[10]   Peter Luff, Press Release through Mid Worcestershire Conservatives, 13 December 2006.

[11]   *Worcester News*, 25 October 2007.

level, and this supported the contention that chaplaincies were being targeted to a disproportionate extent compared with other NHS services. Worcestershire had become the lightning-conductor for this wide-ranging anxiety about cuts because it involved the redundancy of whole-time chaplains. Unwittingly, the Worcestershire Trust had set itself up as a national 'test case' for the whole issue of publicly-funded chaplaincy in the NHS. In a short space of time, all the key players in defence of chaplaincy were united in their determination not to let the Worcestershire decision stand. The Trust received letters from the President of the CHCC, the Chair of the Multi-Faith Group and the Archbishop of Birmingham. The unspoken belief that fuelled the criticism of the Trust by every means available was the suspicion that a domino effect would follow if the Worcestershire decision went through. Judging from the comments made by the Archbishop of Birmingham on *The Jeremy Vine Show*, it was also a debate about an NHS wholly driven by a mechanistic approach to the body (and the financial bottom line) over and against a view that affirmed technical care but wanted it informed by a pastoral and compassionate ethos.

Officers at the Hospital Chaplaincies Council worked behind the scenes to try to resolve the situation and the HCC Chief Executive Edward Lewis was present when the Archbishop of Canterbury met Lord Warner. In part, the activities of the HCC at this point reveal the continuation of its traditional practice in regard to the use of influence. Set in Westminster, the HCC was well placed to draw on political networks and deal with the Department of Health to voice concerns. When the local church leaders met with the Worcestershire Trust, the HCC Chief Executive was also present, advising and informing the discussions as they took place. In contrast, the CHCC began a very public campaign of letter writing and lobbying through the media. The President of the College wrote to all the Anglican bishops in the House of Lords and encouraged CHCC members to write to their own MPs. With the media, the College worked to balance a secular *versus* religion debate with broader comments about spiritual care and the professional standing of the chaplain. At the same time, the College sought to advise chaplains about potential risks to their work, issuing a paper from the CHCC National Professional Committee in November 2007. By means of an article in *The Church Times*, the CHCC President endeavoured to equip chaplains with the best available arguments in making the case for professional – funded – spiritual care in the NHS.[12] Privately, all the chaplaincy leaders knew that Worcester had been a close call – and that in its hour of need the gaping hole of argument and data needed to underpin chaplaincy in the NHS had become painfully apparent.

---

[12]   Chris Swift, 'Cutting chaplains will cost the NHS', in *The Church Times*, 18 August 2006.

The Theos Survey

One of the responses to the crisis in Worcestershire took the form of a systematic study of chaplaincy staffing levels across England. The research by Theos 'the public theology think-tank' attempted to answer the question of how accurate the suspicion was 'that hospital chaplaincy in the NHS as a whole has been subject to serious cuts'.[13] It follows that the chief aim of the work was to produce a comprehensive picture of chaplaincy post reductions across England, rather than focus just on one very public example. Theos, sponsored chiefly by the Church of England and the Roman Catholic Church in England and Wales, asked questions of all NHS trusts in England using the Freedom of Information Act (2000). This was a shrewd move as it placed a legal responsibility on the trusts to respond. The questions which Theos asked were designed to garner comprehensive data about what was happening in trusts across England. While events in Worcestershire had enabled a public discussion about the threat to chaplaincy, the Theos findings gave a far more detailed analysis of the changing nature of English chaplaincy.

Despite the use of the Freedom of Information Act as a tool of enquiry, only 85.7 per cent of trusts responded. Theos expressed its surprise at this as the Act places a legal obligation on NHS organizations to respond within a specific period of time. Even so, in many other respects the response rate is perfectly good for formulating a credible picture of change within English chaplaincy departments.

The cuts experienced across the NHS were by no means evenly spread and fell most heavily on a limited number of trusts. Only one-quarter of trusts that responded reported any cut in the level of funded chaplaincy work, but of these trusts Epsom and St Helier had lost 77 hours per week and the North Bristol and Oxford Radcliffe organizations had cut 49 hours and 38.5 hours per week respectively. The report also noted eight trusts which had frozen posts, although for each one it was stated that eventual appointment was a 'reasonable expectation'.[14]

When the researchers looked at the proportion of trust budgets allocated to chaplaincy, a more complex picture emerged. While 23 per cent reported a cut to budgets, 22.7 per cent reported an increase. The authors of the study report explain this in terms of chaplaincy remaining a constant proportion of budget at a time of overall reductions. However, this is not cross-referenced to existing NHS and trust data, and other factors are likely to have caused these findings. Theos undertook its study at a time of major changes in the way NHS staff were remunerated. A new pay system (*Agenda for Change*) was introduced on 1 October 2004 across the NHS. Many trusts took time to implement the full implications of the new pay policy and this was especially true for chaplains, who, for the first time, became entitled to on-call and call-out payments as a matter of national rather than local

---

[13] Theos, *NHS Chaplaincy Provision in England: Theos Research Paper (Interim Findings)*, (London, 2007).

[14] Ibid., paragraph 4.2.4, p. 14.

agreement. It is therefore highly likely that cuts to chaplaincy establishments could have nevertheless been accompanied by a rising proportion of trust expenditure.

When they were published, the Theos findings were judged to be dramatic. They revealed that for a 24-month period between 2004 and 2006, funded chaplaincy across the NHS in England had fallen by a total figure equating to the loss of nineteen hours' work each and every week. This surprised some commentators because only Worcester had attracted very much attention. The Theos findings, however, paint a subtle picture of incremental cuts spread largely across vacancies, the ending of part-time chaplaincy posts and voluntary redundancies. In the case of Anglican part-time chaplains, this process may have met with little resistance because the individuals concerned probably sent the income directly to the Diocese.[15] For this reason the cuts would have made no difference to the stipends of clergy attending the hospitals alongside their parochial duties. At a time when the size and number of churches allocated to stipendiary clergy was increasing, the prospect of losing hospital duties may have appealed to many part-time chaplains.

The report published by Theos contained the interim findings of the study, and it was argued in the report that further research was needed to understand fully all the factors affecting these changes. There were also some methodological concerns about the approach of the study from individual trusts and chaplains. The report acknowledges the difference between 'direct costs' and the full value of supporting chaplaincy within the hospital environment (what are generally termed 'on costs').[16] In addition to this, the Theos questionnaire had asked for data based on calendar rather than financial years and this may have led to variations in the way trusts responded to some of the questions. Furthermore, the delayed impact of Agenda for Change pay arrears, within the years about which Theos was asking for comparative data, may have distorted significantly the accuracy of the picture that emerged. No reference is made to the new pay structure anywhere in the report.

It is not altogether unexpected that the Theos study suggests that there are 'a number of areas where more research can be undertaken'.[17] What emerges is largely a quantitative account of change within chaplaincy departments during a period of fiscal tightening by NHS management. The report does, however, give some attention to the views of chaplaincy held by a selected number of other NHS staff, and this serves to support the overall contention of value implied by the report. On average, Theos found that the proportion of trust budgets spent on the salaries and non-pay expenditures of chaplaincy departments amounted to just 0.09 per cent of budget. If Theos wished to make the case for value more strongly, then further research would be essential.

---

[15]   Normally Church of England part-time NHS chaplains opt to receive a fixed stipend and commute any additional income to the Diocese.

[16]   Theos, (2007), fn 11, p. 8.

[17]   Ibid., section 3.8, p. 9.

It would be fair to say that the Theos report is accurate in the general proposition of unusually high budget cuts across chaplaincy in the English NHS. However, the strength of the report is limited by its lack of consideration for major influences such as Agenda for Change. While the writers were successful in arguing that the experience of the Worcestershire Trust was not unique, they were less convincing when it came to considering the relationship between budgets and staffing levels. Enquiries by the CHCC, although less extensive in scope, established that on average chaplaincy departments were judged by team leaders in 2004 to be at just 61 per cent of the levels advocated by the Department of Health. Taking this into account, *any* cuts potentially placed a huge burden on fewer and fewer staff and were achieved only at the expense of the well-being of individual chaplains. For example, the Theos findings gave 88 per cent as the proportion of trusts operating an on-call rota. To sustain such an availability in a climate of reduced staffing warrants further study.

Conclusion

The changes which occurred to chaplaincy under the first decade of New Labour were extensive and, in the case of the Worcestershire Acute Hospitals NHS Trust, came to be characterized by conflict in the public arena. Without doubt, the impact of a Government drive for better financial management in the NHS led many trust chief executives to respond with draconian changes. No doubt some of this was done with deep reluctance and the fear of either dismissal or the appearance of an emergency management team. Chaplains were not the cause of overspending in individual hospitals but they appeared to be an answer to prayer when it came to decisions that might suddenly contribute to financial balance.

What followed in the wake of the decisions in Worcestershire demonstrated that chaplains and their supporters were far removed from any kind of sitcom stereotype. Caught between a strong campaign from the chaplains' main professional body – backed by the union AMICUS – and the interventions by the Roman Catholic and Anglican Churches (acting by agreement on behalf of their ecumenical colleagues) at a ministerial level, the Trust was confronted by a formidable array of criticism. Despite some differences of view about chaplains between the faith communities and the chaplains' own organizations, the attack on chaplaincy produced a strength of response common to all. What emerged was a debate wholly disproportionate to the relative size of chaplains as a staff group in the NHS. This may in itself reflect issues of identity, and anxieties about secularization (whether accurate or not), which served to promote chaplains as a rallying point for a range of causes. In Worcestershire, the cuts would only have affected Christian chaplains, but other faiths could see that if funded chaplains were excluded, then there was little hope for faith diversification among chaplains as a group. Against this coalition of criticism, the NHS Trust concerned appeared to have only the National Secular Society as an ally. For some, the extreme language used by the NSS will have simply acted as an incentive to support the chaplains' cause ('these chaplains are parasites on a service that is there first and foremost to provide medical treatment and health care'[18]).

The experience of public debate over a single chaplaincy department fuelled a wider consideration of chaplaincy across the NHS – manifested in the research conducted by Theos. Other responses included the further strengthening of ties between all the UK's professional chaplaincy organizations and the formation in 2007 of an All-Party Parliamentary Group for Chaplaincy in the NHS. These strategic changes have been welcomed by chaplains, but there is also seen to be a pressing need to furnish those prepared to support chaplains with the data and evidence that speak to the cultures of both Government and the Department of Health. This is the less newsworthy but most important piece of work to be carried out in the twenty-first century. It is widely agreed that this is a difficult and costly requirement for chaplaincy, but the price of non-engagement with research into spiritual care may ultimately be far greater.

---

[18]   http://www.secularism.org.uk/ posted 16 November 2007.

Chapter 5

The Chaplain Today: an Auto-Ethnography

Introduction

There is a great danger that any discussion of the role of the chaplain will run all too quickly into abstract notions or diffuse aspirations. As we saw in Chapter 2, one of the criticisms which can be made of public expressions of Christianity in England after the sixteenth century is that faith (especially 'approved' faith) was driven into the mind – an observation supported by the decision at Bedlam to exclude chaplains from an institution for the insane. In order to engage more directly with the experience of chaplaincy, this chapter will draw on auto-ethnographic texts to reflect on the particular activity of a chaplain. As one of the aims of ethnography is to make the familiar strange, it is a technique well-suited to the task of identifying the differences between the public statements about chaplaincy and what is going on in the practice of spiritual care at the start of the twenty-first century.

For some readers, the use of ethnography will raise questions about the role of qualitative research and its suitability for chaplains in the NHS. Ethnography makes a virtue out of what would be anathema for many quantitative researchers. It is particular rather than general, is open to its uncertainties rather than frustrated by them, and is carried out with an awareness of the researcher's own agenda, experiences and involvement in the fieldwork.

In this chapter, a general discussion about the nature and suitability of ethnography as a tool for gaining greater understanding of the contemporary chaplain will be followed by some examples of auto-ethnography. This background discussion will be linked with a consideration of the methodological approaches used by Michel Foucault. It is not unique to make this connection between ethnography, Foucault and chaplaincy – even if it is still unusual.[1]

---

[1]   F. Norwood, 'The Ambivalent Chaplain: Negotiating Structural and Ideological Difference on the Margins of Modern-Day Hospital Medicine', *Medical Anthropology* 25/1 (2006): 1–29. Chris Swift, 'Speaking of the Same Things Differently', in Helen Orchard (ed.), *Spirituality in Health Care Contexts* (London, 2001) pp. 96–106. N. Adams and C. Elliot, 'Ethnography is dogmatics: Making description central to systematic theology', *Scottish Journal of Theology* 53/3 (2000): 339–64.

Ethnography

In recent years, those working in the field of practical theology have pursued a course of growing attention to the description of situations, events and experiences. While the use of case studies is useful in this, there is the danger of 'cherry picking' the unusual or the extreme and overlooking the mundane and routine. Ethnography offers a more structured approach for researchers and has the capacity to identify what is absent with the same scrutiny as it attaches to what is obviously present. Rather than the sudden noting of an event believed by the researcher in the field to have been important, ethnography is a prospective research method – uncertain as to what will (or will not) transpire within its field of observation. For Scharen, 'Ethnography ought to be a means of doing theology'.[2] This turn to structured description as a tool for theology owes much to the epistemological concerns of the late twentieth century about the role and abuse of meta-narratives. The links between Foucault and ethnography emerge out of this concern and combine to stimulate a far closer attention to lived experience and the detailed re-consideration of the history out of which our present subjectivity emerges.

Although he never used formal ethnography, the French intellectual Michel Foucault drew on existing writing to carry out a similar task. In his apparently historical enquiries (what Mitchell Dean terms 'critical and effective histories'[3]), Foucault disturbed the fiction of the present. This had the effect of generating 'a transformation of the relationship we have with our knowledge'.[4] In an interview conducted in 1981, Foucault went on to emphasize the personal nature of this process:

> Every time I have tried to do a piece of theoretical work it has been on the basis of elements of my own experience: always in connection with processes I saw unfolding around me. It was always because I thought I identified cracks, silent tremors, and dysfunctions in things I saw, institutions I was dealing with, or my own relations with others, that I set out to do a piece of work, and each time was partly a fragment of autobiography.[5]

Foucault uses the language of literature – novel, fiction and autobiography – to allude to the character of his work. It is *like* these forms and yet these forms do not fully capture his intention. His accounts of the construction of Western knowledge appeared to be set in the past, but on publication were seen to be critical of

---

[2]   C.B. Scharen, '"Judicious narratives", or ethnography as ecclesiology', *Scottish Journal of Theology* 58/02 (2005): 125.

[3]   Mitchell Dean, *Critical and Effective Histories: Foucault's Methods and Historical Sociology* (London, 1994).

[4]   Michel Foucault, 'Interview with Michel Foucault by Duccio Trombadori', in J.D. Faubion (ed.), *Michel Foucault: Power* (London, 2000) p. 244.

[5]   Ibid., p. 458.

contemporary practice in prisons and medical institutions. In part, Foucault's words answer this paradox, and describe a relationship where observation of present dysfunctions inspires an exploration of epistemology. Of course the past is related to the present: the past is perpetually reproduced in the present, as Foucault's work demonstrates.

The ability to see these 'cracks, silent tremors, and dysfunctions' is the intellectual task which Foucault set himself. As with his exploration of madness and crime, this task is achieved to some degree by the suspension of 'meaning' and the examination of geography, action and discourse as independent facts. For this reason, there are researchers in the field of ethnography who have made links to Foucault, and this has produced work concerned with institutional discourse, including non-discursive dimensions and 'silence'.[6]

The work of ethnography is not to try to identify an 'essence', as some phenomenologists might attempt. It is rather to observe and record events – and objects – so that their relationships can be analysed. Willis makes this point by considering not only the role of language but also the 'sensuous' non-verbal effects of 'artefacts and concrete forms' of daily life. This in turn presents new problems to the task of social observation: 'You could say that the whole ethnographic writing enterprise is such an exercise, a struggle against language in language to produce sensuous reconstructions in the reader's mind.'[7]

The effective ethnographer is therefore engaged in the creation of a text that uses existing signifiers (language) to open up in the reader's mind a new perspective on accepted understandings. Willis describes this as the 'Ah-ha' factor; the grounded observations that open 'up in the new spaces between discourse and experience'.[8] For example, the use of ethnography in medical sociology – amongst a number of aims – is directed at articulating aspects of the patient previously obscured or unobserved: 'The voice of the patient is often silenced, not only in medical practice but also in social scientific research about it. Ethnographic work redresses this silence'.[9]

In short, the present must be disturbed. In order to generate a new fiction which questions the rules governing the body and its functions, the given meanings must (to some degree) be suspended. The ways in which this might be achieved in chaplaincy require an epistemology in sympathy with Foucault, but based on a methodology that draws on his concerns and applies them to an ascetic exploration of present events. Stephen Tyler's work is perhaps the most promising basis for such an approach.

---

[6]   Gale Miller, 'Towards ethnographies of institutional discourse', *Journal of Contemporary Ethnography* 23/3 (1994): 280–306.

[7]   Paul Willis, *The Ethnographic Imagination* (Gateshead, 2000) p. 22.

[8]   Ibid., p. 117.

[9]   K. Charmaz and V. Oleson, 'Ethnographic Research in Medical Sociology: Its Foci and Distinctive Contributions', *Sociological Methods & Research* 25/4 (1997): 461.

In order to 'locate lines of weakness, strong points, positions'[10] in a post-modern world, an observer must bear a number of things in mind. Following Tyler's work, it is clear that the power of discourse must be recognized and that ethnography must avoid the limits posed by both presentation and representation. For Tyler such an ethnography 'makes available through absence what can be conceived but not presented. It is thus beyond truth and immune to the judgement of performance.'[11]

The only way this can be achieved is through 'evocation'. Unlike Enlightenment discourse, which largely assumed that language was fully capable of representing scientific discovery, ethnography doubts the capacity of language to re-present experience. As Foucault set out in his 1968 essay, *Ceci n'est pas une pipe* ('This is not a pipe'), the ambiguities of representation multiply the longer and deeper one considers them. Much of what happens in life cannot be borne by language, yet the experience which it cannot capture might – under certain circumstances – be evoked. Tyler put it this way:

> A post-modern ethnography is a cooperatively evolved text consisting of fragments of discourse intended to evoke in the minds of both readers and writer an emergent fantasy of a possible world of commonsense reality, and thus to provoke an aesthetic integration that will have a therapeutic effect.[12]

Postmodernists, often described as 'ontologically suspicious', would no doubt raise concerns about the therapeutic effect of ethnography. But Tyler goes on to explore the original sense of 'therapy' as a movement towards harmony with therapy acting as a 'ritual substitute' – and therapist as poet. The therapy is therefore a means of disturbing established meaning 'in order to reconfirm it and to return us to it renewed and mindful of renewal'.[13] Such an approach needs to be treated with care, as virtuous intent can often mask a disciplinary function.

Tyler's view of ethnography is of a therapy which has a purpose. If not to create an abstraction of life, then 'to restructure experience'. There are echoes here of Foucault's aspirations to tell a new story, to generate a new experience. This returns to evocation, to the idea that what ethnography generates between text–reader–author(s) is a fantasy, a polyphony of voices which resists the closed nature of traditional discourse. For Tyler as for Foucault, this can only be seen as 'the start of a different kind of journey'.

---

[10]   Michel Foucault, 'Body/Power: interview with Quel Corps?', in C. Gordon (ed.), *Power/Knowledge Selected Interviews and Other writings 1972–1977 Michel Foucault* (Harlow, 1980) p. 62.

[11]   Stephen Tyler, 'Post-Modern Ethnography: From Occult Document to Document of the Occult', in J. Clifford and G.E. Marcus (eds), *Writing Culture* (London, 1986) p. 123.

[12]   Ibid., p. 125.

[13]   Ibid., p. 135.

If this is the approach for a post-modern ethnography, then a model is required to catch those fragments which disturb the normative discourses of the present. For Tyler, the most effective approach to this lies in the work of Clifford Geertz. Geertz takes the term 'thick description' used by Gilbert Ryle to elaborate a method for an ethnographic technique.

Ryle[14] described the problems of attaching different meanings to the same event or, more precisely, the danger of choosing one explanation for an action when a number of alternatives also exist. In anthropological writings, Geertz noted that 'what we call our data are really our own constructions of other people's constructions of what they and their compatriots do'.[15] At the root of this lies the problem that description, however much removed from interpretation, simply cannot avoid the attachment of meaning to action, because language exists as a collection of inter-related referents. The only way even to begin to address this is by 'thick description', a way of doing ethnography which recognizes:

> a multiplicity of complex conceptual structures, many of them superimposed upon or knotted into one another, which are at once strange, irregular, and inexplicit, and which he must contrive somehow first to grasp and then to render.[16]

This organic picture is the antithesis of laboratory conditions. Ethnography fully implicates the researcher, fails to offer clear boundaries and endeavours to evade the limitations of language. Like a two-dimensional floor plan, a text can tell us much about the space it describes. But what it is like to live there, to move within its boundaries – to move beyond them – can only be evoked. It goes without saying that ethnographers can never know what their 'thick description' achieves with the reader. Yet for some a new perspective will be opened up, and unexpected possibilities begin to form: a new journey begins.

Ethnography arose within anthropology as a way to write so that the experience of indigenous communities could be successfully evoked within texts. It has since extended to embrace the notion that all social discourse can be made alien to some degree – and open to be newly experienced – by the same ethnographic approach. If what appears 'natural' in human relations is disturbed, questioned, re-viewed, then it can seem increasingly strange. Brewer[17] describes it as follows:

> Ethnography is the study of people in naturally occurring settings or 'fields' by methods of data collection which capture their social *meanings* and ordinary activities, involving the researcher participating directly in the setting, if not

---

[14]   Gilbert Ryle, *Collected papers* (London, 1971).

[15]   Clifford Geertz, *The Interpretation of Cultures* (London, 1993) p. 9.

[16]   Ibid., p. 10.

[17]   J.D. Brewer, *Ethnography* (Milton Keynes, 2000).

also the activities, in order to collect data in a systematic manner but without meaning being imposed on them externally.[18]

Hospitals have often found it difficult to generate research or audit that effectively describes the role of chaplaincy. Although the word is seldom used, many chaplains seem to feel that the 'transcendent' aspect of the work makes it hard to apply the normal criteria of outcome measures. Or at least that is perhaps the reason why many chaplains struggle to describe their core tasks.[19] There are those who may think this is an excuse – a way of avoiding rigorous examination and its conclusions. However, the fact that many chaplains choose to use story rather than statistics to speak about their work may indicate an affinity with ethnography. They may be saying that chaplaincy interactions can be 'evoked' far more authentically by the isolated event than by the kinds of generalized and abbreviated accounts often found in hospital audits. It is an experience which might come out in carefully-crafted texts: it needs to come alive at the point where the ethnography engages with the reader's imagination.

Ethnography and the Observation of Faith Communities

One area that is worth considering in slightly more detail is the application of ethnographic methods for research into religious practice. This is not an extensive field, but it does contain some accomplished contributions.[20] While these works focus on the United States, Jenkins has used ethnography to make a study of religion and everyday life in England. The American texts offer a much more critical and a deeper analysis than that of Jenkins, who is too apt to accept uncritically the definition of religion 'as the expression of the human aspiration to flourish' while ignoring its disciplinary characteristics.[21]

In their introduction, Becker and Eiesland note that interpreters of religion 'have increasingly shown an interest in analyses situated in particular places, mapping territory close at hand'.[22] This accords with Bernauer and Carrette's contention

---

[18]   Ibid., p. 6.

[19]   H. Mowat, *The potential for efficacy of healthcare chaplaincy and spiritual care provision in the NHS (UK)*, (Aberdeen, 2008) p. 50.

[20]   J.F. Hopewell, *Congregation: stories and structures*, B.G. Wheeler (ed.), (Philadelphia, 1987). R. Wuthnow, 'The Cultural Turn: Stories, Logic, and the Quest for Identity in American Religion', in P.E. Becker and N.L. Eiesland (eds), *Contemporary American Religion: An Ethnographic Reader* (London, 1997). Courtney Bender, *Heaven's Kitchen: Living Religion at God's We Deliver* (London, 2003). P.E. Becker and N.L. Eiesland (eds), *Contemporary American Religion: An Ethnographic Reader* (London, 1997).

[21]   T. Jenkins, *Religion in English everyday life: an ethnographic approach* (Oxford, 1999).

[22]   Becker and Eiesland (London, 1997).

that theology from a Foucauldian perspective involves a rigorous attention 'to practice rather than belief'.[23] Becker and Eiesland have made a compelling case for the relevance of ethnography as a method to investigate situations that are – by common agreement – multi-faceted, complex and located in a particular context:

> Ethnography, we argue, provides an excellent set of tools for developing more adequate narratives of religious change, a more nuanced understanding of the differences between individual belief and practice and organizational culture and process, and a map that refines our knowledge of religious cleavages and religious experience.[24]

Furthermore, they go on to note the particular suitability of ethnography for 'analyzing periods of rapid social and institutional change'. It is a methodology that is capable of generating new perspectives which challenge conventional beliefs, and produces data that is emergent, fragmentary and at ease with contradiction.[25] In the same book, Wuthnow commends the rich texture of ethnography, its reliance on an imaginative relationship with its audience, and the strength of theories that do not have to construct claims of universal application. He also puts forward the case for the suitability of ethnography in studying the range of spiritual and religious expression, which appears to take many different forms depending on factors as diverse as location (church or hospital bed?) and audience (researcher or minister?). Like Becker and Eiesland, Wuthnow sees the strength of ethnography lying in its attention to practice. In ways that find resonance with a Foucauldian framework, this approach seeks to distance observation and interpretation, enabling new perspectives to emerge through the rigorous analysis of ethnographic texts.

In Courtney Bender's study of volunteer work in a non-religious context, there is an attempt to capture the place and operation of 'lived religion'. Moving beyond both formal religious spaces (such as churches) and structured religious outreach (such as church social projects), Bender goes elsewhere to identify religious articulation. Bender describes the complexity of interpretations that can be given to seemingly singular acts. Hence a marriage is at once a religious, economic, political and familial event – to name but a few of its dimensions.[26] An effective ethnography of events that includes a religious dimension should not be blind to these other considerations. This is the nature of the kind of thick description and dense texts that ought to arise from an ethnography that encapsulates the 'socio-symbolic' qualities of a given situation. It is an approach that Willis uses to describe the differences between linguistic signifiers and materiality. It inevitably points to the richness of scenarios in which the interplay of language and concrete artefacts is brought into relation with a wide range of theories.[27]

---

[23]   J. Bernauer and J. Carrette, *Michel Foucault and theology: the politics of religious experience* (Aldershot, 2004) p. 4.
[24]   Becker and Eiesland (London, 1997) p. 17.
[25]   Ibid.
[26]   Bender (London, 2003) p. 9.
[27]   Willis (Gateshead, 2000) p. 114.

Silent Tremors: Exploring the Role of the Chaplain Through Auto-Ethnography

Auto-ethnography is the branch of this research which most seriously questions the assumptions of objectivity and the dialectic of 'them' and 'me'. Here, the researcher is fully implicated in the situations researched: indeed he or she may give rise to them. Developing traditional ideas of ethnography in anthropology, the auto-ethnographer is invited to see himself or herself as 'strange'. It is a feat achieved through painstaking attention to detail: to words, wallpaper and waiting. In the limitations of time and space, this observation is always provisional and circumscribed – a good ethnographer might conceivably spend a year describing a moment – but it generates texts which permit later analysis and deconstruction. It may be at this point that what was considered 'ordinary' suddenly takes on new significance. As Willis argues, reflecting on the data gained is 'to give yourself the chance of being surprised'.[28]

Ethnography might, as Goffman's[29] unique work demonstrated, subvert existing expectations and public confidence in the role of institutions. For readers who engage with his analysis, the effect can be quite startling. Maanen[30] sums up the nature of ethnography as 'the close study of culture as lived by particular people, in particular places, doing particular things at particular times'. Furthermore, Manning argues that the fragmentary and diverse sourcing of postmodern ethnography is a reflection of its rejection of meta-explanations. Its ability to describe events that appear 'meaningless' is a strength rather than a weakness. This approach struggles to avoid those frames of observation which pre-judge significance, or, at the very least, to be aware that such frames exist and to acknowledge them: 'Chance and indeterminacy, not causality or correlation, are central to explanation.'[31]

It is an approach which demands much of 'intuition and insight, knowing and reporting what is unsaid and perhaps *unsayable*'. The inherent problems in such an approach are clear – especially to anyone more familiar with traditional forms of research. Who is to say what is unsayable? What authority can fieldwork and writing claim for such statements? This, surely, is the final part of any ethnography: the 'headwork'. Reception of the texts and recognition of what they describe is some measure of their validity. Does the text allow the reader to see through the ethnographer's frame and recognize something familiar in a new way?

This last point is one addressed with considerable success by Okely and Callaway's ASA monograph of 1992. In developing their study of autobiography

---

[28]   Ibid., p. 113.

[29]   E. Goffman, *Asylums: essays on the social situation of mental patients and other inmates* (New York, 1961).

[30]   J. Van Maanen, 'An End to Innocence: The Ethnography of Ethnography', in J. Van Maanen (ed.), *Representation in ethnography* (London, 1995) p. 23.

[31]   Peter K. Manning, 'The Challenges of Postmodernism', in J. van Maanen (ed.), *Representation in ethnography* (London, 1995) p. 250.

and anthropology, they focus on the participant-observer, and the implications of that role in relation to ethnographic texts. Rejecting the 'objective' claims of early anthropology, the contributors to their book argue for the recognition of the fieldworker's 'total' involvement. This is in contrast to what they identify as a split between data and interpretation that has characterized much of male academia. Both Okely herself (in a chapter titled 'Participatory experience and embodied knowledge') and Kristen Hastrup identify an 'in-betweenness' in ethnography:

> It is not the unmediated world of the 'others', but the world *between* ourselves and the others … Our results are deeply marked by this inbetweenness and there is no way, epistemologically, to overcome its implications.[32]

The idea of this 'in-betweenness' has much to offer those wanting to research chaplaincy. For one thing, it is relational rather than isolating, recognizing a dimension beyond the individual participants. As we shall see in a moment, betweenness occurs on many levels in the auto-ethnography of a chaplain's encounters. There is the sense of something emerging both between people and also between their lives before and after a critical event – in a brief space of time, new understandings of self and of others are being forged.

Methodology

The notion of a 'frame', a bounded and distinct perspective, is essential in ethnography.[33] It alerts the reader to the author's prejudices and predispositions (what might be ruled in or out) and acknowledges the limitations of the work. It has been argued convincingly by Fox that definition of the research field is fundamental to any meaningful ethnographic research. A seemingly unlimited number of factors influence frame, or field, construction. For example, Callaway[34] argues for the importance of gender in the perception of the ethnographer. A hallmark of valid research becomes, for writers such as Fox,[35] its ability to challenge and subvert the accepted norms – elements of discourse to which social research itself has very often contributed.

As a chaplain doing auto-ethnography, I understand that there are a number of aspects to my 'frames'. I am implicitly sensitive to religious ideas and language. The male cleric can represent a powerful archetype, and this affects my own

---

[32] Kristen Hastrup, 'Writing ethnography: state of the art', in J. Okely and H. Callaway (eds), *Anthropology and autobiography* (London, 1992) p. 117.

[33] Nick Fox, *Beyond Health: Postmodernism and Embodiment* (London, 1999) p. 25.

[34] J. Okely and H. Callaway (eds), *Anthropology and autobiography* (London, 1992)

[35] Nick Fox, 'Practice-based Evidence: Towards Collaborative and Transgressive Research', *Sociology* 37/1 (2003): 81–102.

perceptions as well as the ways that others might respond to my presence and actions. On the other hand, because I am removed from the scientific disciplines and medical training, there are many aspects of the hospital environment that I experience as a (partial) stranger. I believe that chaplains have a contribution to make in health care and, although I am also sensitive to counter indications, it is only fair that the reader should be aware of my particular perspective. Lastly, I have worked to identify material within the frame which is not simply an arbitrary collection of 'good stories', but a carefully-structured observation of what happens around me. This is perhaps the most significant factor about what follows.

I should say at the outset that the method I have chosen is neither the most imaginative nor innovative approach from the traditions of ethnography. I attempted to capture a 'day' of my chaplaincy work. It is a day viewed uniquely from my perspective, although I do attempt to hear the alternative and contesting discourses that emerge through the experience of self-observation and writing. But it is not the many-handed work produced by some ethnographers, or the seven-authored creation of 'Beryl Curt'.[36] The challenge was to find a methodology for collecting contemporary data on practice that did not disturb unduly the very work I wished to observe. An ethnography of another chaplain's work would lead to changes in practice and, for those who have some previous experience of relating to clergy, the assumption of one-to-one care would be changed. A third party would alter the dynamic in ways that other professional encounters, which have a less clear patient expectation of the manner of care, might more easily accommodate. In other words, if a patient was told authoritatively by a practitioner that it was routine to have an observer/researcher present, the patient's unawareness of normal practice might elicit acceptance. However, through both the media and personal experience, patients have an expectation that spiritual care is not generally observed, and usually occurs in a one-to-one encounter.

Having undertaken my auto-ethnography, I feel that such methods could find a place in chaplaincy, and perhaps my foray into an unfamiliar field will encourage others to follow. I believe that further work – especially in the encounter between religion and medicine at the site of the sick body – could follow the creative paths taken by some in the world of medical sociology.

Construction of the Field

In order to capture a 'slice' of my own chaplaincy practice, I decided to use an approach that allowed sampling of progressive periods of time over successive days. This recording of consecutive hours on different days (day one 08.30–09.30, day two 09.30–10.30, and so on) created texts resistant to the simplistic story of a single day. In effect, I wanted to disturb the kind of reflective narrative that

---

[36] Beryl Curt, *Textuality and tectonic: troubling social and psychological science* (Milton Keynes,1993).

draws the events of a day to a particular conclusion. By developing a kind of 'sliding day' I also hoped to access the events that belonged to different parts of each day, including times of lesser and greater activity. The auto-ethnography of call-outs at the weekend provided additional material more tightly defined by the sudden appearance of each call and the ending of attendance with my return home. Planning to do an hour a day over the course of eight working days allowed the option of providing a break or pause shortly after the hour to enable writing up, or dictation. Furthermore it ensured a greater representation of options for observation (for example, I would generally only wear one kind of clothing to work per day; the approach which I have chosen enabled reflection on a number of types of attire).

The decision to observe and collate the observations of different hours over a number of days proved manageable. It is true that it presented greater opportunity to manipulate what occurred in each slot, but my commitment to do this over a number of uninterrupted and sequential days meant that this risk was restricted. This approach produced a text that 'juddered' in the sense that its progress shifts at the end of each hour in terms of both geography and activity. Hence one piece of ethnography describes events leading up to the funeral of a child – but ends standing at the chapel door. This effect may be confusing or distracting, but it prevents the smooth telling of the ethnography as a self-contained story. On reflection, I think this method of creating the field of study is well suited to evoking the complexity of the chaplain's presence and interactions.

One potential weakness of the decision to develop a staggered day lay in the fact that, even with good planning, a space could not always be left clear at the end of an hour for immediate writing up. This is particularly evident when the hour ends at the chapel door before the funeral of the baby. In this instance and, when necessary at other times, the recording of observations was completed at the next available gap. The use of a hand-held dictating machine enabled verbal information to be recorded in the car at the end of the funeral – just thirty minutes after the ending of the observed hour. These recordings could then be drawn on once I had arrived back at the office, and served to ensure that there was a consistency in the collection and transfer of data into my notes of the 'day'. Research ethics approval for the study was granted and the project proceeded soon afterwards.

Auto-ethnography of a Chaplain's 'day' and weekend call-outs

The function of this ethnography is intended to generate questions and identify absences within the work of a chaplain in such a way that the contention of a current 'crisis' would be both tested and also, if present, exposed in greater detail. Inevitably the texts produced by this method are large and highly detailed, and for the purposes of this chapter it is only possible to cite some of this material to a partial extent. However, I believe that it is possible to identify within this material aspects of the crisis experienced by chaplaincy in the first decade of the new millennium. It locates the theories, tensions and nature of chaplaincy within the minutiae of practice as it occurs in the hospital.

Ethnographic Text 1

A written referral from the Bereavement Office requests that a foetus in the mortuary is blessed prior to its burial. The parents don't wish to attend the blessing – there is a stock chaplaincy certificate for me to complete and hand to them before the funeral.

> I phone the Mortuary to arrange this, and agree a time to visit. There is some difficulty identifying the foetus. It has an unusual name and when I arrive it is clear that the mortuary attendant thinks it is Muslim (in fact, Hungarian Christian).
>
> He takes me to where it is and pulls out a plastic drawer. 'There it is'. Pause. 'Do you want it here or …?'. 'Here' is just the drawer in the freezer.
>
> 'Would it be possible in the Chapel of Rest?' (a part of the facility).
>
> 'Yeh. OK.'
>
> He takes me into the ante-room to the Chapel and places the box on a chair. 'Will it be all right there?'
>
> I agree. He hesitates. 'I'll just be a few minutes', I say. He leaves.
>
> I sit on a chair by the box. I wear a short sick-communion stole, white side out. I say short prayers for the baby and parents. I finish with the Lord's Prayer.
>
> It takes about five minutes. I go back to the attendant, leaving the box where it is. I say goodbye.

In this text we can note a range of issues. The chaplain is asked to say prayers with the deceased baby of a couple who do not wish to be present (for reasons unknown) but who will be present at the funeral which the same chaplain will later conduct. It is not clear from what circumstances – or from which tradition (if any) – the idea for a blessing has arisen. Nothing is known at this point about the beliefs of the parents as there was no chaplaincy involvement prior to this request. The chaplain may have been able to contact the parents to discuss the blessing, but there is some sense of urgency as the body would soon be moved from the hospital to the funeral parlour. In the contact that will follow in order to make the funeral arrangements, the chaplain may be asked to give an account of the blessing.

The initial encounter in the mortuary suggests that the attendant is either used to chaplains conducting a blessing by the storage unit or simply wants to avoid any unnecessary work. Many factors may have influenced his reticence to move the body but it is likely that the absence of any family – and maybe even a view about the personhood of the baby – govern his actions. The chaplain is not content with this arrangement and makes a clear request for the baby to be placed in the chapel of rest. This is acceded to, but even here there is some suggestion that the attendant still wants the chaplain's presence to be brief. It is noticeable that the attendant refers to the baby as 'it'. In some cases, the loss of a baby at an early stage of pregnancy means that there can be a delay in knowing the gender. However, using 'it' could equally well be a way that the attendant distances himself from the human implications of the work he does.

In praying in the presence of the deceased child, the chaplain is fulfilling the wishes of the parents. Little is known about the parents, other than that they are Hungarian. Issues of denomination and tradition do not appear to concern them as no specific request was made about the chaplain to perform the blessing. It may be that the parents have thought subsequent to the loss of the baby that they would have wanted a chaplain there and a blessing said. The request now may meet their need to know – and be able to tell others – that the baby was blessed.

In the brief service of blessing, the chaplain wears a stole in addition to his clerical garb. It is a sign of the wider Church and of his authority as a priest. The prayers themselves are simple, but include the Lord's Prayer – the form of words most frequently repeated throughout a range of liturgical events, including baptisms and funerals. Not all chaplains would wear a stole for this, and many chaplains would not be wearing clerical attire in any form. In the context of the hospital, the formality of the Church appears to be attenuated.

Ethnographic Text 2

Entering the ward, I went to look for the first patient in a bay near the nursing station. He was not in his bed. I approach a member of staff and enquire where the patient is. I am told that he is away from the ward having an x-ray. I make my way to the side room to see the second patient.

The patient, Ms B, is lying on the bed and appears to be uncomfortable: her face contorts at times. She greets me ('Hello Father'), indicating with a gesture a chair against the opposite wall. I move it nearer the side of the bed and sit down.

Ms B explains her discomfort. 'I was trying to pull myself up a bit; hell it hurts'.

'I'm just in so much pain; they say they can't give me anything more.'

She seems to settle a little, recovering from the effort to move.

Ms B 'I could have done with you last night.' She smiles and reaches for a Bible. 'I wanted a verse – and I couldn't find it. Not in there (she indicates a Gideon New Testament and Psalms) but a nurse helped me find it in this one (holds a complete Bible); I got it from your arch rival the R/C chaplain!' She laughs a little. 'Look at it.'

It is a verse from the Book of Isaiah (ch. 40 vs. 28/29)

Chaplain 'It's a lovely verse'. Ms B puts the Bible down.

Ms B 'I just don't know what to think. Mr X (the surgeon) said I would get back to work – after a while. But yesterday his registrar came.'

She asks me to close the door. I shut the door and sit down. Ms B continues: 'I said to him about getting back to work. He said he didn't think that was going to happen – not for a long time. That got me thinking. Later a Macmillan nurse came. I thought, 'I'll try it on'. I said to her: 'I'm not going to get through this, am I?' She agreed with me. I asked her how long – three years? 'Oh no', she said, 'not that long'. 'Well, how long?' I asked her. 'Oh', she said, 'it's impossible to say'. 'But if it's not three years then they must have some idea. I just want the truth'.

Her eyes moisten and she appears distressed.

'After she'd gone, I told a nurse what had happened. She didn't disagree. She went back and they must have discussed it. A nurse came back and gave me a hug. She went and then another one came in and asked if I was all right. Then, like the pantomime demon, the registrar came in. He kept saying, "It'll be all right – everything will be fine". He seemed to want me to agree with him, but I wouldn't. Eventually, he asked me what I thought. I said I didn't know if it would be all right, I didn't know what to think. He went after that.'

She appears to be in pain again. 'I've called for the nurse' and Ms B nods her head towards the red light on her buzzer.

'Would you like me to speak to them when I go – to ask if there's something more they can do for the pain?' I ask. She nods.

Ms B 'I just don't know what to think. Why can't someone tell me the truth?'

Chaplain 'These days they should tell you.'

Ms B 'What's going to happen to me?'

We sit in silence for several minutes.

Chaplain 'I'll call again tomorrow. Remember to call me at any time – the staff will page me. Would you like me to say a prayer?'

Ms B 'Yes'

I place my hand on top of the hand of Ms B on the counterpane. She closes her eyes as do I.

Chaplain 'Almighty God, we pray for B; asking that your healing presence may be with her; that you may grant her strength in all that lies ahead. And may B be filled with the knowledge of your constant love for her. We ask this in the name of Jesus Christ. Amen.'

We sit in silence for a few moments.

Ms B 'Thank you Father.'

I get up and place the chair back against the wall.

Chaplain 'I'll remind the staff that you need them.'

Mrs B 'Thank you. God bless'

I raise my hand in farewell, and leave.

In this instance we see the chaplain paying a return visit to a patient who is known to the team (possibly by a referral) and who is being visited on a regular basis. The opening of the encounter is characterized by the silence of the chaplain.

The patient pours out the story of the previous night. She wants to be told the truth but feels that those with the information are refusing her request to know it. The chaplain's presence appears to create the context for the telling of this story, and the chaplain is invited to support her moral contention that she has the right to the truth of her own condition. In the patient's account, there are fascinating examples of how the patient challenges the staff's evasion and manipulates them in order to access the information or opinion she feels they are denying her. When her behaviour leads to the return of the registrar, she resists his invitation to agree with his assurances.

In his relative silence the chaplain is – perhaps consciously – choosing not to emulate the behaviour of the medical staff. He offers no assurances but supports her view that she should be told what is happening – or what is thought to be happening. Ms B's request for the chaplain to close the door suggests that she is fully aware of her subversive actions and wishes to describe them in confidence. For her, the chaplain is not seen as being in cahoots with the ward staff.

The fact that Ms B refers to the chaplain as 'Father' indicates that she is from a High Church tradition. She is used to drawing on the Bible as a means of comfort and guidance as her search for a particular verse the previous evening makes clear. While Ms B refuses to collude (as she saw it) with the assurances of the registrar, her choice of Bible verse is precisely about assurance and trust in God as the creator of all and source of strength for the weary. It is difficult to say for certain whether the chaplain ended his encounter too speedily. His decision to leave follows a period of silence, which may have been uncomfortable but might perhaps have led to further reflection and the emergence of deeper spiritual needs. Equally, it may have formed a natural point at which to end the visit, and there is no request for him to stay once the offer of prayer has been accepted. Prayer is employed in a range of ways in the work of a chaplain, and closure of a meeting is just one example. Care is taken in the prayer not to be prescriptive, but to draw on the idea of love and strength already indicated by the Bible verse quoted by Ms B. On occasion, a chaplain might ask the patient if he or she wanted to voice a prayer, but this can sometimes create a burden of expectation which would be unhelpful. As it is, the chaplain needed to make a judgement about this, and chose to lead the prayer himself.

Ethnographic Text 3

This text arises from one of three emergency call-outs at a weekend nominated in advance to be part of the study. It is the first one, and came in on a Saturday lunchtime when I was at home. The request came from the neonatal unit and was described as 'very urgent'. I arrived on the unit just 20 minutes after receiving the call.

A nurse greets me and is about to take me into the screened-off section of the ward when I begin to ask some questions.

'Is the baby still alive?'

She pauses and we walk back outside the ward. She speaks in a quiet, confidential tone.

'Yes, it's still alive.'

'Have they chosen a name?'

'Yes, Gareth, mmm ...' The nurse appears to rack her brain.

'Don't worry if they've chosen a middle name – I'll ask them. Who's there?'

'The mother and father, and the mother's parents.'

'How old is he?'

'Three hours.'

'OK, shall we go in?'

'Do you want me to introduce you?'

'Yes, my name's Chris.'

We move towards the screens. Another nurse comes from behind the screens and speaks to the nurse with me: 'He's just passed away.' We go in.

This initial part of the field notes contain a scenario familiar to many chaplains working in acute hospitals. What to do when a request for baptism is made and the baby dies before the request can be fulfilled. In this particular case, the arrival of the chaplain appears to coincide with the moment of death. What follows later challenged my own understanding of the situation and made me reflect on the kind of certainty that those trained outside scientific disciplines are often too eager to ascribe to clinical statements. Being introduced to the family as 'Chris', rather than simply 'the chaplain' or 'the reverend', may represent an attempt to get alongside the family instead of operating from a position of formality and authority. The absence of a religious title suggests that the first impression the chaplain wishes to create is one of personal encounter. In the opening exchange, the request for baptism is affirmed by both the mother and grandmother of the baby. Nursing staff have set out the equipment for the baptism and there is a high expectation that the service will be performed.

The mother is sitting up in a bed cradling her baby. The father is half sitting on the bed on the far side. The mother and the father of the baby's mother are standing on the near side of the bed. They shake my hand, as does the baby's father. The mother doesn't have a free hand but looks up and half smiles. The nurse has left. A metal trolley by the bed has been covered in a white cloth. There are two small silver candlesticks on it, a cross, and a small silver bowl and spoon.

'So this is Gareth? I'm so very sorry that this happened.' I have half knelt by the bed in order to better look at the baby: I speak to the mother. The mother simply carries on looking at the baby. 'Will you baptize him?' she asks.

'Yes, of course I will.'

> I stand up. The grandmother adds 'She really wants him baptized.'
> The grandfather: 'We're not great church people or anything, but ...'
> 'It's OK, that's not a problem', I reply.

It is not uncommon for those meeting a chaplain to express some sense of apology or account for their lack of church involvement. In two other places in the ethnographic material, similar statements are made, including remarks which imply that people involved in events are far from certain of their capacity to believe in what the chaplain might represent. Just before a funeral in a crematorium, a grandfather of a deceased baby mentions that one idea for music in the service was 'Knock knock knocking on heaven's door'. He goes on to say that perhaps that would have been all right 'if you believed in that kind of thing'. In another call-out, the father of a young man dying from cystic fibrosis says, 'we're not church-goers. I'm not even sure what we believe. But now it's come to it, we just thought it couldn't do any harm.' For the parents of Gareth, the baptism is clearly wanted, but what it will convey or mean for them is less certain. As the situation unfolds, a request is made by Gareth's mother to have *Footprints* read during the baptism. This creates some delay as the chaplain does not have it to hand and a nurse agrees to transcribe it from the internet. Apparently, the mother was once herself seriously ill when still of school age and during the most critical stage of her illness the school held an assembly in which she was prayed for and *Footprints* was read. As the chaplain waits in the office for the nurse to complete the text, a doctor casually asks what is going on:

> I tell him why it is meaningful to the mother. The doctor says, in a very quiet voice: 'So long as she doesn't expect the baby to start breathing!' I look surprised. 'Well', he goes on, 'stranger things have been known.' And, to the nurse, the doctor asks, 'The baby's not moving at all?'
> 'No'. The doctor raises his eyebrows and leaves.
> I take the poem back to the ward, thanking the nurse: 'Anything we can do that might help' she says. 'Yes', I reply, 'I think it will.'

One of the key questions arising from this text is whether, or to what extent, the chaplain may be fulfilling an expectation by staff and family, but going against the doctrines of the Church. This is an important question because one of the themes throughout this book concerns the extent to which some commentators believe the chaplain is forced to accommodate his or her theology in order to meet the requirements of the institution. Would a refusal in this case have generated passionate feelings on the ward, the breakdown of the mother and a serious complaint against the hospital? Could it be that the integrity of the chaplain is undermined by a departure from the norms and understandings applicable to Christian baptism? Careful examination of this ethnographic text is required in order to discern whether more complex understandings of what has occurred can be generated.

The dialectic outlook produced by the Enlightenment does not favour the significance of what is liminal. Liminality implies an uncertain and transitional state, difficult to classify. One example of this relates to the time and clarity by which a person passes out of life and is deemed 'dead'. As Getz argues, before the advent of scientific methods those present at the time of death were modest in their claims of certainty about the event.

Northern Europeans, especially, tended to see the post-mortem dissolution of the link between body and spirit as a gradual one, typically taking a year. During this time, the body decomposed bit by bit, but retained what Katherine Park has called its 'selfhood':

> Thus the selfhood of the corpse persisted (though ever more tenuously) in the transitional year after burial, during which the body gradually reduced and decomposed. While in this liminal state, this selfhood did not depend at all on the body remaining intact.[37]

Intriguingly, Park also describes a practice in Northern Europe from the late fourteenth and fifteenth centuries where 'religious shrines that specialized in the temporary resurrection (for baptism) of stillborn infants'[38] proliferated. This suggests that the approach of the Church to the popular demand for baptism in the case of still-birth has been far from consistent. No doubt these practices stemmed in part from the less than certain boundary between the living and the dead which gave rise to the difficulty medieval people had in determining whether life had actually left the body irretrievably, in the modern sense. One chronicler remarked that revival of the dead after a couple of days was not unusual in England, but that after seven days it was very surprising.[39]

Traditionally the Church lived with this uncertainty – as did all people. Because of this ambiguity, actions which might be done to the living could be done to someone who appeared to have died. Today, the popular image (confirmed by many television dramas) is that death has a precise time. A brief search round the internet reveals a number of articles in learned journals which seem far less convinced that death can be pronounced swiftly and with absolute certainty.[40] However, the Church appears to have adopted the popular view with little critical attention. Professor Oliver O'Donovan at Oxford University has provided the theological note which accompanies the liturgical website dealing with baptism in such circumstances:

---

[37]   Katherine Park, 'The Life of the Corpse: Division and Dissection in Late Medieval Europe', *Journal of the History of Medicine and Allied Sciences* 50/1 (1995): 119.

[38]   Ibid., p. 117.

[39]   F. Getz, *Medicine in the English Middle Ages* (Chichester, 1998) p. 92.

[40]   V. Adhiyaman, S. Adhiyaman and R. Sundaram, 'The Lazarus phenomenon', *Journal of the Royal Society of Medicine* 100/12 (2007): 552–7.

You cannot baptize someone who is dead: in any case, to do this would open up enormous areas of debate at the other end of the age-scale. Nor is there provision for baptism *in utero*: not only is it difficult to consider as baptism an event in which water does not touch the person being baptized, it also raises problems about how the decision is taken as to which babies to baptize in this way.[41]

This is not, of course, contrary to what has been the earlier practice of the Church. But it shows no appreciation that knowing with certainty when someone is dead is not always clear, even with the aid of modern technology.

I have raised this issue because such considerations are a part of the chaplain's response to the on-call request for baptism. He experiences the inner tension of the theological structure sustained by a denomination and his wish to support what is perceived to be a pastoral need. There are many in the Church who would be unhappy to baptize under these circumstances, and might also think it was wrong on this occasion. The nursing staff support the baptism because it is seen as helpful, 'giving them what they want/need'. But would a request from the parents to put up a drip be considered in the same light? In all likelihood, that request would be seen as a denial of what has happened, and would be refused. Could the request for baptism be seen equally as a form of denial about what has occurred? On the other hand, it may be that the request for baptism illustrates that death is not a single event but a many-faceted process which, for this family, has just begun.

It seems unacceptable to the chaplain from a pastoral perspective to try to dissuade the parents from this request. Although one nurse has told another that the child has 'passed away', the family continue to cuddle and love him as though he were still alive. In the conversations which take place with the family, there is the language of loss but not the separation which consigns the baby to the care of pathologists and mortuary staff. And, significantly, there is the note of uncertainty about the death struck by the duty paediatrician: 'stranger things have been known'.

In this situation, the chaplain's role addresses the liminal and changing status of the baby. He is passing from life into death, and the baptism (whatever it means for the family) seems to give weight to his having been here – and also to make the opportunity for letting go. The presence of a religious figure at such a moment – what could be termed a rite of passage – is not unusual. Fox's work notes the traditional tripartite structure of such rites (separation, liminal phase, reintegration) but argues that the liminal has been overstated. Fox prefers to note the crucial aspects of separation and reintegration, particularly as they relate to the master of ceremonies who controls the 'truth' about what is happening.[42] Paradoxically, by affirming the existence of a life – even one primarily lived in the womb – the chaplain may be presiding over the spiritual and social counterpart of the physical loss.

---

[41] Oliver O'Donovan, 'theological note' listed on the Church of England's Common Worship website (2000).

[42] Fox (London, 1999) p. 38.

In this case, there is considerable shaping of the ritual by the mother in particular. She has a passage in mind which she would like to be read at the baptism. The chaplain knows it but does not have it, but a member of staff is happy to look for it. The parents have chosen the baby's names. It is their request to have him baptized: it is not part of the policy operated by the department to have all babies baptized, although it would be policy to offer spiritual support to all parents in these circumstances. The chaplain brings things to this situation. He has his stole, words from the Gospel of St Mark, water and a blessing – and the mother has her story, the reading and the baby's names.

Using the analysis of a rite of passage, it is possible to suggest a number of possible similarities to other ceremonies. The separation of the baby from life was imminent when the chaplain was first called. This is a service of farewell, although it is made through a service normally understood as one of welcome (baptism). When the chaplain arrives, the baby dies, yet the baby continues to be present both through the parental care he receives (he is treated as though alive) as well as the remaining appearance of sleep (normal for a baby so newly-born). His sudden departure is staged and allows the possibility of a formal service and the inclusion of words chosen by the mother. Once this is completed, the mother kisses the baby, as though in farewell. The baptism, as a service for the living, has narrated his passage into death – which is now accepted. After the baptism the following exchange occurs:

> As I sort out the table and find the baptism register (on the shelf below), they take photographs. The grandfather helps me with the details I need in order to fill out the register. I go and retrieve my jacket. The grandfather speaks to me:
> 'You just wonder how He can allow it to happen: it doesn't make sense.'
> 'No, I agree. It doesn't seem to make sense. No one can blame anyone for asking that question', I reply. We look at the baby.

The grandfather's questioning of the death indicates a different view of the baby once the baptism is ended. Despite the early declaration that they are not a church-going family, there is evidence of both belief and expectation. Perhaps here there is a mirror of the earlier exchange between the chaplain and the paediatrician. Just as a populist view of science was suddenly brought into question, it now appears that a particular view of God has been equally problematized by this experience of loss. In questioning how God could 'allow it to happen' the grandfather is alluding to a view of God's activity perhaps best described as 'governance'. While God may not have caused the death of the baby, he has not prevented it: the death has been permitted. The grandfather cannot understand this and the chaplain agrees with the difficulty of making sense in these circumstances and affirms the appropriateness of the grandfather's question.

It is useful to situate this piece of ethnography within a frame offered by Fox to view the dynamics of transitional rites: 'What seems important is the emphasis on rites which will put right what is seen as a dangerous breach of cultural norms.'[43] A dead baby is not the normal expectation of pregnancy, especially at an advanced stage of development. It can be accompanied by a sense of failure by the mother/ parents, as well as grief or anger by close family. It does not, as the grandfather says, seem 'fair'. For medical staff it is also failure, and their eagerness to help in finding the poem might be seen to aid their sense of usefulness at a time when medical and professional resources are futile. Although permitted to stay for a while, there will also be pressure to remove the dead baby – and to free space for those who are the purpose of the unit: ill but living children. As such, the presence of the dead baby breaks the cultural norm of the ward and provides an unwelcome reminder of the uncertainty of life.

As rite-master, what authority does the chaplain wield? He is able to baptize the baby but this is also a function which can be carried out by any baptized person in an emergency. The 'problem' of the dead child might be addressed by baptism in two ways. First, as a means of recognizing the emergency and death and, second, by affirming the reality and value of his life. It is also conceivable – if seldom indicated – that parents see baptism as ensuring that the baby's soul will be recognized and received in heaven after the physical death of the body. After the baptism, those involved appear to have permission to move on. The baby is integrated into the Church (that is what baptism does) and also translated to the realm of those beyond this life (he is kissed farewell).

This dramatic and moving event reveals both the professional role called out of the chaplain by the family and also the kind of function the chaplain might fulfil for the ward. There is a potential tension between the wishes of the nursing staff to support the family, the knowledge and practice (theology etc.) informing the chaplain's role, and the beliefs, doubts and expectations of the family. By paying structured and close attention to the practice of one chaplain, larger questions are raised about the relationship between science and theology as well as the link between the chaplain and the knowledge that informs his actions. To adapt the language of the culture in which the chaplain works, it might be said that this approach to larger issues through the narrow aperture of a single event is a kind of 'keyhole theology'. The absence of advice geared to the situations which chaplains face highlights the problematic world of ministry in hospitals. Like the unlit candles set out on the trolley for the baptism somehow formal theology in this context is questioned and challenged by clinical uncertainties and pastoral needs. The chaplain is required to make an attenuated use of Church resources chiefly designed for quite different contexts. If the service had been in a chapel the candles would have been lit. This lack of direct engagement between the Church (centrally) and the experience of chaplaincy enables theology to remain largely silent about the unique and complex situations which chaplains face. In turn, this

---

[43]   Ibid., p. 39.

runs the risk of both turning hospital chaplains into ministerial mavericks and also leaving mainstream theology unchallenged by the realities of pastoral care as it occurs in secular and scientific contexts. There is some evidence that this is beginning to change,[44] but whether there will be a full engagement between liturgical scholars and chaplains remains to be seen.

To explore some of these shifting approaches to mortality and ministry I shall turn to Foucault's exploration of discourses, archives and genealogy.

Discourses, the Archive and Genealogy

> The archive cannot be described in its totality; and in its presence it is unavoidable. It emerges in fragments, regions, and levels, more fully, no doubt, and with greater sharpness, the greater the time that separates us from it.[45]

Foucault's description of the archive – of that which permits statements to be made as unique events – concerns the differentiation of discourses and their duration. I believe, however, that the crisis in which chaplains are immersed stems in part from their reference to an historic archive outside the dominant systems of the present. I believe that chaplains operate to varying degrees on the basis that their discourse claims its validity from an earlier pre-Enlightenment archive. In effect, chaplains are bound to the archive-fragment they carry internal to their institutions (for example, churches), while at the same time facing the question of their role in the NHS according to the episteme of late modernity. I call it an archival – or epistemic – fragment because it is more than a single discourse, and reproduces in its diminished state the character of the former episteme. However, it does so within the context of modernity, which in itself shapes the way the fragment is used. In what follows, I shall discuss the ethnographic data in such a way as to permit the possibility that chaplains experience tension as their epistemic fragment encounters the dominant archive on which contemporary health care practices claim validity.

Examination of the ethnography shows that the elements of the text that suggest this tension between a relationship to a past episteme and the contemporary archive include things such as costume and artefacts. I have not invented a new way of dressing, but made a choice from existing options. The stole, baptismal kit, oil and office equipment all have precedents. They lend authority and significance to the role the chaplain performs on certain occasions, and it is useful to reflect on what effects they have on the performance of the chaplain and how his or her presence is received. Without doubt, they relate to a popular image, and while the operation of the chaplain may be restricted (as by ward regulations on the lighting of candles), there remains an accepted territory for the chaplain to authenticate what occurs.

---

[44]   Liturgical Commission of the Church of England, *Transforming Worship: Living the New Creation (GS 1651)* (London, 2007).

[45]   Michel Foucault, *The Archaeology of Knowledge* (New York, 1972) p. 130.

The chaplain as priest is shown to mediate traditional forms of religious practice at moments of transition. As with one of the on-calls, those requesting the presence of a chaplain may not even be clear what it is they want: the patient's father is not sure what they believe. In the Sister's introduction when I arrive on the unit, any mention of funeral planning might indicate a possible link to the request for my attendance. Once again, the grandfather positions the family as non-attending, uncertain, yet still seems to be one of those who might look to the Church at a time such as this for something they cannot fully articulate. While the contemporary archive speaks of this moment as failure, it is possible that those requesting a chaplain are looking for 'true' statements that only the former episteme can effect: life beyond death; hope in personal disaster.

It may be that the principal resources for chaplains in these circumstances are the prayers and scriptural passages which are carried in books or in memory. There is also the element of theology and Church tradition, most of which was formed in a time when the archive largely consisted of an assemblage of these discourses. However, the situations encountered in the ethnography also call for a degree of ingenuity and adaptation which move away from set forms. For these reasons, what follows is structured under the two headings of power and contested boundaries.

> As can be demonstrated in the role of many professional language constructs, inaccessibility can be seen to establish the 'carer–cared for' relationship in order to strengthen the power of the former.[46]

For example, what theological significance is given to prayers and blessing before death – and what discourse gives the action authority. Most strikingly from the ethnographic material there is the theological question of baptizing a 'dead' baby.

Power and Contested Boundaries

Foucault noted that regimes of power are sustained by the regular patrolling (or pushing forward) of boundaries. Within this is the concept of organizational space as finite, and something which cannot allow equal expansion for all. Crowded around the patient's body, the professions stake out their territory, and each claims space for the exercise of its own discipline. In turn, the relative status of carers fluctuates depending on how effectively they can sell their story of success to other disciplines and political masters: how well they can situate their discourse as part of the archive. An acute hospital, like Goffman's mental hospitals, can be seen in this way to serve the requirements of staff who need to earn a living and pay a mortgage.

At several points, this facet of power is demonstrated in relation to the chaplain. As the earlier chapters about the chaplain's role in relation to hospital patients have shown, chaplains are at times squeezed out of the inner circle

---

[46]   Fox (2003) p. 84.

round the patient, their spiritual view of the patient often passing for little more than amateur psychology. As a profession, we have not created the kinds of language and measures which have purchase within the NHS. In the postgraduate libraries of major UK hospitals there is no 'Journal of Spirituality in Healthcare'. The systems which lend status to professions in health have been neglected by chaplains and – not surprisingly – no one has pressed us to adopt them. An empty space round the patient's bed is someone else's opportunity.

Without the appearance of an objective discourse to claim authority over aspects of the patient (such their heart, lungs, psychological state and so on), chaplains become increasingly dependent on patient need. I would not be called to the cot of a dying baby unless the mother requested it. There is no clear quantitative evidence to suggest that having a chaplain there has any effect one way or another, and the wider studies about prayer are inconclusive (see The Cochrane Library on the internet).

Yet there remain historic elements to chaplaincy – like the aging chapel – which can still give authority. Clothing might be one example. When the chaplain wears clerical costume, there is a sense in which this is informed and permitted by history rather than clinical need or organizational effectiveness. What the chaplain wears may – like all uniforms – minimize individuality and signal that the patient might expect some common traits no matter who the chaplain is. However, the diversity of Christian clergy and the multiplicity of training routes that lead to ordination, may leave many people with a lack of clarity about what the chaplain will bring. Other kinds of garb in the NHS harness the discourses of infection control, safety and accountability. The latter point may apply to chaplains in the sense that they are sometimes seen to be accountable for God (because what has happened is unfair), but in other respects religious attire may conflict with the claims of the medical world. This is perhaps most striking in a debate that has arisen between the Muslim requirement to keep the body modestly covered and the NHS drive to reduce the rate of hospital-acquired infections. In the meeting with the mortuary technician, there appears to be reluctance to move the baby to the chapel of rest, but what little hesitancy there is seems to evaporate in the presence of the officially-attired chaplain and in the face of the parents' request. The ambiguity about the degree of power the chaplain has might be of assistance in some situations: 'we're not quite sure whether we should do what he wants – but we don't know who the chaplain relates to in the organization'.

In exploring the material used by a chaplain from biblical and theological sources, the role of language was considered. Language is a significant element of power and of the way in which boundaries are established and tested. This is achieved not only by the words themselves (as an educated middle-class cleric, I can construct language so as to be persuasive), but by the whole nature of the discourses which the chaplain employs and within which he is immersed in the hospital.

Although it is difficult to describe the phenomenon fully, biblical language conveys by its construction and tone a formality and spaciousness which may affect the events involved. However trivial it may seem from other perspectives, the means of description make them portentous. It is a way of speaking which most people, even those with no knowledge of the Church, would recognize and respond to as narrative that is separate from the routine or normal. It may even be that it connects with what I earlier referred to as an epistemic fragment, the remnant of a former archive still resonating in the English language. Like certain forms of music used in films, the poetic qualities of the language unconsciously steer our emotions.

Put simply, the chaplain's epistemic fragment has potential to confer gravitas and significance onto events which could be described in quite different terms. Until fairly recently, a baby miscarried up to a certain stage of gestation would eventually be classed as 'clinical waste' for the purposes of disposal. Only with growing public concern about these matters have NHS Trusts begun to change both the language and the means of burial or cremation. Viewed in this way, it could be argued that the chaplain's involvement and endowment of value to the child stems from connections made between aspects of historic religious discourse and an alliance with new notions of patient rights and moral authority.

This ability to handle ancient words (and invent a few new ones on occasions!) is a tool in the preservation and extension of power. Others in the health care setting would not know how to do this. Creating the sense of different time (eternity?) and intrinsic value enables the chaplain to shape events into a form which permits – or appropriates – release. The very fact that a chaplain has been called marks a threshold in a family's understanding of the events in which they are immersed. It is possible to suggest that the chaplain is the visible sign of the 'limit' and, as such, his or her appearance on the scene expresses what cannot be apprehended by normal activities.

Concluding Analysis

> The notion that religion tunes human actions to an envisaged cosmic order and projects images of cosmic order onto the plane of human experience is hardly novel.[47]

The use of ethnography in this chapter is intended to provide data from the minutiae of daily practice that could help articulate more clearly any sense of 'crisis' which may be affecting chaplaincy. What is perhaps surprising about the ethnography is the degree of negotiation around what takes place and, by implication, little agreed clarity about any 'cosmic order' being imposed. This is not to say there are no fragments of such an order – or that the chaplain lacks 'power'. But we do sense the underlying tensions of the role, where even death is an uncertain and an unfolding event rather than a theoretical or clinical 'moment'.

---

[47] Geertz (London, 1993) p. 90.

The chaplain may, as Bloor[48] recounts in his consideration of the literature, be a part of the hospital's transition of the patient from life to death *via* the performance of 'last rites' – contributing to the creation of a social death corresponding to the physical events. In particular, drawing on the auto-ethnography, the question begins to emerge as to whether the chaplain is not only operating in the liminal territory between Church and medicine but also within the brief space betwixt life and death. The auto-ethnography supports an emerging picture of the chaplain as someone operating within an insecure and uncertain landscape. In the baptism service, the unlit candles are iconic of the constraint placed by the clinical environment on the work of the chaplain. And this restriction extends to liturgical and theological considerations as well. It is puzzling that the Church which licenses ministry in these marginal places does not make a greater effort to learn from these experiences about the nature of personhood, pastoral care and the sacraments. In Chapter 7, further thought will be given to these questions – leading to some surprising conclusions as to why the experience of chaplaincy in the NHS is drawn on so little within the wider life of the Church.

The final key area that emerges from the ethnography relates to the whole question of what sustains chaplaincy alongside other hospital discourses. As I have just indicated, chaplains appear ambiguous in comparison with other staff when the nature of their 'intervention' is so open-ended and little defined. The chaplain may be called in when the patient has moved beyond the scope of medical discourse – that is, through death. Unlike all other referrals, including to psychology, the decision regarding the intervention of the chaplain is uniquely that of the patient or the patient's carer. A chaplain might be offered by members of the staff, but they very rarely seek involvement without the prior consent of the patient. In other words, there is no 'threshold of grief', no trauma scale where at a given level staff say, 'we can't cope – let's call a chaplain'. Such a care pathway might suggest that a chaplain is *offered*, but at present the patient remains in charge of the choice. However, even in the case of patient consent, it should be borne in mind that religious expectations may have been implanted from youth. In other words, the patient has arrived at a particular experience of life that triggers a need for a minister to be summoned. The religious discipline to which they have been exposed may incline some patients both to seek and to welcome the imposition of religious interpretations of their experiences.

From the perspective of other staff in the hospital, it appears that the chaplain can be recruited to ease the acceptance of a medical procedure. Yet the spoken and recorded nature of these roles seems very minor within the overall context of health care. What has the chaplain 'done' and how does the organization manage that *doing* and its effects? This is a much more difficult question, with the nature of the chaplain's authority seeming to stem from the communities considered to be 'outside'. How operational legitimacy of such a role survives in the NHS following

48   M. Bloor, 'The Ethnography of Health and Medicine', in P. Atkinson, A. Coffey, S. Delamont and others (eds), *Handbook of Ethnography* (London, 2001) p. 180.

developments beginning in the late 1990s will therefore require further comment before the end of this book. However, there still remains an historic referencing of artefacts and texts which enable the chaplain to function within a modern hospital. At particular times and in given contexts, the chaplain is permitted to act with authority, and the ethnography indicates that these occasions often arise in the gaps where a medical solution is no longer offered.

The creation of a 'rolling-day' auto-ethnography and its post-modern analysis brings to the surface three basic issues about the role and operation of hospital chaplains:

Accommodation

There is a sense in which the epistemic fragment reproduced in the chaplain – and his or her various strands of narrative – is limited, or accommodated, within the discourse of the hospital. A candle is present at the baptism of the neonate – but not lit. The baptism takes place, but the theological tradition might be compromised by the wish to meet what are understood as pastoral needs. It follows that the chaplain is required to accommodate what he or she does in response to the dominant values of the hospital in ways different from the conduct of similar services in a church building. The chaplain's discourse must adapt to the powerful concepts of risk management and the construction of 'patient-centred care'.

Multiple Worlds

There is much evidence in the ethnography that the chaplain moves between at least two distinctly different worlds of meaning. This is obvious in the subject of attire, where in a single day a chaplain might switch from dress that is centuries old and ecclesiastical to the modern day garb of the manager. The chaplain also has to mediate the language of the hospital with the vocabulary of his faith community. It may well be the case that far more than two worlds can be described. Yet the ethnography supports the view that there are two distinct assemblages of discourse, and the friction of an epistemic fragment with manifestations of the present archive is evident at several points. Of course the present archive permits the expression of the other – but largely by its own inability to (yet) address certain limits and voids.

This issue of shifting between different structures of meaning can be set alongside the official statements about the chaplain's 'home' that will be discussed in Chapter 8, but is also present in the examination of chaplains at moments of historic reconfiguration (Chapters 1 and 2).

Role

The role of the chaplain is perhaps the most significant of the issues picked up in the auto-ethnography and relates to the two previous points.

The chaplain is part of conversations about different theories of his role (generic *versus* faith-specific care). There is the implied challenge in the mortuary about the 'need' to remove the baby's body. It appears at times that improvisation is required in adapting the formal rituals of faith in the context of the hospital. And the register filled in at baptism reminds us of an age when legitimacy and religious validation were vital things to record for reasons ranging from entitlement to burial in certain places to marriage and employment prospects.

At various points, it is possible to reflect on what the chaplain 'comes for', and how the role is re-shaped or remains resilient in the face of different challenges. This flexibility represents both opportunity and also uncertainty for the chaplain, and is indicative of the 'crisis' which I identified at the opening of this book. Even if it is not a crisis so much for the chaplain or the patient, it is a difficult issue for those managing or commissioning chaplaincy work.

The ethnography has developed in greater detail the general thesis of crisis set out in this study. The tension between the basis of the chaplain's power to act, and the dominant archive in which the hospital is set, suggests that the appearance of the chaplain denotes the emergence of an unorthodox space in the fabric of care. It is a space supported by the religious or spiritual disposition already present in the patient, but contained and managed by the wider truth of the institution. This containment and constraint has not been a constant in the history of hospitals and, as we have seen, different eras have seen wide variations in the chaplain's capacity to act. In the twenty-first century we can see in the detail of the chaplain's practice the presence of alternative worlds of meaning which have yet to establish an agreed form of coexistence.

Chapter 6
Religion, Secularization and Spirituality

Introduction

It is a central idea of this book that chaplains occupy an unusual and interesting place in British society. I would further contend that their position has the potential to yield a depth of insight and breadth of perspective which is at odds with their significance to either medicine or the Church. It is possible that a study of chaplains presents the opportunity to do 'keyhole theology', entering the complexity of belief and popular imagination through the narrowest of apertures in order to understand something of what is occurring deep within. In particular, as they are paid for by the State, licensed by the Church and employed as NHS staff, chaplains know more than most about the conflicts of expectation and accountability that accompany multiple belongings. In order to situate the discussion that will follow in subsequent chapters it is necessary at this point to give a fuller consideration to the context of faith and secularity in twenty-first-century Britain. This is needed not least because chaplains are affected by a wider sense of concern/relief that society is embarked upon an inevitable path of secularization. The truth or otherwise of this analysis is seen to have a significant bearing on what chaplains now do and whether they will continue to be present in the NHS in the future. Furthermore, at a more implicit level, how chaplains view the direction of travel of society may be silently informing their activities and investments in a particular process of change. It is my contention that chaplains owe it to themselves – and to those they care for – to make explicit the beliefs which are now motivating their actions.

In order to have this discussion about the insights and experiences of chaplains, it is first necessary to gave consideration to the current state of secularization theories. To do this, I shall discuss the work of Charles Taylor, set out in *A Secular Age*,[1] first because it is a comprehensive and historically-situated study, and second because it offers a more dynamic and nuanced view compared with other – more static – accounts of secularity. In this chapter the work of Taylor and other academics in the field will be closely related to the chaplain's experience and anxieties about the emergence of 'spirituality' as a post-religious concept of what they are about.

---

[1]   Charles Taylor, *A Secular Age* (Cambridge, MA and London, 2007).

Decline in Religious Observance

The number of people who attend activities such as worship has declined in England since the 1950s. Callum Brown[2] and others have charted these changes in detail, and it requires little effort to find statistical data that supports the scale of the members lost from the weekly life of the mainstream churches. For example, the widespread Christian consensus which framed the outlook of Church leaders such as William Temple was set to change to an extent few could have imagined in 1948. Yet the decline in religious observance has not been matched by a corresponding decline in the numbers of chaplains in the NHS: quite the reverse. In 1948 there were estimated to be just 28 whole-time chaplains in the NHS while today the figure is just 350. Of course this in part reflects a growth in hospital staff across all disciplines as well as a reduction in hours for individual staff, more holidays and training leave, as well as a greater need to plan and record activities. It is also the case that some of the increase in chaplaincy staffing reflects the diversification of society and the NHS's commitment to meet more fully the needs of groups previously ignored when it came to spiritual care (such as Roman Catholics and Muslims).

Nevertheless, the relative rise in the number of chaplains stands in some opposition to what might otherwise be regarded as a secularizing period over the last 50 years. Grace Davie's analysis of this change as a shift to 'believing without belonging'[3] has captured the imaginations of many, but has also met criticism. For Voas and Crockett,[4] Davie's thesis is only accurate in so far as it identifies a vague populist sense of 'something out there' rather than any serious, structured or sustained set of beliefs. They argue that there is little value in identifying a religiosity that has melted into the 'mission statements' and other pseudo-religious features of modern society. Their paper suggests that the growth in interest in spirituality and New Ageism is generally pursued by those exiting orthodox religion and is in effect a manifestation of religious decline rather than a sign of a new band of believers springing from a secular landscape.

It is perhaps the consequence of post-colonial views that the decline in personal belief in any orthodox sense is viewed by some in the academic and ecclesiastical worlds as a single story of decline. Around the world this is not the picture with many areas experiencing growth in activity within organized religion. Even within Britain the changes that are taking place are more variegated and sophisticated than many commentators allow. In Dewsbury, for example, more people at the start of the twenty-first century attend religious services there than at any point in the town's history. This change is not the result of a Christian revival but of the influx

---

[2] Callum Brown, *The Death of Christian Britain* (London, 2000).

[3] Grace Davie, 'Believing without Belonging: Is This the Future of Religion in Britain?', *Social Compass* 37/4 (1990): 455–69.

[4] David Voas and Alasdair Crockett, 'Religion in Britain: Neither Believing nor Belonging', *Sociology* 39/1 (2005): 11–28.

of Muslims, with their daily prayers in the mosque. Some observers have now come to characterize this situation as 'European exceptionalism',[5] challenging an assumption that somehow the rest of the world would eventually 'catch-up' with the decline.

The reality of changed patterns of religious belief in Britain is something chaplains encounter on a daily basis. Even in the few fragments of ethnography included above there is only a limited sense of the formal authority of the chaplain. Throughout hospitals across much of England there is no uniform group of Anglican patients to lend the chaplain a commanding role. What transpires involves negotiation and creativity rather than the standard application of a procedure. In the case of the Worcestershire NHS Trust we saw in black-and-white the vulnerability of chaplains when an organization in financial turmoil tried to discover hard evidence for the need and function of the clergy it employed. All this can be described as the waning of religious authority and the Church's social status in public institutions. The response to this both in chaplaincy and the wider health care community may in itself be a manifestation of secularity: 'spiritual health care'. This emerging phenomenon will be discussed in greater detail after a consideration of one of the most extensive attempts to interrogate the broad concept of what some might continue to describe as a secular age.

A Secular Age

In his magisterial tome, Charles Taylor refers to secularity within the heritage of Latin Christendom in three related but distinct ways. Firstly, as the retreat or expulsion of religion from public institutions and practices; secondly, as the decline of public belief and worship (falling church attendance); and thirdly as a change in the context and social attitude towards belief. Taylor sees this third category as a significantly different experience of secularization when compared with the first two. It concerns the shift from a society where belief in God was effectively present in all social interactions, to one in which faith has become one option among many alternatives. It is this third understanding of secularization that attracts Taylor's attention, and he examines its origins over an extended historical period. For Taylor the various events grouped under the heading 'Reformation' mark a growing disenchantment with everything construed as magical – including religious practices. The new emphasis is on the here and now, with an accompanying incarnational theology, all of which enables the possibility of a 'purely immanent world'.[6] In effect, the way people imagined themselves, and the way in which they imagined the whole of society, was steadily 'disembedded'. A new individualism emerged alongside a growing political project intended to manage and discipline

---

[5] Peter L. Berger, 'Reflections on the Sociology of Religion Today', *Sociology of Religion* 62/4 (2001): 443–54.

[6] Charles Taylor (London, 2007) p. 145.

populations. Taylor argues that it is no longer the default position in the West to see the world as 'purposefully ordered'[7] although religious practices such as meditation may enable life to be seen this way. This is not simply a repetition of the theory that science displaced faith, but an attempt to grapple with the question as to how this way of seeing the world became our first – unmediated – response. From the perspective of chaplaincy, while it is not possible to estimate the prevalence of this view, it is certainly the case that many chaplains encounter expressions of a latent expectation that life *should* have a purpose and meaning. A typical example of this would concern questions of fairness and justice that are alluded to by a family following the death of a baby. However, even here the articulations are frequently in the negative, that is, 'why is the world not like this (fair, just)?' It is manifested as a sudden and desperate desire rather than the disappointment of an expectation that had been largely assumed. Even the request for a chaplain to attend can be seen as part of that longing for a connection that the family themselves are unable to make. The chaplain is looked to in order to lend meaning/hope to an event of awful and life-changing magnitude.

In his examination of the loss of an implicitly religious world view, Taylor notes the rise of spirituality. Often accused of being trivial, eclectic and individualistic[8] Taylor believes that these caricatures are too simplistic. The spiritual quest for many people in the contemporary West arises from dissatisfaction with the idea of delegating moral authority to the Bible or Pope as much as with disillusionment in the inauthentic promises of the consumer society. The contrast between spirituality and religion lies to a degree in the primary decision either to accept authority and have a 'supervised' journey or explore without authority – or between authorities – as a way of discerning whether any single authority is fit to be accepted above and beyond or alongside personal experience. It is not Taylor's view that human longing for 'religion' is flagging, but that these drives now inhabit a less defined and more individual quest for spiritual fulfilment. Yet in the public arena, at times such as the death of Princess Diana, there is no meaningful corporate alternative to the offices of the Christian Church. We live in a post-Christendom age, but the practices and presence of that history remain. They are not the default of day-to-day thinking but return to view when an event needs to be marked as a continuation of our main community story. Within chaplaincy this occurs at the family level when significant or sufficient family members see themselves as retaining a nominal Christian identity. Whether or not this is a transitional phase, or is open to other interpretations, lies at the heart of the secularization debate.

There can be no doubt that the changes generated within the sixteenth century altered fundamentally – or created the environment for the alteration – of our subjectivity. A workplace conversation beginning 'Do you believe in God?' is scarcely imaginable prior to the Reformation: what would the question have

---

[7]   Ibid., p. 325.

[8]   Jeremy Carrette and Richard King, *Selling spirituality: the silent takeover of religion* (London, 2004).

meant? By the late twentieth century, it is only difficult to imagine because the idea of discussing religion at all had become a victim of a widespread social taboo, with the possible exception of extraordinary prompts such as mortality. David Hay's research[9] provides significant evidence for this – although he notes a shift in recent years to a greater willingness to express experiences as having a spiritual quality. Yet within all this is a longing for something *other* which is persistent and may even be growing. The success of art exhibitions such as *Seeing Salvation*, as well as the hordes of post-religious tourists who flock to Europe's cathedrals, all point to a desire 'to live while dreaming of being elsewhere, or in another stream of time'.[10] At one level, this experience is dismissed by its critics as the obstinate craving for some sense of providence outside human agency. It is the comfort blanket we have never found the courage or occasion to discard.

In Taylor's thesis, science is recruited by the 'death of God' proponents to bolster the inevitability of their claims against religion. Taylor does not believe that the story of causation between modern science and decline of religious belief stands up to scrutiny. In a way he sees atheists as the unconscious creators of their own version of 'providence'; an inevitable growing up for humanity in which the demise of religion is an important and necessary stage. This is not to say that science is unimportant in our modern episteme, in the way of knowing ourselves and the world around us. In fact the power of materialism can be described as the effectiveness with which it combines scientific narratives with a particular moral outlook. This outlook is the product of the way our ability to see and understand ourselves within the picture of the modern age has come about. We do not see the underlying construction of this view but lay hands on the 'inevitable' moral outlook which it affords us. Taylor here appears to be arguing a similar line to that made by Foucault – that the ideas which govern our subjectivity consist in various reincarnations of power, such as the change from religious confession to modern psychiatry.[11] Foucault is perhaps more inclined than Taylor to see the shifts in epistemes as ruptures in which the implicit apparatus governing the production of statements and legitimating knowledge collapses and is replaced. This perspective is a starker view than Taylor's description of related but competing epistemes that co-exist in the same time. And in as much as the narrative of consumption in the contemporary West appears to control the vast majority of resources it is fair to say – as Taylor does – that his picture is not one of balance but of epistemic positions that are accepted or responded to in changing degrees.

In Taylor's view there is a kind of happenstance which ought to sound alarm bells for wise atheists: they are seeing what the apparatus of knowledge tells them they *ought* to be seeing. This is not – and may never be – the precise inverse of

---

9   David Hay 'The Spirituality of Adults in Britain – Recent Research', *Scottish Journal of Healthcare Chaplaincy* 5/1 (2002): 4–10.

10   Charles Taylor (London, 2007) p. 552.

11   Michel Foucault, 'Christianity and Confession', in S. Lothringer and L. Hochroth (eds), *The Politics of Truth* (New York, 1997).

the medieval workplace conversation: the unimaginability of one person asking another if they are an atheist. However, it does support a thesis I proposed some time ago that religious belief in the West constitutes a form of *epistemic fragment* lodged within modernity. It may be, as Taylor suggests, that this fragment is a necessary part of modernity because it enables groups and individuals to define themselves against it. In place of the meta-narrative of Christendom emerges the master story of secularization, defined by its act of defeating and excluding the childishness of religion.

The condition of modern Western living is defined for Taylor by 'the immanent frame', the idea that everything in our experience, relationships and public structures is understood entirely in its own terms – without reference to the transcendent. It is not difficult to see how this is applicable to chaplaincy as the NHS makes implicit, and sometimes explicit, demands on chaplains to produce evidence of value and efficacy. The health service is not asking chaplains how many souls they saved, or how often their worship appeased the wrath of a God justly angered at our sins. There is an increasingly dominant view – supported by the Churches – that the value of chaplaincy must be contended within the scope and assumed benefits of the here and now.

Increasingly, chaplains encounter those who neither accept a narrow materialism nor embrace a religious orthodoxy. Those who have made a conscious decision to depart from the teachings of a faith community seldom seem inclined to embrace again what they have rejected. But this does not imply they are therefore happy or satisfied with the kind of materialism and immanent frame referred to above. It is this group of patients who are generally categorized as expressing 'spiritual needs'. Although no longer inclined to frame these within traditional belief, these patients attribute to their experience of illness meanings and trajectories that have implications of the transcendent. In both the materialist camp and among those who recognize an unorthodox transcendence there is a belief in the broad idea of the 'fullness of life', albeit understood in very different ways. It is not that the advance of science and the emergence of strident materialism have dispelled belief in the good life, but that the dynamics of virtue have been appropriated in order to redefine what it means to live fully and hopefully. A simple but effective example of this can be seen in the dominance of medicine as the way to maximize pain-free, independent and prolonged life. The weekly journal reports picked up by the media do not say that x treatment will extend life for this category of patients by six months: they say that therapy x will 'save' y number of lives each year. Salvation has become immediate, pressing and temporarily obtainable.

The present debates about modern subjectivity are suspended – in Taylor's view – between the extremes of atheistic materialism and the rigidity of orthodox belief. In fact they require these extremes as points from which alternative positions can be defined. The dominance of this middle ground, unwilling or unable to give full allegiance to the opposing poles, has been emerging for many years. For many people concern about moral and spiritual surrender to *any* ideology became focused by the world wars of the twentieth century. The experience of living in

Europe through events of the Second World War was captured with insight and economy in 1941 by the Dutch Jewish war-time diarist and victim of the Nazis, Etty Hillesum. She writes:

> Everything is chance, or nothing is chance. If I believed the first, I would be unable to live on, but I am not yet fully convinced of the second.[12]

And a little later:

> ... I feel like a small battlefield, in which the problems, or some of the problems, of our time are being fought out. All one can hope to do is to keep oneself humbly available, to allow oneself to be a battlefield. After all, the problems must be accommodated, have somewhere to struggle and to come to rest, and we, poor little humans, must put our inner space at their service and not run away.[13]

This moral and ethical approach to the problems of the modern age is picked out by Taylor in his consideration of the violence which both Christians and humanists appear unable to solve. What Hillesum describes in 1941 is echoed in Taylor's description of the actions of Nelson Mandela after his release from prison in South Africa: it amounts to the 'renunciation of the rights of victimhood'.[14] It is a stance that offers the self, sacrificially, as the place in which the cycle of violence is broken. In the case of Hillesum, this arises not from a convicted and strict religious belief, but from a new position somewhere in the middle ground which is closely concerned with the human condition while seeking for some kind of spiritual integration that is authentic.

The emergence of new positions is, however, hotly contested by both extremes. In the final book of Philip Pullman's *His Dark Materials*, a character who was once a nun recalls the impact of her decision to renounce her belief. From her family, priests and Mother Superior she came to feel that their disappointment arose in part from a kind of threat that her renunciation imposed on them – as though their believing was dependent upon hers.[15] To leave the spiritual home at a time when the storm is beating at the door can feel like a most painful betrayal: the act says, 'there is no future here'.

Taylor posits that within the two poles, between which we experience 'cross pressures', there is a common desire for life to be lived fully, with a sense of values and beliefs beyond the immediate. In fact both contemporary Christianity and modern secularism are children of the same parents found in Latin Christendom and the period of Reformation. It is not that materialism has emerged from a wholly

---

[12] Etty Hillesum, *An interrupted life: diaries and letters of Etty Hillesum 1941–1943* (London, 1999) p. 29.

[13] Ibid., p. 31.

[14] Charles Taylor (London, 2007) p. 710.

[15] Philip Pullman, *The Amber Spyglass* (London, 2001) p. 447.

different world-view from that of Christianity; it is simply trying to achieve its own vision of human salvation and fullness of life by other means. In particular, as we have seen since the Reformation, much of the religious construction of the individual in the West has moved into the mind – creating a kind of fracture with our lived experience as bodily beings. Many of the new positions emerging between the poles of orthodoxy and materialistic atheism seek to overcome this divide. It can clearly be seen in many of the New Age approaches that require the full involvement of both body and mind.

For Taylor, one of the chief problems for the modern age lies in its relationship to time. We noted earlier, in Chapter 1, the medieval emphasis on the cycle of the year, marked by religious festivals and parades. It was also a time when people were connected at a conscious level with the 'saints who have gone before' in the growth of chantry chapels and the evolving doctrine of purgatory. In the present societies of the West it can be argued that there is a lack of connection in many people's lives between past and present, and between one stage of life and another. If rites of passage provided a Christian narrative of personal continuity then the modern vogue for personal re-invention (of appearance; job; relationships; or community) cuts across that in a definitive way. It may well be that the growing numbers of people attending Christmas church services, visiting galleries and cathedrals and doing family genealogies, are demonstrating the deficit left by the absence of sacred time.

The question of secular and sacred time is inevitably bound up with the question of meaning. For materialists the idea of meaning is not irrelevant – it is simply that religious accounts are judged to be another manifestation of childish wishful thinking. Yet the evidence shows time and again that human beings experience meaning as something beyond themselves. This is why the death of a loved one produces such profound grief and loss. With them has departed a certain kind of meaning, a connection with the past and – through their legacy in the world, be it children or art – a contribution to a continuing chain of significance. In Taylor's view, this reveals a human trait that does not emerge as a product of a particular faith view but signals a fundamental desire for meaning that exists apart from religious enforcement. With the absence of an implicit belief in eternity, it is no wonder that many people struggle to know what to say to those who grieve. True, this silence or hesitation has replaced what many felt to be platitudes ('he's in a better place') but the alternative is hardly satisfactory. In the hospital, the approach of death, and especially the cues from terminally-ill people that they would like to talk about their impending death, may be missed in a culture that has ceased to know what to do with mortality. If death has little or no meaning, it is best kept out of sight. This is a far cry from those times when death enabled a person to share in the victory of Christ or allowed the community to re-tell the story of salvation in the life of one of its members. Not that I am unaware of the abuses that could be perpetrated in the extremities of this approach to death: there are many, including an over-eagerness to renounce the virtues of actually being alive! But this does not diminish the potent critique of our muted response to the prospect of mortality. The conditions of meaning in the West do not, by and large, allow for a confident and meaningful discourse in the face of close personal loss. Time and again chaplains enter those situations where death has occurred and meaningful speech becomes a significant challenge. Very often the experience is met largely with silence and the potential use of ritual acts present the possibility of meaning (eternal peace; love; happiness) in the face of an otherwise nihilistic experience. While responses inevitably vary, out of this silence will come for some a new departure in their understanding of meaning in life – a moment which Taylor argues can be 'the paradigm gathering point for life'.[16] Death can become in certain instances – perhaps not at the time of the funeral but later – a kind of 'immanent transcendence': a significance for life that emerges out of the grave.

Taylor's analysis of the present state of post-Christendom secularity is complex and multi-layered. Given the significance and range of our present world view this is as it should be. There are no simple answers to the numerous facets that make up our immanent frame. Taylor argues persuasively that even the greatest proponents of atheistic materialism are creatures of the same religious heritage shared by modern Christians. And between the poles of these related extremes stand the vast majority of people, unable to accept the view of the past yet not wholly persuaded by the austerity of 'here and now and nothing more'. What we call secularization is the creation of the two poles: an anti-religious characterization that suits religious fundamentalists as much as it does ardent materialists. The purity of my position requires me to draw a definitive line between 'me' and 'you'. In fact my view of the world is only tenable because it excludes you and those like you. By contrast Taylor notes those moments in the lives of individuals and communities when something beyond the present frame comes into view and has a transformative effect.[17] Arguably, it takes great intellectual effort, personal holiness, or artistic inspiration to be able to see something outside the constructed inevitability of what is before us and written into us. It requires a kind of personal earthquake, a shaking of the epistemological foundations, and this may be why death is one occasion when the possibility of something beyond the frame comes into view.

Part of the difficulty for the task of spiritual care within hospitals is that it meets head on a fetishism of regulation and bureaucracy that Taylor (drawing on Illich) sees within a corrupted frame of modernity born out of a secularized Christendom. The systematic emphasis within this society on rational rules leaves little space for instinctive compassion and *agape*. It is a collective way of being that chooses retribution over mercy precisely because retribution lends itself to legal calculation. Not only does an over-emphasis on social codification negate what it cannot include, for example compassion, it usually also fails to see that its acceptance and power within people comes in large part from their metaphysical longings. Law is accepted because we long for justice; the NHS is supported because we want to be cared for irrespective of our social class or circumstances.

[16]   Charles Taylor (London, 2007) p. 726.
[17]   Ibid., p. 731.

For Illich and Taylor, the ubiquitous experience of modern life with its many codes requires something more – requires a spiritual life beyond the legal and needs supporting by a connectedness that is more than a set of contractual relationships.

The crux of the problem discerned in this approach is the violent totalizing dynamic of a certain kind of Christian – and post-Christian – ideology. There must be a single answer: we must reinstate Christendom or assert the domination of materialism. Only the weak suggest any kind of co-existence, those lacking the moral will to commit to the exclusive alternatives. Taylor proposes another path for Christianity, as the 'loyal opposition'.[18] Unlike the use of that term in politics, it is not to be a temporary position waiting for the moment of a return to power. It is akin to Runcie's view of the Church of England being in critical solidarity with the institutions of society. This position requires acceptance of an inevitable and constant tension between the nature of faith and the requirements of the world: but it is not a call for Christians to become exiles from material realities or the questions of their time.

In considering how secularity might change in the coming years Taylor rejects the view of Bruce[19] and others of an exponential decline which will only level off when a vestigial number of irrational people continue to practise their religion in spite of the blindingly obvious. Instead, Taylor renews the theme present throughout his argument that the human desire for transcendent fullness is a response to a transcendent reality.[20] If he is right, then this is not going to go away. At the extremes of both poles, where there is a notable lack of epistemological humility, it is impossible to countenance this kind of transcendence. Certainty breeds its own kind of poverty – and violence. If Britain moves more decidedly down the road of secularization, Taylor's thesis is that it will become increasingly apparent that immanent materialism neither solves the ills previously attributed to faith nor meets the deep need for fullness within people. Consequently, the balance between the two poles of atheism and faith will shift towards faith for a time. Yet there is nothing to stop the equilibrium moving the other way when Christianity suppresses aspects of transcendence in reaction to other faiths or narrow issues. Taylor is thinking, in particular, of what he calls 'excarnation' – the disembodiment of spiritual experience he sees as linked to the present worldwide divisions over human sexuality. In effect we might say that faith has provided space for secularization because it was all too eager to retreat from a positive understanding of the human body, and of all the implications of incarnation.

In Chapter 1, we saw how religion in the hospitals of the medieval period was the binding purpose for the activity and ordering of a hospital. From the centrality of the chapel in the architecture of the hospital to the routines of prayer and sacrament, the presence of religion was inextricable to the life of the institution. Even after the reformations of the sixteenth century, and the re-casting of hospitals as civic

---

[18]   Ibid., p. 745.
[19]   Steve Bruce, *God is Dead* (Oxford, 2002).
[20]   Charles Taylor (London, 2007) p. 769.

spaces, the presentation of care as a Christian activity remained in place. In this sense, the events in Worcestershire in 2006 demonstrated just how far the hospital has been secularized. Furthermore, if we apply Taylor's second criterion to the experience of chaplains, we can track a similar tale of secularization. At St James's Hospital in Leeds in 1954, a single Anglican chaplain gave Holy Communion to 3,560 people during the course of his duties.[21] In 2004, with a team of four whole-time ecumenical chaplains, the figure was 967, in the context of bed numbers that had changed very little. While these figures can be interpreted in a number of ways (such as the reduction in longer term patients and the routine attendance of nurses at services in the chapel) this would only lead to a modification of scale – not of the central fact. As church attendance statistics have fallen in the last fifty years, so too has the number of NHS patients requesting Holy Communion. Far fewer people now express their spirituality through participation in the rituals of religion. Finally, regarding secularization in Taylor's third sense, it is more difficult to establish with precision the extent to which chaplains either experience personally or find in patients an assumption that religion is no longer a natural subject to raise. However, a study conducted in Leeds in 2006 produced findings which support Taylor's view that it has become increasingly difficult to raise religious matters in public life. The study explored nurses' attitudes towards recording religious data, and sought to establish what factors facilitated good recording and what issues might be obstacles to this task.

All NHS hospitals are required to collect basic data about patient's religious and spiritual identification. Some areas will collect more sophisticated information about spiritual needs, but this is not yet obligatory. While it may appear that increasing secularization would diminish interest in this data, a contradictory emphasis on discrimination has heightened the need to ensure the information is accurate. In other words, the NHS cannot defend itself in the face of a charge of discrimination against a particular group unless it has the data to confirm or refute what is alleged. This in itself suggests that there are some counter-currents beneath any assumption of uniform and unidirectional secularization. It may well be that what remains after a period of religious decline are more clearly defined and defended religious minorities, increasingly set apart from the outlook of the majority population.

The way in which spirituality will change in Britain in the coming years is a matter of intimate concern for those interested in the future of chaplaincy. Apart from any sense of concern for professional preservation, many chaplains would argue that the lessening of orthodox religious expression has generated a greater need for chaplains who are prepared to listen openly, and respond creatively, to personal spiritualities. Even for those writers who express positive view about the expansion of spiritual beliefs at a time of religious decline, the trajectory of secularization suggests that the prevalence of Christian fragments within those beliefs will gradually lessen. This presents a real challenge to Church of

---

[21] Chaplains, *Half-Year Report Book* (Leeds, 1927–).

England chaplains because their external appearance will often be taken to imply a commitment to the maintenance of 'religion' even in the face of personal experience. This is seen most clearly in the present attitude of the Church – both nationally and internationally – to issues of human sexuality. As research has shown,[22] chaplains are often those making a virtue of necessity in their vocation – entering the health service in part because of a wish to live with greater integrity the realities of sexual orientation and ministerial calling. This is not just an issue for gay clergy, but also for those who find themselves on the edge of church life for a range of reasons including clergy couples, where a diocese might only pay one, or one and an half, salaries as a matter of policy. Another reason may be those clergy whose liberal or radical theology is no longer in favour. This research is perhaps the clearest indication that chaplains themselves are 'refugees' from certain representations of religion, and this may predispose them to honour similar feelings in the patients and staff whom they encounter. If the gap widens in the coming years between a tighter orthodoxy in Anglicanism, and further dissipation of Christian fragments in society, chaplains will experience the ensuing tensions more than most. It is a future that is all too easily imaginable:

> The language and symbols of Christianity will become increasingly remote to most people, but the 'nagging instinct' for a belief in 'something there' ... will remain. The danger is that, without a shared language, spirituality will continue to be privatized.[23]

This is the world in which chaplains work to some extent now, and are likely to encounter far more in the future.

Once upon a time, the story of religion in Western Europe appeared to be very simple. Rising standards of living, better education and a weakening of ecclesiastical influence all pointed towards the long withdrawing roar of religion. In its wake, new spaces emerged where belief was only present as a private and individual matter: corporate activity was secular. Leaving aside the simplicity of how the terms 'secular' and 'religious' came to be used, it is fair to say that this general understanding of social change is no longer the view of the majority of academics.

---

[22] Graeme Hancocks, John Sherbourne and Chris Swift, 'Are they Refugees? Why Church of England male clergy enter health care chaplaincy', *Practical Theology*, 1/2 (2008): 163–79.

[23] K. Hunt, 'Understanding the Spirituality of People who Do Not Go to Church', in G. Davie, P. Heelas and L. Woodhead (eds), *Predicting Religion: Christian, secular and alternative futures* (Aldershot, 2003) p. 168.

Religious Care

As we have seen in previous chapters, chaplains have been distinguished in the hospital community chiefly by their role of providing religious care. From the medieval mass at the bedside to the biblical instruction and comfortable words of the Reformation, chaplains drew on religious tradition and Scripture to fulfil their duties. Without doubt there were lapses in the fidelity of providing ministry, as well as examples of chaplains doing less clearly religious tasks – as can be seen in the medieval records and in the hospitals of the post-Reformation era.[24]

The idea of binding lies in the etymology of the word 'religion'. Religions bind people together; bind individual and communities to a higher being; and faith can be seen to mark a religious contract with the author of ultimate values such as love, justice and mercy. The anthropologist Clifford Geertz[25] has described religion as a way to pass agreed ideas of meaning between the generations. Religious leaders can be seen as those who manage the interpretation of this legacy in the face of new situations and experiences. In response to a collective questioning after plague, holocaust or famine, clergy and theologians have been required to reconcile the religious legacy with the horrors of human experience. While all too often this is witnessed on a grand scale, chaplains encounter similar situations on a daily basis when tragedy affects an individual or the micro-community of a family. Time and again chaplains walk through doors into rooms that are filled with a world of personal sorrow and the accompanying question for which there is no sensible answer: 'why?'

In many respects, the most visible elements of the chaplain's religious practice in the hospital have been in decline. Whereas once the chaplain led corporate prayers for nurses in the chapel on a weekly basis the only religious service that attracts large numbers of staff in many places is the Carol Service. As we have seen, the number of patients receiving Holy Communion has fallen over the years and requests for other specific religious provisions in the Christian community have declined in similar ways. In a climate of increasing patient rights, complaints about all aspects of care and the growing diversity of belief, some of this change may lie in the chaplain taking a less assertive role in promoting religious activity. While once it could be assumed that an entire ward would be almost exclusively made up of patients who were nominally or actively Christian this is not the case now. The chaplains must take great care not to impose their beliefs on others and this has become reflected more strongly in the *Code of Conduct* published by the UK's three professional chaplaincy bodies:

---

[24] In 1592, St Bartholomew's 'hospitaller' demanded extra payment from the governors because of his pains in 'setting the bones and joints of xii persons' (N. Moore, *The History of St Bartholomew's Hospital* (London, 1918) p. 446. It may be that here we are seeing a manifestation of the chaplain's desire to gain a recognition that religious duties alone could not accord him.

[25] Clifford Geertz, *The Interpretation of Cultures: selected essays* (London, 1993).

Spiritual abuse is the imposition of a chaplain's values and beliefs on those in their care, proselytism, and a failure to respect their spiritual interests.[26]

The concept of 'spiritual abuse' is relatively new within chaplaincy and reflects the rise in successful litigation against religious leaders who have used their position and the relationships that arise from it to commit offences. This in turn feeds into the secularization debate in the sense that religious *leadership*, rather than religion itself, has become suspect. The rise of spirituality can be interpreted as a means of retaining aspects of religious belief and value without making oneself subject to the influence of potentially discredited religious authority. Drawing on the work of Heelas and Woodward,[27] John Reader[28] sets out the view that most religious groups are facing the choice between entering the market place of ideas as equal 'traders' or retreating into self-defined certainties that reject any engagement that may lead to self-change. In the market place, successful authority is charismatic, is authentic to experience, and is conferred by popularity. In the place of religious certainty – let us call it the palace – authority arises from tradition, structure and exclusivity. Both forms of authority are present across the range of denominations and faiths involved in chaplaincy, and in some cases the forms can overlap. In the case of Church of England chaplains, there is evidence that most of them see their ministry within the former model of engagement. The personal experience of many of these chaplains suggests that they share, to some degree, a suspicion of authority with those occupying the market place. Due to their personal circumstances as gay clergy or as clergy couples, up to half of the whole-time chaplains appear to have sought refuge in the NHS following experiences that have weakened their confidence in traditional religious leadership.[29]

Spiritual Care

'Spirituality' has become the vogue word in the majority of the chaplaincy and nursing literature in place of religion. The term is attractive because of its plasticity (a reason why some appear to dislike it) as well as its refusal of external authority. For both these reasons spirituality has become notoriously difficult to define. In Harriet Mowat's exploration of research into chaplaincy and spiritual care, there is a delightful image that captures the nature and frustration of the quest to define authentic 'spirituality': 'Defining spirituality and distinguishing it from religion

---

[26]   AHPCC, CHCC and SACH, *Health Care Chaplains Code of Conduct* (Sheffield, 2005) p. 8.

[27]   Paul Heelas and Linda Woodhead, *The spiritual revolution: why religion is giving way to spirituality* (Malden, MA and Oxford, 2005).

[28]   John Reader, *Reconstructing Practical Theology: The Impact of Globalization* (Aldershot, 2008).

[29]   Graeme Hancocks, John Sherbourne and Chris Swift (London, 2008): 163–79.

may turn out to be a room with no doors.'[30] However, this view is at odds with those writers, mostly linked to nursing, who have posited the idea of a portable, individual and non-religious form of personal support focused on beliefs, values and the search for meaning.

Those in favour of identifying a non-religious spirituality as a facet – or unifying theme – of patient care are published widely throughout the nursing literature. In theological circles, there is a divergence of view between those who see spirituality as a form of filleted religion with ideas of prophecy and onerous demands removed, and those who judge it more positively as a striving for connection with non-material realities. However, it is not necessarily helpful – as Mowat suggests – to dwell too much on the distinctions between what is religious and what is spiritual. In fact, I would argue that one of the key differences between the two concepts lies in the issue of religious authority. It may be that spirituality represents a flight from religious authority, from the idea that religion with a capital 'R' requires an outward conformity which is inauthentic to inner belief. Is spirituality simply the religion of our time?

It is easy to see that there is a lot about spirituality that attracts the postmodern, therapy culture, of modern Western living. It aspires to congruency and to honesty. But is this enough? The American scholar Kenneth Pargament has argued strongly that spirituality must be more than a hobby and pleasant thoughts. He dismisses the idea that vegetarianism can be defined as a spirituality, saying that in order to be seen as such the vegetarian's actions would need to be a response to the Sacred, which in some cases they may not be. This approach is interesting, not least because it challenges the idea prevalent in NHS chaplaincy literature that all people have a spirituality. In view of Pargament's analysis, it is possible to see the claim that all people have a spirituality as either a political or ideological assertion rather than a view based on systematic evidence.

Pargament[31] offers a useful analysis of the developing tensions between religion and spirituality. However, he sees these tensions to be felt most strongly at a theoretical level – rather than in the lives of individuals. While the context from which he speaks (the USA) has its particular characteristics there is a lot in his work that is applicable to the UK. In much of the academic and professional discourse, Pargament sees an overly simplistic dichotomy between 'bad' religion and 'good' spirituality.[32] He sees this approach as setting out a contrast between the institutional and the personal, the static and the dynamic. But the US research into personal experience contradicts this perception. Pargament cites research suggesting that most people in America see themselves as both religious *and* spiritual. Given the fact that in the 2001 census, 75 per cent of people in the UK

---

[30]   Harriet Mowat *The potential for efficacy of healthcare chaplaincy and spiritual care provision in the NHS (UK)* (Aberdeen, 2008) p. 38.

[31]   Kenneth I. Pargament, *Spiritually integrated psychotherapy : understanding and addressing the sacred* (New York and London, 2007).

[32]   Ibid., p. 31.

voluntarily identified with a religion – vastly greater than the numbers attending religious services – it is possible that religion and spirituality are similarly entwined in the British psyche.

David Hay's research into spirituality in Britain provides the clearest evidence to support this close but not coterminous understanding of religion and spirituality. Hay notes the response rate in a survey in the year 2000 which estimated that 75 per cent of the population were aware of some spiritual dimension to their experience.[33] This was around 60 per cent higher than the figure when the question was asked 13 years earlier. The fact that the census question about religion in 2001 scored exactly the same percentage suggests that these terms live very closely together in people's self-understanding. Looking at the ways in which spirituality is understood, Hay identifies 'meaning-making' as the most common characteristic. Both good and bad experiences are seen to be part of 'an unfolding transcendent meaning' which is not of people's own making. However, Hay notes that on the whole people want to distance their experience 'from any formal religious interpretation'. Once again, we return to issues of religious authority, definition and representation – and the capacity of the individual in secular space to resist what may be felt to be an inauthentic rendering of their experience.

Within the health care literature, spirituality has been a topic that has generated considerable interest in the nursing profession. However, in 2008 a fierce debate about the foundations of spirituality was ignited by an article taking a reductionist approach.[34] The philosopher John Paley argued that much of what had been written in the nursing literature about spirituality was vague and unsupported. Citing Principe,[35] Paley noted that 'spirituality' in a generic sense is an invention dating from the 1950s, although the widening scope of its usage has also been accompanied by Christians developing spirituality as a more contemporary way to present religious practices.[36] More generally, once spirituality escaped the confines of a particular religion it widened its terms of reference at an astonishing rate. For Paley, this new conception of spirituality becomes 'a sort of giant conceptual sponge' absorbing everything. This view of spirituality further argues that despite its universalistic rhetoric, in practice spiritual care remains firmly anchored to Christianity. In a spirited fashion, Paley rebuts what he sees as the ungrounded and ill-conceived project of spiritual care.

Paley's article was published in the journal *Nursing Philosophy* and it is addressed chiefly to the basis of knowledge upon which writers about spirituality make their claims. In its own way, Paley's interrogation of spirituality is an

---

[33]   David Hay (2002).

[34]   John Paley, 'Spirituality and nursing: a reductionist approach', *Nursing Philosophy* 9/1 (2008): 3–18.

[35]   Walter Principe, 'Toward defining spirituality', *Studies in Religion* 12/2 (Toronto, 1983): 127–41.

[36]   Richard K. Young and Albert L. Meiburg, *Spiritual Therapy: How the Physician, Psychiatrist and Minister Collaborate in Healing* (London, 1961).

academic counterpart to the reductionist thinking that informed the Worcestershire Acute Hospitals NHS Trust's decision to axe its chaplaincy. In the world of modern health care, spirituality looks propositional and illusory, lacking the kind of basis in research which any other discipline would be required to demonstrate. Even Mowat's 2008 review of efficacy suggests the gaping omission of volume and quality about research into spiritual care in the NHS.

One of the foremost challenges for chaplaincy in this culture is to discern and agree what it is that enables a judgement about the efficacy of spiritual care to be made. Against what is the contribution of spiritual care to be calibrated? For Paley, the issue is straightforward:

> the main aim is to reconfigure the spirituality-in-nursing debate, and to position it where it belongs: in the literature on health psychology and social psychology, and not in a disciplinary cul-de-sac labelled "unfathomable mystery".[37]

Earlier we saw the resentment and frustration caused by the total lack of accountability to the workhouse management of the Victorian workhouse chaplain Pocock. This chaplain appeared to work with a kind of ecclesiastical exemption from the demands placed upon other members of staff. I have suggested that this kind of separation – still present in some measure – arises from the chaplain's continuing relationship to an epistemic fragment that predates the Enlightenment. For almost all their history chaplains have been required to 'save' the sick, whether by sacraments or moral argument, and this has meant the chaplain working to conform the patient's behaviour or language to the spiritual expectations of the time.

While Paley offers a wake-up call for nurses and chaplains complacent about their use of spirituality as a meaningful construct, his provocation fails to engage with the work of authors such as Pargament. Paley appears to be overly enamoured of psychological interpretations of the illness experience, without recognizing the artificial nature of Western psychological discourse or its debt to much older religious ideas either by adoption or rejection. In the West, it is hardly surprising that the literature about spirituality is linked to Christian theologies and frameworks. For this not to be the case, the whole of the English language would have required reinvention. It is to be expected that generic spirituality will be linked to deeply Christian concepts – because in many cases spirituality is a term applied to those who reject religious *authority* rather than all the beliefs attributable to the religion. This change in attitude to religious leadership has already been noted. Neither do all commentators suggest that *everything* is an expression of spirituality: Pargament is one who makes rational and persuasive criteria for boundaries. However, I believe that Paley is right to question the alacrity with which spirituality has been seized on as form of non-religious belief. It may well be that generic spirituality is seen to offer a more malleable and politically-convenient construct for a society in which religion has ceased to be an implicit part of day-to-day life. Certainly, chaplaincy

---

[37]   John Paley (2008) p. 11.

leaders have acted quickly to try to catch the benefits of a prevailing wind, with a number of chaplaincy departments re-branding themselves as centres for 'spiritual care'. Yet as my auto-ethnography illustrates, scratch below the surface and the reality of what chaplains do appears to remain resiliently religious – albeit in a more fragmented and less prescriptive manner.

The changing relationship between pastoral care and subjects such as psychology has been recognized by a number of authors. Paul Goodliff contends that in the twentieth century many clergy adopted aspects of 'new-psychology' uncritically in order to bolster their credibility.[38] A few even moved out of Church employment to work as therapists. The attraction of ascendant disciplines such as psychology and sociology appeared to stand in stark contrast to the more muddled and divided state of professional Christian ministry. For those trying to establish a mode of Christian care in a late modern (or postmodern) context it has been necessary to engage with the dominant forms of contemporary thought. It could be argued that the fruit of this religious union with current paradigms is 'spirituality'. In this view spirituality would be understood as the post-orthodox dispersal of religious ideas characterized by the fragmentation, eclecticism and contradiction, but united in a resistance to the right of religious authority to conform individual conduct. As we saw in earlier chapters chaplains in previous eras were officially seen as those empowered to promote compliance with ideas of moral behaviour and godly conversation. They were intended to be part of what reformed patients, making them duly grateful and – if possible – socially useful. It is feasible to suggest that the growth in attachment to the idea of spirituality is influenced to some extent by a flight from clerical authority and what some will have regarded as the oppressive nature of organized belief. The restrictive aspects of religion are associated for some with hypocrisy and a failure to bring into meaningful relationship the inner self and required public behaviour. So, for example, the latter part of the twentieth century saw major changes in the acceptability of homosexual expression and relationships in England when compared with previous generations. To describe this process more positively we might say that the modern vogue for the spiritual is a drive towards authenticity and integrity rather than simply the abandonment of a benign religious belonging.

If nothing else can be said with certainty, then it appears that spirituality as a burgeoning discourse in the literature and practices of health care remains both partial and contested. In the following chapter, more attention will be given to this in relation to theological concerns. For chaplaincy, I would wish to simply raise the question as to whether, like multi-faith discourse, spirituality has been mobilized as a vehicle for protecting and advancing forms of chaplaincy which have in reality remained largely unchanged. This hypothesis is supported to some extent by the fundamental requirement – even in departments which have re-titled themselves as providers of 'spiritual care' – that chaplains are authorized

---

[38]   Paul Goodliff, *Care in a confused climate: pastoral care and postmodern culture* (London, 1998) p. 18.

ministers of recognized Churches, mosques and synagogues. John Paley's critique of a spirituality hiding in Christian clothes cannot and should not be dismissed lightly. For nurses, the interest in spirituality may offer a helpful way to value and affirm less technical aspects of care which are still felt to be important but some believe to be under attack in the target driven culture of the NHS. A secular spirituality, or at least one constructed from religious elements, may enable some nurses to assert more strongly the idea of 'vocation' at a time when the term appears unfashionable. For chaplains, it is interesting to consider whether, as a professional group, spirituality offers a way of working and talking across religious divides within chaplaincy teams. However, in Chapter 3 we explored the contention that multi-faith chaplaincy has been written about to a greater extent than it has been enacted, and it may be that what Paley is identifying leads to much the same hypothesis. Perhaps in order to influence the Department of Health, and harness NHS resources for the continuation and development of chaplaincy, we are witnessing the rise of 'the myth of spiritual care'.

Conclusion

It is quite possible that the churches in the West have been complicit in the story of secularization that holds sway in the popular – media – imagination. It has been widely accepted that a decline in forms of religious observance in 'church space' throughout Western Europe amounts to the decline of Christianity as a faith that is meaningful in postmodern times. It is difficult to evaluate this fully, in part because historic Christian affiliations did not always have much to do with free will or personal choice, as we have seen in the history of the chaplain. Chaplains were part of the disciplinary apparatus of the hospitals and religion mattered to those who financed these institutions because of a desire to see moral improvement amongst the poor and in part to assuage the conscience of a Christian society. The loss of disciplinary utility for the hospital administration has been seen to contribute to the perceived vulnerability of chaplains as a group. However, drawing on most of the contemporary accounts of secularization there should be ample opportunity for chaplains to strengthen their case. While the auto-ethnography set out earlier is in no way capable of generalization it does accord with the observations of Taylor and findings of Hay. In a world where religious belief prevails over atheism, and where such beliefs are fragmentary, the need for skilful interpreters must surely be in the ascendant. In other words the data available about the nature of secularization strengthens rather than weakens the case for professional chaplains. Dealing as it does with questions of life, death and suffering, aspects of the Christian faith continue to be expressed in the world of the NHS. David Martin has commented that the 'future of Christianity depends not on what scientific advance may show, but on whether the Christian drama continues to make sense'. I would suggest that based on the auto-ethnography, and drawing on other accounts of chaplaincy, there is a considerable and continuing role to be played in bringing the Christian drama to meet the powerful experiences that arise in health care. It may well be that chaplains themselves need to do far more work to explore those parts of the Christian drama that resonate with the experience of patients. There is good reason to believe that faiths which embody narratives of suffering, loss, death, hope and love should be able to say – and do – meaningful things within hospitals. The changed social context of modern Britain with its postmodern characteristics means that there is an opportunity for such an argument to be heard. However, whether chaplains can engage effectively with this context will depend on their charism and authenticity far more than on their institutional or historic privilege. Strategically this analysis of secularization further emphasizes the lessons of Worcester that chaplains must articulate a stronger case for their presence in healthcare if they are to survive. It is no longer either desirable or tenable to rely for professional security on the social influence of religious leaders. The broad picture of spirituality emerging in the twenty-first century demands a chaplaincy that is self-aware; open to the experiences of others; and able to articulate a theology that is of practical relevance.

Chapter 7
Theological Voices and Ventures

Introduction

In the examination of the chaplain at moments of historic change, we noted the political and ecclesiastical influences that have reshaped the understanding of what the chaplain 'comes for'. Through an analysis of a small amount of ethnographic material, we have witnessed the pressing and potentially controversial nature of the chaplain's pastoral role. And in the analysis of what followed the Worcestershire Acute Hospitals NHS Trust's decision to axe its chaplaincy, we saw how various arguments were mobilized from different quarters to attack or defend the presence of chaplains in the health service. Theological considerations have been largely implicit in these various strands, but we now come to consider directly the contribution that practical theology can make to interrogating, interpreting and comprehending more fully the role of the contemporary chaplain. This latter task will be done in relation to two particular areas of concern: the person of the chaplain and the spaces within the hospital set apart for prayer, reflection and spiritual care.

Practical Theology

Practical theology has become the normative theological approach to pastoral care and what are termed the 'sector ministries' of the Church. However, as Paul Ballard has noted, 'practical theology is problematic'[1]. It has been a problem within academic circles because it so embedded in Church and ministerial practice. At the same time it is methodologically eclectic and runs the risk of becoming other things by inhabiting other clothes (sociology; psychology; postmodern philosophy). Like chaplains themselves, practical theology may appear merged, accommodated and altered by its willingness to embrace forms of enquiry borrowed from other disciplines.[2] It is not a theology for those seeking purity. The risk of acculturation within other disciplines is real and requires careful negotiation. However, many of those committed to practical theology believe that these potential compromises are counterbalanced by the richness and insight that critical engagement with

---

[1]   Paul Ballard and J. Pritchard, *Practical Theology in Action: Christian thinking in the service of Church and society* (second edition) (London, 2006) p. 11.

[2]   Martyn Percy, *Engaging with contemporary culture: Christianity, theology, and the concrete church* (Aldershot, 2005) pp. 8–9.

other disciplines and faiths can bring.[3] Practical theology is neither narrow in its focus nor remote from the experiences of people and events. It is opposed to that characteristic we saw described in Chapter 6 by Charles Taylor as 'excarnation'. Practical theology is concerned with the lived experience of spirituality, the embodied nature of humanity and the detail of human relationships. A theologian in this tradition attends to the work of groups such as chaplains on the basis of Anselm's classic definition of theology as faith seeking understanding. Schleiermacher was the first to use the term in the sense it continues to possess today, and he saw it as an activity and area of study rooted in the Church.[4] Alastair Campbell notes that in Schleiermacher's understanding the Church was 'the fellowship of those who share in God-consciousness',[5] although this still appeared to leave practical theology chiefly concerned with how pastors might best serve those who met behind church doors. Practical theology has come a long way since Schleiermacher, but it has not arrived at any position of certainty or security within either the Church or the secular academy. It appears that practical theology is bound by its endeavour to occupy a place between the alternative worlds of the prodigal son and his brother: lost in the world or limited by the boundaries of the familiar. For Campbell it is the unique genius of this kind of theology to tread 'a difficult path between practical relevance and theological integrity'.[6]

The tensions which arise in the pursuit of practical theology are identified by Paul Ballard to lie between 'its roots in the community of faith and its freedom of enquiry'[7]. Similarly, Lyall refers to those ministering 'in the tension between the story of the Christian community and its tradition and the particularity of individual life stories'.[8] As we shall shortly go on to see, for those intent on pursuing this understanding of practical theology in the context of the NHS a problem may emerge concerning the significant number of chaplains who find themselves estranged in some measure from the community of faith. Chaplains are formed in the story of faith, but they also come to do theology with their personal life stories.

It is in practical theology that scholars are most engaged with questions of professional identity and role. Here we see a sophisticated recognition of theory embedded within practice, and this is well suited to a methodology such as ethnography. Using tools that detail activities and absences, practical theology

---

[3]   Ian S. Markham, *A theology of engagement* (Oxford, 2003) pp. 7f.

[4]   Friedrich Schleiermacher, James O. Duke and Howard W. Stone, *Christian caring: selections from Practical Theology* (Philadelphia, 1988).

[5]   Alistair Campbell, 'The Nature of Practical Theology', in J. Woodward and S. Pattison (eds), *The Blackwell Reader in Pastoral and Practical Theology* (Oxford, 2000) pp. 77–88.

[6]   Ibid., p. 86.

[7]   Paul Ballard and J. Pritchard (London, 2006) p. 14.

[8]   David Lyall, *The integrity of pastoral care* (London, 2001) p. 61.

offers the prospect of a conversation that runs practice–theory–practice.[9] Among other things, practical theology draws on critical correlation theory and develops concepts of practical wisdom that may help chaplains both articulate and analyse their experiences. It is a form of theology that offers political critique, and calls into question some of the accepted claims of both churches and the contemporary health community. Pattison, for example, argues that the popular focus on 'wholeness' obscures the lived experience of those for whom fragmentation is a daily and seemingly permanent condition.[10] However, Lyall questions the extent to which chaplains can effectively challenge institutions along the lines Pattison draws out from liberation theology.[11] In some measure, this comes back to both who employs chaplains and the potency or desire with which the faith communities are prepared to engage fully with what chaplains do. In the work of David Tracy, the political dimension of practical theology is taken further, and the question of those excluded from the production of theology itself is addressed. Tracy identifies Foucault as a 'real master' in his ability to challenge our complacent understanding and sloth in easily accepting what lies in front of us. While wary of some of the conclusions drawn by postmodern philosophers, Tracy nevertheless recognizes the value of their methodologies. Allied to practical theology the political theologians: 'achieve their journey of intensification into the concrete by means of an unyielding critique of the illusions and ideologies embedded in the concrete situations and structures of both society and church'.[12] It is not difficult to see the elements of common ground between practical and political theology and the work of Foucault. In fact, so promising does the dialogue appear that some social scientists have been surprised by the lack of engagement in the analysis of religion from the perspective of both his work on confession as well as on governmentality.[13] In this book I have suggested at a number of points that a methodology inspired by Foucault enables a politicization of the role of chaplain within a much wider context of professionalization, health care and the competing claims and priorities of faith communities.

While there is evidence of much to hope for in the engagement I am describing, a note of caution needs to be struck. By its nature, the ethnographic and Foucauldian approaches inevitably question the forms of knowledge and belief that underpin practical theology. It is an encounter that might be far from comfortable, and the silences to which this research points may have roots in the historic systems of thought that have privileged established discourses over others. In order to take

---

[9]   Don Browning, *A fundamental practical theology: descriptive and strategic proposals* (Minneapolis, 1991).

[10]   Stephen Pattison, *Alive and kicking: towards a practical theology of illness and healing* (London, 1989) p. 77.

[11]   David Lyall (London, 2001) p. 40.

[12]   David Tracy, *Analogical imagination: Christian theology and the culture of pluralism* (New York, 1981) p. 393.

[13]   James A. Beckford, *Social theory and religion* (Cambridge, 2003).

that challenge seriously, the history of pastoral care, and the emergence of practical and political theologies that arise from it, must face stringent critique if they are not simply to replicate dominant ideologies. For example, Carrette has noted the dualism and imperialism of Western Christianity in relation to sexuality.[14] All this implies the need for work to better train and educate clergy and faith leaders in the skills of deep critical reflection. Johannes van der Ven has made an excellent case for such an approach in a call to education for reflective ministry.[15] As different strategies to educate and train chaplains develop, these insights need to inform the debate and question smooth answers to the human complexity that chaplains face on a daily basis. The fruit of an historic consciousness in chaplaincy allied to a more critical and reflective practical theology could be a vital and dynamic spiritual care embraced by the Church as a whole. Such care would not appropriate patients' experience but enable their hospitalization to be received more openly, and allow what it means to live through illness to speak cogently to the theories of care that seek to define them. It is a possible future trajectory for chaplaincy that sees the most significant alliance not with health professionals – but with patients.

In the view of many theologians committed to practical theology, what distinguishes the discipline from other fields is the nature of its questioning and its commitment to the study of concrete situations. Appropriately this point can be illustrated by drawing on the assessment by a theologian of an academic from outside the theological academy. In summarizing the contribution of Michel Foucault the Jesuit philosopher James Berneur noted: 'He left no teaching, but he did engrave a manner of questioning.'[16] A pragmatic approach of this kind in theology worries less about the mode of investigation and more about getting right the question that is being asked. This is not to say that practical theologians are naive about the impact that tools can make upon tasks, but I would suggest that recognizing this is a strength in the approach taken by practical theologians. It follows that the choice of methodology will depend upon the kind of question that is being asked. If theology is concerned with the real world, and examines a confessional claim that God is involved in the diversity and intricacies of life (human and otherwise), then the scope for research is 'infinite'.[17] In order to answer meaningfully different questions, the practical theologian will need to draw on a diverse collection of methodologies.

The methods employed in my development of a practical theological examination of the chaplain draw on the insights from other disciplines. For example, the auto-ethnography used in Chapter 5 was selected due to its well-established place in the

---

[14]   Jeremy Carrette and Richard King, *Selling Spirituality: The Silent Takeover of Religion* (London, 2004).

[15]   Johannes van der Ven, *Education for reflective ministry* (Louvain, 1998).

[16]   James Bernauer, *Michel Foucault's Force of Flight* (London, 1990) p. 4.

[17]   James Woodward, Stephen Pattison and John Patton, *The Blackwell reader in pastoral and practical theology* (Oxford, 2000) p. 8.

field of qualitative research and proven ability to disturb and refresh the approach to what might otherwise seem to be routine subjects. The method has been debated vigorously regarding its epistemology and, as we noted, it has become an accepted tool for examining congregations and forms of ministry. In a similar way the chapters addressing the historical construction of the chaplain were influenced by Foucault's way of problematizing forms of institutional behaviour that generate the impression of being obviously good or evidently necessary. Deeper understanding requires some form of disturbance to the world we are encouraged to accept; otherwise we simply make an idol of our present knowledge.

Even within the relatively small world of health care chaplaincy, there are many aspects of the chaplain's work that would benefit from a greater engagement with the methods and insights of practical theology. As the chaplain is placed at the intersection of issues that remain significant in society (illness, health, secularization, belief, professionalism and so on), there is a richness in the experience of this ministry which often seems ignored by the Church at large. Within the scope of this book, and my desire to make this richness and complexity more apparent, I shall now consider two very different aspects of the chaplain's presence in the hospital: who the chaplain is, and the particular place with which he is identified.

Who are Health Care Chaplains?

The question of what the chaplain 'does' in the modern hospital cannot be separated from asking the question as to who the chaplain *is*. This is important because – if practical theology is to do with what is incarnate – then the person of the chaplain is a proper subject for study. As I have attempted to do earlier, it is important to distinguish between the rhetoric of public statements about the chaplain (caring; called and committed) and the more detailed reality of some chaplains' experience (rejected, marginalized – a transformer of necessity into virtue). The voices of chaplains need to be heard if we are to take seriously the nature of the chaplains' pastoral encounters and their role within the health service. Following this exploration of the chaplain I shall turn to a consideration of the spaces set aside for spiritual practice and prayer within the hospital.

Ostensibly, health care chaplains are clergy and religious leaders sent or mandated by faith communities to take part in the spiritual and religious care of patients and staff. In this book, it is furthermore important to say that the chaplains I am concerned with are employed directly by the National Health Service. According to the strategy document developed between the NHS and Multi-Faith Group in England chaplains:

> are representatives of their faith communities which require them to live out the commitment of those communities to the wider world, in this case in a healthcare context. They must therefore be learned in the ways of the faith group

and knowledgeable about the basis for its decisions and guidance. In this role, chaplains are accountable to the faith group for embodying its ethos and teaching appropriately. A regular checking-back and refreshment of this representative role is necessary.[18]

This statement in an NHS guidance document gives prominence to the faith communities' control over the deployment and sustention of chaplains in the health service. While no doubt supportive in many respects it raises the question as to what would happen if a church or synagogue suddenly decided that an individual chaplain's representative role was impaired and incapable of being 'refreshed'. Reflecting on this official statement identifies the potential tension for the chaplains who inhabit a world of secular employment rights alongside their relationship to a church or faith group exempted from many laws designed to prohibit inequalities and discrimination.

In what follows, my concern will be with whole-time chaplains, those who have made a decision to move out of daily work with the local religious community in order to devote themselves to full-time work in the health service. Almost without exception it is these chaplains who fuel the professional debate about spiritual care, attend local and national meetings about chaplains, and publish research and opinion about the direction and development of chaplaincy.

Research published in 2008[19] provides the most detailed account of who Anglican chaplains are and how they have come to be in chaplaincy. The work was restricted to whole-time clergy of the Church of England because they are the largest single group of chaplains working in the NHS, and also because the study sought to compare ministerial experience pre-chaplaincy employment and subsequently.[20] Reasons to enter chaplaincy may have been influenced by financial factors including the provision of housing, stipend levels and other benefits. These would have been different in other traditions, introducing a much wider range of variables and decreasing the likelihood of finding meaningful data.

The most striking thing to emerge from the research is the evidence of major influences in personal circumstances for those entering chaplaincy. In a group of clergy whose numbers match those of a major Anglican diocese in terms of staffing (say, Winchester) the 43 per cent response rate found that over 20 per cent

---

[18]   South Yorkshire Workforce Development Confederation, *Caring for the Spirit: A strategy for the chaplaincy and spiritual healthcare workforce* (Sheffield, 2003) paragraph 33.

[19]   Graeme Hancocks, John Sherbourne and Chris Swift, 'Are they Refugees? Why Church of England male clergy enter health care chaplaincy', *Practical Theology*, 1/2 (2008): 163–79.

[20]   The 2007 survey had a 43.5 per cent response rate from England's 260 whole-time chaplains (those in post at the time the questionnaire was distributed). If the statistics for the clergy in same-sex partnerships were true for the whole population then the total number of partnered clergy would have been 43.

of male respondents were in same-sex partnerships. The figure was lower for female chaplains but, if those who responded were typical of the total number, it suggests that out of the 260 chaplains 43 would be in same-sex partnerships. Even more striking were the figures for those chaplains who had a partner (married or same-sex) who was also in ministry. This came out at 27 per cent in the sample, equating to 64 chaplains if the sample was true for all chaplains. Given that 25 per cent of women in the research stated that they were single, this means that of all those with a partner, many are in a relationship with another minister. Furthermore, some of the verbatim comments from those participating in the research make a clear link between a negative experience of the Church dealing with the complexity of placing a married clergy couple in parish ministry and their decision to enter chaplaincy. The same was found to be true for those stating that they were in a same-sex relationship. More than 80 per cent agreed that 'personal circumstances made it easier for me to work in health care chaplaincy'.

The research into Anglican clergy suggests a very high probability that chaplains as a group contain many individuals who feel disenchanted with the leadership and structures of the Church. It is difficult – for all kinds of reasons – to trace whether this has been a persistent factor in the history of chaplains or only a modern manifestation. In the case of clergy married to clergy it is obviously a twentieth-century innovation. The specific issue of homosexuality and chaplaincy is also uncertain, partly because such questions would never have been asked (or answered) in the past. As one comment in the Leeds research put it:

> Is there any correlation between the reasons people go into chaplaincy and their model of chaplaincy. Are those who come into chaplaincy for 'negative' reasons more likely to be theologically liberal and less attached to their church/faith community. Are they 'refugees'?[21]

Certainly the findings support the contention that chaplains are theologically liberal (80 per cent identified with this statement) and in some sense 'catholic' (75 per cent). Evangelicals, seen as the ascendant category in the parochial system, figured as just 16 per cent of the respondents. It would appear that either certain kinds of clergy become chaplains – or that some life-experiences form particular theological outlooks that lead people into chaplaincy. In any event, health care chaplains are an unusual group in the Church of England when it comes to their theological convictions and their capacity to sit outside the mainstream. This analysis may account for the fact that little work has been done on the theology that emerges from the experience of chaplains. I would contend that the general lack of desire to involve chaplains more deeply in the structures of the Church, in its theology and policy making bodies, stems from an array of factors that serve to marginalize chaplains:

---

[21] Ibid.

a. At a time of renewed conservatism in Church leadership, witnessed especially in the Anglican Communion, the liberal make-up of most chaplains is unattractive and appears remote from the desire to establish 'orthodoxy';
b. Given the presence of relatively large numbers of gay, lesbian and bisexual clergy in chaplaincy there are considerable advantages for the Church's decision making bodies and leadership to keep chaplains at arm's length;
c. The pastoral practice of chaplains as clergy is difficult and raises questions about life, ministry and personhood which are much easier to ignore than to engage. A theology developed from chaplaincy is unlikely to be tidy.

I believe that there is sufficient evidence to postulate that it is not simply benign neglect on the part of the Church that leaves chaplains at one remove from the concerns of the Church's central structures: either consciously or unconsciously chaplains are regarded as either dangerous or doubtful and are, therefore, best ignored. The ability for bishops to shepherd problematic clerics into safe positions, with a good distance from the main body of Christ, has been silently viewed as a way for vocations to be honoured while avoiding difficulties in parish settings. It is possible to construct the theory that the Hospital Chaplaincies Council, as the body both representing Anglican interests *and* providing NHS trusts with assessors for chaplaincy appointments, has tacitly managed the removal of problematic clergy from the visibility of the parsonage to the relative privacy of the NHS. In a similar manner – albeit for different reasons – many Roman Catholic clergy who left the Church of England at the time women were ordained to the priesthood now work within chaplaincy. This enables the Roman Catholic Church to utilize a group of married clergy it might otherwise find difficult either to accommodate in a parish or pay a salary of sufficient size to meet the needs of those supporting a family. In both cases the NHS effectively provides the solution to a difficulty faced by the Church authorities. To understand the factors influencing Free Church clergy to enter chaplaincy more data is required.

Having suggested that chaplains are a discrete and unusual group of clergy, it can be argued that a fuller understanding of God's presence in the world will therefore arise from greater theological attention to the chaplains' experience. As we saw in the ethnographic material in Chapter 5, the chaplain is someone working within situations that are complex, liminal and highly charged. To be effective, the chaplain must know herself well and understand the processes occurring within. A number of commentators have noted that the emotional sophistication required for this kind of work is not something the Church has been good at promoting. Pattison argues that theology must not:

> collude in demonising or hiding dimensions of life that, if ignored or repressed, are more likely to be haunting and destructive than they would be if they were acknowledged... Notions of creation, incarnation and bodily resurrection point

to the importance of taking all aspects of embodied human existence, including emotions, very seriously indeed.[22]

This accords with the view of the Royal College of Psychiatrists as expressed in a written consultation response prepared for the Church of England's Listening Exercise on Human Sexuality by Professor King.[23] In it, the College states that: 'People are happiest and are likely to reach their potential when they are able to integrate the various aspects of the self as fully as possible.' It would appear that the struggle to achieve this has led some clergy to enter chaplaincy.

If these facts are collected and presented in this way, then the general characteristics of hospital chaplains make them a potentially dangerous group for those striving to present uniformity and ecclesiastical cohesion. Added to this, as we have seen, the work of chaplains at the limits of life, liturgy and theology presents problems for the smooth telling of orthodoxy. It may be more accurate to say that the Church of England's attitude is not so much benign neglect as intentional remoteness. This may seem a provocative claim, but it is supported by some analysis of the way the Church relates to chaplains. In the last ten years, there has been only one national gathering of Anglican chaplains with the Chair and Chief Executive of the Hospital Chaplaincies Council (HCC). Chaplains are seldom consulted on liturgical matters and even less on theological issues. While at a diocesan level there are periodic meetings for chaplains (usually annual events of a couple of hours in duration), there is a lack of systematic engagement with what chaplains do.

In considering who chaplains are, the image of the 'refugee' seems appropriate to a certain extent. Melvyn Macarthur's study[24] of Protestant prison chaplains uses the biblical metaphor of 'exile' to conceptualize the current situation of the chaplain. He identifies this experience not only within an institution such as the prison but also in the way Church-funded chaplaincy work is often the first thing to go when Churches are faced by financial difficulties:

> Churches in general are reluctant to commit their own financial resources into the chaplaincies, clearly indicating that their priorities are elsewhere. While the rhetoric may deny this, the evidence is overwhelming.[25]

---

[22] S. Pattison, *The Challenge of Practical Theology: Selected Essays* (London, 2007) p. 190.

[23] Michael King, *Submission to the Church of England's Listening Exercise on Human Sexuality* (London, 2007).

[24] Melvyn J. Macarthur, *From Armageddon to Babylon: A sociological-religious studies analysis of the decline of the Protestant prison chaplain as an institution with particular reference to the British and New South Wales prisons from the penitentiary to the present time* (Sydney, 2006) (unpublished PhD thesis).

[25] Ibid., p. 233.

If the Church finds the NHS a useful place to resolve – without financial cost to itself – a difficulty it faces in the lives of clergy whose personal circumstances makes them a problem, it is also important to consider the experience the chaplains have of the Church. Alongside the statistics that enable chaplains to be identified as a highly unusual group of ministers, the verbatim comments captured in the research shed light on the view of the Church formed by the chaplain:

> I think now that I have ended up in health care Chaplaincy by default because of the situation on human sexuality in the CofE. I never envisaged being in full-time health-care chaplaincy... My best ministerial gifts are more suitable to parish life. But ... it is and would be difficult to secure a parish post under the present climate. I had a wonderful curacy with an extremely supportive incumbent and parish. But my experience of looking for a new appointment after that curacy was very dis-heartening and even frightening – when a very unsupportive conservative Bishop simply asked if I had thought of secular employment.[26]

In this research, many chaplains were both saddened and angry about the kind of Church they saw manifested through their personal experiences. At the same time, immersed in a context of ultimate questions and great human need, some chaplains struggle to comprehend how the Church can summon up so much energy for issues that seem increasingly remote from the daily experience of the patients and staff they work amongst. John Hull's brief and cogent theological response to 'Mission-Shaped Church' perhaps best summarizes the frustration with the Church born out of the chaplains' personal experience:

> what we have is a lament over the broken territorialism of the Church of England; ... a church that patronizes the poor, that ignores diversity, clings to an imperial past, and which most disturbingly of all is innocent. We looked for a mission-shaped church but what we found was a church-shaped mission.[27]

In the past decade, as the number of paid parish clergy has declined, the relative size of those funded to provide chaplaincy to public institutions has increased. The armed forces, prison service and the NHS now account for approximately 10 per cent of those clergy employed to provide whole-time ministry. Yet in the Church's selection criteria for ordination training, in synodical structures and in the annual reports of the Church's activities, chaplaincy occupies less than 1 per cent of the agenda. This is in many respects an inexplicable omission given the enthusiasm for 'fresh expressions' and the focus on Christian life outside established Church structures. Chaplains are at the front line of ministry among the imprisoned, the

---

[26]   Graeme Hancocks, Chris Swift and John Sherbourne (2008): 172.

[27]   John M. Hull, *Mission-Shaped Church: A Theological Response* (London, 2006) p. 36.

sick and young people serving in the armed forces. Probably no other group of clergy is so aware of social change, faith diversification and the spiritualities of modern Britain. Yet the experiences and insights of chaplains as a group appear to be drawn on both superficially and fitfully.

The crisis in Worcestershire in 2006 provided further evidence of the general disengagement that has characterized Church leadership and sector chaplaincies. At the height of national publicity about the proposed reduction of posts, the Archbishop of Canterbury sent a letter to all hospital chaplains. The opening sentence of the letter reminded the recipients: 'This is the first time that the Archbishop of Canterbury has written directly to Hospital Chaplains.'[28] In the same letter, the Archbishop went on to say that the work of chaplains is 'at the forefront of the mission of the Church'.

Standing outside Church employment, hospital chaplains occupy a position which enables them to ask searching questions about the Church's public stance on issues such as human sexuality. This is not just a matter of voicing their personal experiences but stems fundamentally from the nature of their work. As I have suggested in the ethnography of Chapter 5, theology written out of intensive care may well look somewhat different from that emerging out of academia. By and large, the diversity of this experience and the issues which it raises are unacknowledged by the Church's public statements and teachings. This may be benign neglect – but it may equally well be a determination not to hear complex and challenging thoughts and experiences: a rendering into silence of dangerous voices.

The examination of chaplains undertaken in Chapters 1 and 2 suggested that there were disparities between the public story of the chaplain told by the Church and the care experienced by patients. In some instances cast as the friend of the poor, the chaplain nevertheless remained a figure of the Establishment. The chaplain operated among some of the poorest and least powerful in society and was intended to contribute to moral improvement and the grateful acceptance of public charity. In the axis between social order, virtuous poverty and spiritual conformity, the chaplain remained a useful figure until the founding of the NHS. Since 1948, the utility of the chaplain in terms of the social and political agendas of governance has undoubtedly diminished.

If many chaplains for one reason or another feel detached from their sponsoring church or faith community, this is likely to be significant in their theological outlook and development. There are chaplains whose experience of the 'Church' – in the sense of hierarchy and dogmatic stances – is systematically oppressive and operates to deny emotions that are central to their core identity and personhood. It may be that the awareness of these feelings has grown and changed since ordination; the image of a denying and punitive God succeeded by a more embodied realization of community, commitment, faithfulness and divine love made flesh. The insight and understanding that this then offers to the

---

[28]   Letter from the Archbishop of Canterbury to all Hospital Chaplains dated 3 October 2006.

experience of ministry is met with silence by the custodians of Church order. It is not surprising if many chaplains are happier speaking about the Kingdom of God more than the Church. From this perspective, the Church as a community with which the chaplain is required to 'check-back' may feel far from supportive or affirming. The apparent ease with which the Church distinguishes between orientation and practice fractures wholeness of human living and creates artificial categories that impose meaningless burdens on those singled out for lecturing. As one colleague once commented to me regarding this dichotomy, 'I don't want to be a theoretical gay man.' Despite the promise of dialogue and genuine listening, little attempt has been made to understand the on-going human cost for those encouraged to deny key aspects of their personhood. The Church's approach to human sexuality remains largely excarnational and dispassionate. In some cases, repeating its history in a modern guise, the Church appears be utilizing the NHS as a comfortable ghetto into which it can dispose of those clergy who complicate the tidiness of doctrine and Church discipline. From the chaplain's perspective making untidy the questions of human being, love, suffering and hope is what makes the questions real.

What the Chaplain Comes For: Licensing Sermon 1997

While the experience of many chaplains may be of marginalization by the Church, there is one occasion in particular when the leadership of the Church is required to make some public statement about the chaplain. The arrival of a new chaplain in a hospital is traditionally celebrated as part of God's activity in the world, sending pastors to care for the vulnerable and those associated with them. While relatively little of any depth has emerged from the Church in recent years about the role of the chaplain, one occasion when some articulation is usually required occurs at the licensing of a new chaplain. For this reason, I now wish to examine in some detail a licensing sermon from 1997.

    While such events are routine in the NHS, I believe that this sermon is significant in that it was given by the bishop appointed to be the Chair of the Church of England's Hospital Chaplaincies Council. The context for the licensing itself was the 75th anniversary of the dedication service for the Barnet Hospital chapel. For that reason, it begins with reflections on the changing nature of ideas and language, including the 'deferential' tone still used by the local media in 1927 to describe a formal religious occasion. The Bishop then proposes what might be described as some 'hypothetical ethnography', asking what kind of words would be used in the day-to-day life of a hospital in 1997. He identifies the language of business and the higher speed of conversation indicated by acronyms. In observing this culture he concludes that all this 'leaves chaplaincy in a difficult situation'. The Bishop's hope about how chaplaincy might act in these circumstances is that it will see itself to possess 'a defiant language system'. He is quick to avoid the implication that this means chaplains should be rude or ill-mannered:

What I mean by a 'defiant language system' is that they should not be able to be fitted into any of the technical or professional, or managerial or medical language groups which exist in all hospitals.[29]

It is in the counter-cultural language of 'passivity', when the chaplain is alongside the patients enabling them to 'to recreate their self-understanding in the light of their illness', that Christian chaplains fulfil their role most effectively. Like the still and silent chapel, chaplains are there to 'make the question of God inescapable' and ensure that issues of personal and universal meaning are not avoided. Of course, whether – or in what sense – these questions exist is a matter of conjecture. The Bishop sees the purpose of the chaplain to be both a potential instigator of this kind of reflection and also an enabler of the patient's discursive redefinition in the light of faith. Furthermore it is a role which he sees to be necessary in the chaplain's relationship with the staff.

Towards the end of his sermon, the Bishop speaks of the chapel as needing to have about it 'the smell of starlight' and, like the chaplains themselves, it should be the space where 'eternity is glimpsed' – 'the intersection of the timeless with time'. This is all a strongly poetic and philosophical use of language that it is quite impossible to imagine being employed in other areas of the hospital. By its nature, it raises the problem of putting into words qualities and effects of a silent building and the chaplain's 'presence'. However, both the occasion and the chapel itself could be seen to provide a sustainable platform for the Bishop's comments – and it may be that staff present could recognize there what he was seeking to describe. Unfortunately, no follow-up work was done to assess the effect, if any, that his words had on those present.

A sermon at the licensing of a chaplain cannot be very long, is not referenced, and does not always stand up to reproduction in a journal. However, on one of the first occasions at which he could give an address in a hospital since becoming Chairman of the HCC, Bishop Herbert sets out an authoritative and thoughtful view of the chaplain and the significance of religious space in the NHS. His reference to a 'defiant language system' can be seen as a call for chaplains to resist assimilation into medical and managerial discourse. It is a vision of the continuation of chaplaincy within the NHS while retaining a distinct, determined and useful role in enabling staff and patients to value vulnerability and understand passivity.

Despite this, it is a sermon that looks almost exclusively one way. The virtue of the chaplain is extolled, and the Bishop's approach is understandably supportive of what the chaplain has to offer the hospital. With the patient the presence of the chaplain raises a question and, conveniently, the chaplain is there to help the patient develop answers about purpose, meaning and hope. There is no consideration in the address as to what the chaplain might offer to the Church, or how the experience of

---

[29]   Christopher Herbert, 'Barnet General Hospital Address', *Journal of Health Care Chaplaincy* (February 1998): 25–7.

being a priest in this context might enable the Church to understand more deeply its ministry in some of the most testing places of our society. In suggesting that chaplains develop a 'defiant language system' for the culture of the hospital the Bishop avoids the corollary that the chaplain's experience might come to develop a resistance to Church language that may be life-diminishing, partial or abusive.

Theological Engagement

In Britain, Don Cupitt has been an influential theologian in the criticism of a Church that lives in the paradigm of Christendom chiefly in order to maintain social conformity and the privileges of those in charge of it.[30] Cupitt is persuasive in his appeal for a theology that takes seriously the practices of belief rather than the abstraction of metaphysical discourse. For him, the theologian is there to 'ask what jobs the word "God" does now, and in what ways we can use it in building our world and lives'.[31] This focus on application reaches the same conclusions as those theologians labouring in the very different circumstances of Latin America. For Gutierrez it is:

> In the deed our faith becomes truth, not only for others, but for ourselves as well. We become Christians by acting as Christians.[32]

In the context of the ethnographic material used earlier, this seems a meaningful and illuminating approach to take in order to understand the interaction of chaplains and those they care for. For some people, Cupitt will sound excessively certain about his non-realism, the kind of certainty Charles Taylor sees at the poles of the religion–atheism divide. It is true that Cupitt is not dismissing the potential value of religion – although he is focusing its value entirely within the here and now. He is dismissive of the metaphysical focus held in the Church's interpretive control of the Christian message. For him the Gospel is concerned with the Kingdom of God in *this* world. I would not suggest that all or even most chaplains would subscribe to this kind of theology. However, the disenchantment with the institutional Church that chaplains have experienced at a personal level over issues such as human sexuality disposes them to recognize what Cupitt is saying. Around the hospital, chaplains encounter forms of post-metaphysical spirituality that bear good fruit and may be interpreted as betokening the Kingdom of God ('cure the sick who are there, and say to them, "The Kingdom of God has come near to you"'[33]).

---

[30] Don Cupitt, *Is Nothing Sacred? The Non-Realist Philosophy of Religion* (New York, 2002).
[31] Ibid., p. 51.
[32] Gustavo Gutierrez, *Power of the Poor in History: Selected Writings* (Maryknoll, 1983) p. 17.
[33] Luke 10:9.

Contrasted with what Cupitt sees as the ecclesiastical captivity of the Christian faith, the creativity, immediacy and vision of the Kingdom of God offers a far more fitting hermeneutical prism for places such as intensive care. In hospitals that have shifted from the altar-centric design of the medieval period, the lessening of structure and formality in the chaplain's work may constitute a largely untapped theological seam. However, as I have already suggested, the lack of excavation may be largely intentional.

Those who are regarded by their peers as successful chaplains are often those able to survive and flourish by attending to the reality of patients' experience while remaining at ease with their own ambiguity. A study drawing into the experience of chaplaincy interns in the Unites States (what would be termed 'trainee' or placement chaplains in the UK) combined ethnography with theories of Foucault and Good. In her research, Frances Norwood[34] confirms the marginalization of chaplains; the uncertainty felt by some staff concerning what the chaplain comes for; and the fact that chaplains have 'inherited contested ground' between science and religion. This study observes how the technical and specializing tendencies of medicine have added to the uncertainties of chaplaincy. As the centre of the hospital has progressed down this road, the chaplains, simply in order to survive, have needed to inhabit more deeply the dominant culture of their host institutions:

> Chaplains are coming to see and practice in the language of hospital medicine and, in order to survive, must at times alternatively embrace or distance themselves from competing discourses of religion and medicine.[35]

In other words, if chaplains present a potential source of anxiety for the Church they constitute a different kind of concern to the health care authorities. As we have seen, in the evidence-based world of health care, chaplains offer little that connects them to the central priorities of the modern institution. Gone is the hospital's central privileging of religious discourse – the management of the morals of the poor, and the role of the chaplain in raising funds. Apart from the unexpected need for chaplains generated by organ and tissue retention at the turn of the century, the professional has become largely removed to the sidelines of the NHS. In some respects, the chaplains present an implicit challenge to their employers by the counter-cultural nature of their endeavours. Despite moves to standardize matters such as data recording, chaplains probably have the least systematized form of working of any group in the health service. Consequently, there is a remarkable range of models in a professional grouping which is one of the smallest in the NHS.[36] This does not sit easily with management expectations

---

[34] Frances Norwood, 'The Ambivalent Chaplain: Negotiating Structural and Ideological Difference on the Margins of Modern-Day Hospital Medicine', *Medical Anthropology* 25/1 (2006): 1–29.

[35] Ibid., p. 5.

[36] H. Orchard, *Hospital Chaplaincy Modern, Dependable?* (Sheffield, 2000) p. 90.

or the general picture of what chaplaincy is about across the UK. Furthermore, the physical facilities associated with the chaplain (chapel, prayer room) replicate the organizational ambiguity found in the chaplains themselves.

Michael Wilson's research into the hospital chaplain sprang out of a request by the Queen Elizabeth Medical Centre's development unit in 1966 for advice about 'certain specifications for a possible hospital chapel'. However, the request for advice about the chapel was met with the suggestion for a different approach 'namely to consider first the role of the hospital chaplain and then to examine what architectural provision should be made for this'.[37] As late as the 1960s, the approach taken was that the first priority for a chapel was that it should accommodate the role of the chaplain rather than the needs of the patients. Chapels provided clear demarcation about the place and behaviour of the chaplain and the laity. As the illustrations in this book demonstrate, the incarnation of the chaplain's function within the fabric of the hospital has changed. Inside the two structures we see how a single religious focus has given way to an absence of religious imagery. The telling of a story in figurative glass, angelic carvings and incremental progress towards the sacred, has acceded to a tale of postmodernism: anonymity, curved walls, and an abstract glasswork installation.[38] In the former, the chaplain knows (and others know) his place. Even at times of personal prayer, when no service is being conducted, the individual is reminded of religious leadership through the unfilled places that elevate and privilege the operation of priesthood. In the prayer room of 2008, there are no visible cues suggesting that a chaplain is required either individually or corporately. The architecture has adapted to the perceived spiritual needs of the modern hospital – but has the chaplain?

Heterotopias as a Conceptualization for the Chaplain's Space

In earlier chapters, I explored the silent presence of history in the operation of contemporary chaplaincy. The chaplain is experienced as a figure linked to history to a degree that is unusual in the hospital. From a base in the workhouse chapel, and the occasional appearance of seventeenth-century clothing and liturgies, the chaplain's role is enacted at various points within the broad range of internal hospital spaces – as well as connected to external locations such as the crematorium. The ethnography has demonstrated that the presence of the chaplain is frequently experienced as the incursion of religious space into the clinical world. The makeshift altar in the neonatal unit, complete with cross and

---

[37]   Michael Wilson, *The Hospital – A Place of Truth* (Birmingham, 1971) p. i.

[38]   Keiko Mukaide, the Japanese artist who created the installation, 'intended to develop work that would support prayer, meditation and reflection. The work reflects light and in all religions light is an important symbol of the divine presence and the spirit. The floating circles represent ideas of unity, the passage of time and the eternal' (the artist's text).

candles, encounters restriction (the candles cannot be lit) but also uses these visual symbols and liturgy to provide a sense of religious definition and continuity. In other words, the temporary space accesses a number of 'real' spaces that have particular meanings and historic associations.

In considering the kind of space that exists, either as a permanent physical presence in one part of the hospital or as a temporary experience in multiple locations, it is useful to examine Foucault's work on 'other spaces'.[39] It is an idea that begins with utopias – unreal places that represent society in either a perfected form or as the precise opposite, a world turned upside-down. Foucault develops this idea with reference to the mirror; the 'placeless place' that enables us to see ourselves where we are absent – over there. Yet, at the same time, the mirror also functions as a 'heterotopia', because the mirror does exist and is the place that makes visible the observer's relationship with all that lies around. As the conceptualization of spaces that reflect our presence and relationships, heterotopias are described by Foucault as chiefly falling into two categories.

Foucault drew a distinction between 'crisis' heterotopias and heterotopias of 'deviation'. The crisis heterotopia describes the kind of privileged space seen in the early hospitals. In the consideration of the early hospital, I used the idea of immersion to describe the placing of a patient within an intense field of religious images, language and ritual. Within that field, the patient is made aware of his or her religious deficit – the need to repent and so on – but is also permitted to contemplate the images of perfection that may await should confession be effective. Patients are invited to see themselves where they are not (heaven/hell), and through the management of that experience they are promoted to conform to certain standards of conduct. At the same time, the distinctive and separate nature of the hospital space removes the crisis of death from the home and enables a semi-public religious significance. It is a stable space set in a hierarchy of places – sacred, profane, celestial and terrestrial. In the history of English hospitals, it is a space that underwent dramatic change in the sixteenth century, and once the principle of fundamental change had been established, the place religion occupied became but a provisional point in a world set in motion. For Foucault, that is the chief consequence of Galileo's discovery; that after the medieval period the appearance of stability only amounts to 'movement infinitely slowed down'.

The second type of heterotopia concerns an exclusion of certain sites from the main social body. Foucault takes the example of the cemetery, but it could equally well apply to the modern movement of hospitals away from city centres. The places to which deviance was consigned were therefore separated from the body politic because they were dangerous. They should not be held in public view and, in the case of hospitals, the intimation of mortality should not be held before the sane (healthy). These 'other spaces' were therefore relocated from the centre of civic life to its extremities.

---

[39]   Michel Foucault, 'Of Other Spaces', *Diacritics* 16/1 (1986): 22–7.

Foucault summarizes the principles of the heterotopias as their ubiquity, their reinvention within a society during the course of history in order to function differently, and thirdly their capacity to juxtapose 'in a single real space several spaces, several sites that are in themselves incompatible'.[40] This is evident in hospitals, where the struggle to preserve premature birth is juxtaposed with late terminations only a matter of metres away. The modern hospital is a small city in which the whole of human life is played out, but it is also a place segregated from 'normality'. The fourth principle relates to 'heterochrony', the multiple presence of alternative time frames – of which museums and libraries are the strongest example. However, even here, with its chapels, plaques and memorials, a hospital encompasses many different connections with time. And in the activities of the chaplain, numerous strands link the present to fragments and places of the past.

The fifth principle Foucault sets out for heterotopias is the necessity for there to be some rite or ritual of entry. In a hospital, this might take many forms, not least exchanging clothes and submitting to the authority of medical examination. At the same time, what occurs in the heterotopia is permitted yet obscured, 'absolutely sheltered and absolutely hidden'. Despite the increasing presence of closed-circuit television cameras in all areas of the hospital, this latter point has until recently been true of the hospital and all its various compartments for observation, cutting, testing, repairing and dying.

The last characteristic of heterotopias concerns their general connection to other spaces. They either create a space of illusion exposing the remaining real space as even more illusory, or they actually embody a real space that models a particular kind of perfection. Certainly the latter could be seen in much hospital history, although the frequent failure of the institution and its officers calls into question its ability to be a site inversely mirroring the imperfection of other sites. The debates that occur externally to the hospital (about its role in worship or social reform) serve to illustrate that heterotopias are also political spaces in which the priorities for the exercise of power are enacted with greater determination than might be possible elsewhere.

I have raised the idea of Foucault's heterotopias because they provide a useful framework for some of the central concerns of this book. While the chaplain may be a figure within the hospital, he is also the custodian of various temporary and permanent places. A repeated question to chaplains when they visit patients is 'where is your church?' Chaplains seem inevitably associated with a building, and this gives shape to the perception that patients have and implicitly questions any separation of the chaplain from a religious location. Using the concept of heterotopias it is possible to make the following points:

1. While the nature of heterotopias was one of crisis (and this would apply to early hospitals), the shift to deviance has been shown to develop strongly after the Reformation. Hospitals were one element of a system of other spaces

---

    40   Ibid., p. 25.

to which people were consigned and where ideals of moral improvement were practised with intensity. The chaplain as 'Sunday gaoler' protected this space and separated its religious life from that of the wider community. If the chaplain was to be a 'light burning and shining', he was clearly being instructed to set an example: to use the space of the hospital, its physical attributes and scope for pastoral conversation, to inspire conformity, and acceptance of both the cosmic and social orders.

2. There is no doubt that, while appearing to convey continuity, the historical study in Chapters 1 and 2 have demonstrated that hospitals have functioned in strikingly different ways across the centuries. While the overall formation of knowledge on which the hospital operates has changed both in the chapel and in the temporary religious space of the ward, the chaplain's presence utilizes and affirms elements of heterochrony. For example, ministry is seen to be done partly 'in remembrance' and this connects the chaplain and the traditional chapel to religious history; the Reformation; the monarchy, and much more. While this sense of other times may be increasingly implicit it is nevertheless true that the chaplain is seen to be constructed by tradition.

3. The idea that hospitals in fact contain a range of contradictory spaces is not difficult to accept. The art-work of a hospital proclaims a clean and optimistic culture founded on science, but the chaplain is often drawn into situations where events stand in opposition to that story. Within the overall discourse of healing and repair, the use of pills and procedures, those places where the chaplain emerges in the ethnography are seen as unorthodox. The inability to cure leaves a silence that sits uncomfortably within the dominant story of improvement and progress.

4. The issue of time in the hospital heterotopia has a further dimension in regard to what Foucault called the 'quasi-eternity' of places like a cemetery. Wards are often perceived by patients and staff as a 'timeless' space – where light and lack of external views give little indication of days, hours or seasons. Yet the experiences which occur in hospital, and with which the chaplain is often involved, mark certain dates in ways that remove them from the general progression of time. It was the day my baby died; the day we were told he would need to go into a home; the day I was given the all-clear. In other words, the chaplain may sometimes move through a chronologically-undifferentiated space yet become involved in moments that require liturgical recognition as enduring and connected to eternity.

5. At one time the chaplain was a key figure in the process of admission to hospital, and part of the ritual of prayer and purification which went with it. This is no longer part of the chaplain's remit, and the role can only be partly seen in the movement out of the hospital of a patient who has died. This aspect of the heterotopia serves as a reminder of how other staff

now control and monitor the process of entry, and the intervention of the chaplain is delayed until the patient (or a relative) seeks contact.

6. If the hospital is a space in which the person is dismembered by a process of medical classification (departments for noses, knees, brains and so on), it is also the space where the myth of medical order and mastery is constantly re-stated. As I have argued, the chaplain can be seen to act in order to regularize those events that stand in contradiction to this dominant myth, especially with regard to death. The heterotopia therefore projects its perfection by enabling the subject of death to be managed and contained – drawing on the chaplain's expertise to contain the consequences of what may be seen as medical failure.

Foucault's concept of heterotopias is helpful in drawing together both the historic activity and current presence of chaplains within the hospital. To some extent, the crisis of contemporary chaplaincy can be seen in how the purpose of the heterotopia's function has changed at critical historic moments. From techniques that ensured the moulding of a holy soul to practices that involved moral reform and improvement, the chaplain was central to the institution. However, as emphasis shifted to medical dominance and authority in support of neo-liberal economic goals, the role of the chaplain within the heterotopia became more peripheral. Rather than representing the central purpose of the space, the chaplain has increasingly accrued value in the organization by moderating those events that call into question the myth of medical perfection – especially mortality.

Chaplaincy might now be seen as one of the inner contradictions of the heterotopia, juxtaposing an awareness of the limit of life beside a dominant culture committed to the ultimate cure of all our ills. In these circumstances, it is understandable that people ask what the chaplain has come for – and what his or her presence beside the patient is intended to achieve.

While the concept of heterotopias relates to aspects of the hospital and those who work within it I believe it has a special application to the subject of prayer space. If we examine the main chapel at St James's University Hospital (pages 52 and 53) we encounter a space that is rich in its Christian imagery and historic connections. There are plaques remembering former staff of the hospital, including a nurse who died as the result of enemy action in a field hospital in the First World War and two nurses who died shortly afterwards due to the flu pandemic of 1919. In stained glass, the Christian story is told from the nativity of Jesus to the Resurrection. The pews and inner architecture give order to the seating of the congregation and elevate the place of the chaplain. It is a chapel that draws together the history of the workhouse it was built to serve, the children of the poor and, latterly, the children of staff who came for baptism, and the moral purpose of a place ostensibly intended to provide shelter, care and public compassion. It gives the impression of being a place where the poor would have been reminded of their station in life – and have been encouraged to accept it with the prospect of eternity.

The chapel stands alone in the hospital site, untouched by the developments which have occurred around it.

The new Faith Centre in the same hospital makes visible the impact of social and religious change over the intervening one hundred and fifty years. It is tiny by comparison with the older building, and has little to indicate the Christian faith other than a plain wooden table. Unlike the stand-alone chapel, this space is accommodated within the hospital alongside very modern and highly technical areas such as nuclear medicine. The title 'chapel' has gone and been replaced by the heading 'Faith Centre'. In its design, it is distinct from other hospital spaces by its oval shape and its emptiness. A modern glass sculpture art-work runs round the inside of the main prayer room. It is colourful and abstract. The furnishings are few but of high quality and made from natural materials. The room is lit with care, highlighting the art-work and giving largely indirect illumination to the rest of the space. In terms of being a heterotopia, the space is devoid of historic references, and appears likely to remain so. The design does not tell a religious story except, perhaps, that it has become impossible to tell a single public religious story in the twenty-first century. The consequence is space, light and colour to which those present must bring their own resources of faith, reflection or doubt. Religious books and prayer mats are present but hidden – only to be used when someone is there and then put away again. The default setting of the room is neutrality: a space from which both medicine and religion are excluded.

While it would be a mistake to equate the intentions of those who designed the two buildings, there are some key similarities. Church of England clergy were closely involved in the design of each, the spaces are set aside for religious and spiritual uses, and the costs for each were chiefly met from public funds. However, while the chapel of 1861 AD undoubtedly cohered with a widespread public belief in the value of the Christian religion to public benefit and order, the space of 2008 AD is less strident in its sense of purpose. If the chapel contained physical reminders of the place of the chaplain to instruct and minister (pulpit and font), the prayer room indicates no necessity for a religious figure. In many respects, the Faith Centre appears to be a small and tolerated exception to the technical purposes of the hospital, an heretical fragment lodged in the orthodoxy of clinical success and Enlightenment progress. It feels a little like religion hanging on with its fingernails, no longer able to mobilize major resources – but incapable of being entirely excluded.

Conclusion

Chaplaincy is a form of religious practice that lives in the territory of other disciplines. Practical theology offers Christian chaplains the most sympathetic theories and body of work through which to better articulate, discuss and develop an understanding how to be of best use to others. As we have seen in this chapter, there is a great deal in common between this kind of theology and the experience of chaplaincy. Even the marginality of practical theology, and its frequent soul searching, is akin to the dilemmas and doubts that beset chaplains. Practical theology might be said to be on the edge of the discipline of theology which in turn has a rather precarious place in the academic world.[41] Just as chaplains feel the pressure to conform to the dominant culture they inhabit, so too practical theology is mindful of its vulnerability. I would suggest that this persisting sense of vulnerability is in fact a constituent characteristic of what makes for effective chaplaincy and good practical theology.

If the chaplain is 'ambivalent' and self-consciously practises in an age of uncertainty, then it is far less likely that the chaplain's involvement in a situation will constitute some form of repression or domination. Insecurity can breed renewed self-awareness and questioning which, if it is not paralysing, can lead to ministry that is fruitful, relational, adaptive and compassionate. As Elaine Graham has identified, this still leaves a major problem over the role of historic narratives of the Christian faith and 'the relationship of the inherited tradition to the changing context that confronts every new generation'.[42] This all suggests, alongside the demographic data already discussed in relation to chaplains, that we are passing through a period of diminishing popular orthodoxy even as Anglican leaders appear to be re-positioning themselves within it. In Charles Taylor's analysis of secularization, it is possible to view chaplains occupying the ground between the polarities of an excarnational orthodoxy and the self-certainty of modern atheism. Paralleling these changes, the multi-referenced chapel has given way to the ambiguity of the prayer room and its accompanying sense of uncertainty about the role of the chaplain. In all of this, the chaplain continues to mediate the resources of the Christian faith to meet the kind of pastoral situations set out in Chapter 5. While the place of chaplaincy is maintained and managed at a national level by the HCC, there is a tension between the Church's influence on chaplaincy and the life experiences and pastoral encounters of chaplains themselves. Just as the spiritual space allocated to chaplaincy within the hospital has changed, is it now time to re-think the personnel corresponding to that space? In the final chapter consideration will be given to the future shape of chaplaincy.

---

[41]   Matthew Reisz, 'Losing our religion?', *Times Higher Education* 24 January 2008.

[42]   Elaine Graham, 'Pastoral theology in an age of uncertainty', *HTS: Theological Studies* 62/3 (2006): 845–65.

Chapter 8
Conclusion

Introduction

> ... it is our imaginations which shape us, keep us, create us – for good and for ill. It is our stories that will recreate us, when we are torn, hurt, even destroyed. It is the storyteller, the dream-maker, the myth-maker, that is our phoenix, that represents us at our best, and at our most creative.[1]

In this book I have brought together material from several eras and contexts to reflect on the chaplain working in hospitals in England. Inevitably it is an incomplete picture, but it begins to tell a story of the chaplain that reveals considerable complexity and insight into contemporary spirituality. In both the ethnography and the voices that emerged in the media during the crisis in Worcestershire, the chaplain was shown to be a prominent figure in the story-telling that brought the semblance of meaning to experiences of great personal pain and distress. The chaplain's power to enable connections across generations, between life-experiences and to give sacramental recognition to moments of personal crises remains a prominent feature of this ministry. At times when individual narratives collapse, the presence of the chaplain may contribute to the creation of new meaning and the hope of a sustainable story.

The powerful experiences of what Bury originally termed 'biographical disruption'[2] have an immense impact on people's wellbeing and ability to cope in the face of adversity. Yet in a world of productive knowledge and solution-focused health care it can be hard to argue for the necessity of space and silence. In this respect the physical places associated with the chaplain are akin to the interactions that take place at the bedside. Rather than utility we find signs, space, prayer, reflection and (potentially) meaning. According to Heather Walton, a central part of the chaplain's role is to 'speak in signs' with those experiencing trauma:

> Speaking in signs, communicating in the language of silence, preserving the gestures of pain. These are difficult and maddeningly imprecise attempts to describe what it means to let suffering speak... We will need to develop a new sensibility as to how material objects and physical gestures can embody what words may not. We will begin to learn that there are times when it is not right to

---

[1]   Extract from Doris Lessing's Nobel Prize Acceptance Speech, 2007.

[2]   Michael Bury, 'Chronic illness as biographical disruption', *Sociology of Health and Illness* 4/2 (1982):167–82.

make connections, supply meanings or resolutions for others. At points all we will be able to do is preserve the sanctity of their silence.[3]

To this work the chaplain brings sensitivity for the broken stories of others because, very often, they know personally what it is to live in the tension between different narratives. Not only in this respect, but as someone who embodies a membership of multiple communities,[4] the chaplain bears the strains of a postmodern age. For all these reasons, if the experience of chaplaincy is allowed to walk out of the shadows, there is much to be learned from the story of the chaplain.

Chaplaincy in a Time of Change

I have endeavoured to analyse and understand the range of relationships, from historic events to present-day secularization, that resource the character and activities of the chaplain. It has in some ways been a messy enterprise, because there is no established body of work focusing on chaplaincy in England that takes account of the chaplain's connections to history, practice, politics and the shifting nature of modern spirituality. However, even when these accounts of the chaplain have been obscured, they are present in the altered design of chapels and the changing fortunes of the chaplain's place in the hospital and the wider-Church. The chaplain has emerged as a figure at the edge of major narratives about faith and medicine which seem largely oblivious to what chaplaincy is and who performs it. Yet, as I have argued, this marginality – if it is recognized and understood – presents the chaplain as someone skilled and experienced in honouring the stories of the staff and patients who find themselves on other kinds of margins. As we have seen Charles Taylor argue, the vast majority of people in the West are in this territory between the opposing certainties of unbending materialism and religious fundamentalisms. Through collegiality and a growing commitment to critical reflection on practice, chaplains are beginning to draw their theologies and beliefs into an open encounter with the experiences of care for those occupying this middle ground. Within the spiritual care offered in hospital there remains a central mission of compassionate engagement with the experience of sickness that is rooted in the chaplain's pastoral character. The chaplain is a unique auditor of the impact on people's lives that illness makes. It is up to NHS Trusts and to society to determine whether this role continues to be of value. In Worcester at least there was a resounding affirmation that it is wanted, and that in a largely post-Christian society the presence of fragmented belief requires those skilled at weaving the old spirituality with the new. Patients and staff want to be

---

[3]   Heather Walton, 'Speaking in Signs: Narrative and Trauma in Pastoral Theology'. *Scottish Journal of Healthcare Chaplaincy* 5/2 (2002): 2–5.

[4]   Mark Cobb, 'The Location and Identity of Chaplains', *Scottish Journal of Healthcare Chaplaincy* 7/2 (2004): 11.

served by chaplains who know what it means to inhabit uncertainty and change, and there is good evidence that this is a fitting description of the chaplains of today. The erosion of religious authority and episcopal influence has contributed to the creation of a chaplain who no longer rests on privileged certainties. At a moment such as the Worcestershire crisis, these older influences emerged with vigour, but the very novelty of their intervention highlighted the extent of the distance that has grown up in many places between the mainstream Church and chaplains in the NHS.

From one perspective, it is possible to suggest that the loss of an authoritative role, built into the core of personal subjectivity and society's implicit knowledge, constitutes the crisis of the chaplain. The place for the chaplain to stand, quite literally, has been chipped away and reconfigured. There is no longer a pulpit to privilege the chaplain's discourse. If chaplains have survived to date partly because of the historical impetus that projected them into the NHS, it has become increasingly clear that this energy has dissipated. As the auto-ethnography illustrates, chaplains walk through ordinary doors to spend time in rooms with those whose lives have suddenly become immersed in sorrow. As the Anglican chaplain's disciplinary usefulness to the governance of people has disappeared, a new space – perhaps a postmodern space – has opened in which the chaplain is far more available to the reality of the patient's experience than was once the case. As Taylor and others have argued, it is a mistake to equate the decline of religious authority with the demise of religious longings and spiritual desire.

The problems experienced by Anglican chaplains, be they a sexuality-related distancing by religious hierarchies or the fragmentation of traditional spirituality, might in fact be the strength of a profession committed to serve the spiritualities of the sick. For chaplains willing to explore their personal life-journey in relation to the Christian tradition, the outcome will be a practical wisdom that is helpful for those struggling towards their own post-crisis narratives. This is a subject that requires further research and consideration, because the collective experience of this work, its engagement of experience, belief and theology, could become a creative and theologically rich offering to both secular and ecclesial communities. However, in order to do this the hidden factors that inhibit the open discussion of these issues must be revealed and overcome.

The spiritual orthodoxy once embedded in the patient, which lent the Anglican chaplain authority and institutional confidence, is now hardly discernible. Yet in varying measures both the hospital and the Church expect the chaplain to conform to a pattern of legitimate ministry that belongs more to the old world order than to the new. One of the questions facing chaplaincy is that if faith-specific forms of belief are in decline, should chaplaincy continue to be faith-based and denominationally delineated? Just as chaplaincy bodies and individual chaplains describe their role as those able to meet increasing levels of non-religious spiritual needs, the question arises as to why the vast majority of these chaplains are required to be religiously authorized. As time goes on, I suspect that this will become a growing question and one ever more difficult to answer with credibility.

The loss of the chaplain's disciplinary role in regulating conduct and conversation has created the potential for a space of considerable honesty and openness in the hospital. Increasingly, the chaplain no longer comes to colonize the experience of the patient, or build the patient's story into a tool for professional power. This may become a temptation for chaplains as their sense of professionalism grows, but I suggest that it should be resisted. Chaplains need the kind of structure and identity required to remain within health care – but they do not need to recruit patients into a campaign for professional aggrandizement. If that were to be done, they would find that they have lost the marginality that makes them uniquely useful to patients who are exploring what it means to live in a post-Christendom world. Nevertheless, if, as I have suggested, the experience of chaplains has important things to say to the NHS and to the faith communities, then an appropriate form of organization and structure is needed. The chaplains also need these structures in order to hear – and consider together – what Churches, faith groups and health care bodies have to say to them. This relationship needs to be more open, more active and less concerned with the retention of status than has previously been the case. For those looking on, it is beyond question that the changes arising from the work undertaken by chaplains have generated a new grouping of faith leaders:

> A shift for your work as chaplains into a freestanding profession, differentiated from yet related to the Church that heretofore was your employer, is a striking example of one story now becoming two. Your location in General and in Psychiatric Hospitals, Learning Disability Units, Care of the Elderly Units, Mental Health Clinics, distinguishes you from the clergy serving parishes. You are the remnant in the community, in the front line of emergencies of illness physical, mental and spiritual. Your story will be a different narrative, now to be recognised as distinct.[5]

This challenges comfortable assumptions about ecclesial belonging and the right of those with no chaplaincy experience to speak for the profession. As chaplains become more confident in claiming a corporate voice, the need for the Church to understand this and respond positively to the new situation becomes ever more important.

Critical Choices

Chaplains are drawn from communities whose central beliefs are popularly seen as antithetical to the forms of knowledge – and ways of knowing – associated with contemporary scientific thought. While the epistemic fragment on which chaplains have stood may be crumbling, it is far from certain how chaplains can effectively

---

5   Ann B. Ulanov, 'The Space Between Pastoral Care and Global Terrorism', *Scottish Journal of Healthcare Chaplaincy* 10/2 (2007): 3–8.

occupy a new space within the health service of the twenty-first century. Mowat (2008) was tasked by the NHS to make proposals about how chaplains could develop a research agenda and extend the evidence base for health care chaplaincy. Without doubt, this work marks a further step in the inclusion of chaplaincy in the culture and expectations of the NHS. Along with the new national pay structure, *Agenda for Change*, we have seen chaplains increasingly 'owned' by the health service in the early years of the new century. At the same time, this ownership remains tentative and at times ambivalent, as the situation in Worcester served to illustrate. While this was not typical of how chaplains were being considered across the UK, it showed how local decision-making could challenge a service whose provision was assumed rather than demonstrably essential. Without a more proactive engagement of the faith communities with chaplains it is likely that chaplains will continue to address their professional and research agendas to the employing institution rather than to the denominational sponsor.

When chaplains regarded their presence in the NHS as largely assumed and secure, their relationship to the changes taking place in other disciplines was often remote. As this picture has shifted, chaplains have suddenly found themselves exposed to a culture of research and professional debate for which they are often underpowered. At the same time, the chaplains' faith communities have not provided a clear lead in showing how chaplains might cope effectively with this new situation. A *Health Service Journal* article early in 2008 quoted the theological adviser to the Hospital Chaplaincies Council referring to simple data collection and outlining how many chaplains now deeply 'resented this descent into what she referred to as statistics, questionnaires and management speak'.[6] While this view is not supported by research[7] it does reflect an anxiety in the faith communities that chaplains are beginning to work in ways alien to traditional forms of ministry. The view from outside can all too easily be that of able chaplains, keen to be present on the wards, forced by bureaucracy to spend ever more time sitting at desks. Yet an inarticulate aloofness does nothing to enhance the understanding of the chaplain by the organization. Worcester happened not because chaplaincy posts were unwanted by their faith communities but because chaplains were not seen as fundamentally relevant to the practice of health care. In these circumstances, it was wholly understandable that chaplains would reflect increasingly on their capacity to communicate within a culture whose mother tongue is research and evidence. To date, the faith communities have not offered an alternative likely to alter this shift in the chaplains' approach or appease the clamour for evidence within NHS Trusts. While there is considerable hand-wringing of the sort quoted in the HSJ, the idea that chaplains should work without a proper framework for accountability and reflection is in fact deeply concerning. We saw earlier the

[6]   *Health Service Journal* (2008).
[7]   Graeme Hancocks, John Sherbourne and Chris Swift, 'Are they Refugees? Why Church of England male clergy enter health care chaplaincy', *Practical Theology*, 1/2, 2008: 163–79.

extraordinary example of the Revd Frederick Pocock, spending none of his time accounting for his activities and achievements, but leaving a swath of neglect among those for whom he was supposed to care. In fact, the idea of protecting the clergy – chaplains or otherwise – from searching enquiry fails to take adequate account of human sinfulness. Perhaps those who feel no need to account for their activities will visit the sick, but some might equally well do a quick twirl round ICU and head off for a pleasant afternoon's shopping.

The Hidden Dynamics of Healthcare Chaplaincy

We noted earlier research findings in the opening years of the twenty-first century that gave the first quantifiable data about the personal characteristics of Anglican chaplains. This information described a group of clergy who were significantly different from their parochial colleagues. In particular, it supported the view that at least 50 per cent of chaplains were in personal circumstances that would make placement in a parish a difficult option (both for them and for the Church authorities). This would also be true for the high proportion of Roman Catholic chaplains who are married ex-Anglicans with families to support. It is reasonable to postulate that the NHS serves a useful purpose for the Churches by employing clergy otherwise difficult to place. Furthermore, should bishops be pressed to act against any clergy perceived to be living beyond a conservative understanding of a Christian life, it is possible for bishops to protest that they are unable to take action as chaplains operate under NHS employment regulations.

This perception of the utility of the NHS to the Churches leads to a further possibility. Without wishing to suggest that any conscious decision was ever taken, it is conceivable that the role of the Hospital Chaplaincies Council in the latter part of the twentieth century, and the beginning of the twenty-first, has been to manage the transition of problematic clergy out of the parish system and into the health service. It does not necessarily follow that these clergy would perform badly in the NHS, but it is probable that the chief reason for their departure from parishes has in many cases been concealed. Despite a widespread awareness of high levels of gay clergy serving in chaplaincy, not a single course or advertised meeting has been held to explore the spiritual and psychological implications of the situation in which some chaplains find themselves. The same could be said for clergy who have partners who are parish clergy and feel they must abandon a vocation in a parochial setting because the Church, having legislated in favour of the ordination of women, has done little in a systematic way to support the employment of clergy couples. In fact, in some dioceses, the idea of employing two clergy in parish ministry is banned as a matter of policy. From a Church culture which has encouraged the concealment of sexual identity; the frustration of a clergy couple's desire for equal opportunities to serve; and the rejection of a liberal pastoral theology, the hospital has become an accepting and affirming place of truth.

Occupying Multiple Marginalities

Previous researchers, like James Woodward in 1998, have developed the thesis of the chaplain as a figure 'between worlds'. Based on the evidence and arguments developed earlier in this book I would suggest that this is an accurate description, but one which we now know to be more wide-ranging than was previously understood. Not simply on the margins between the parochial system central to dioceses and the medical paradigm that dominates the hospital, but between life and death, gay and straight, a Christendom past and a contemporary spirituality that has rejected the rights of external authority. What follows for many chaplains is a liminality reinforced by the sense of exile tacitly fostered by the Church. Despite occasional comments about chaplains being at the forefront of mission, their experience of ministry at the intersection of many of society's most pressing personal and public concerns remains mostly untapped. It may seem reasonable to argue that chaplains themselves have not done enough to engage the Church or to articulate a theology fashioned by their convictions and experiences. Chaplains certainly need to do more and work harder to integrate their experience and theology with a vision of how chaplaincy might develop. However, given the research findings about who chaplains are, and their experiences as stipendiary clergy, it is likely that their exile has been largely constructed by the Church. Some bishops have been sympathetic and supportive of individual chaplains, but there has been a complete absence of serious corporate engagement. It is hard to avoid the impression that the Church does not want to hear the experience of the chaplains: it is too difficult, too marginal and too raw. The silent exile of the chaplains from the central preoccupations of the Church is based on that most dubious of policies: 'don't ask; don't tell'. Not simply about human sexuality, but in relation to the complexities of pastoral care, what the chaplain has to bring is the messy reality of human travails and hopeful courage. The shift of focus for the Church from pastoral ministry to mission is far more attractive than the dilemmas and uncertainty of the hospital and its myriad of pressing needs:

> My regret is that so few people now seem able to see that this theologically-informed, practically relevant everyday realm is at the centre of mission rather than a peripheral distraction from it. You can't have too much humanity in mission – that is the central message of the incarnation.[8]

For those who spend much time speaking with chaplains – be they in health care, the prison service or the military, these themes are recurrent. The Church is happy that state-funded chaplaincy is there. As we saw in the case of the Worcestershire NHS Trust, various denominations and faiths rushed to the defence of the chaplains when cuts were announced. But it is an ambivalent relationship.

---

[8]   Stephen Pattison, 'Is Pastoral Care Dead in a Mission-led Church?', *Practical Theology* 1/1 (2008): 7–10.

The NHS houses clergy who might otherwise be troublesome or whose personal integrity of life might lead others to call on a bishop to take action. In his study of the chaplain in the prison system in Britain and New South Wales, Melvyn Macarthur notes a similar disengagement:

> Little critical thought about the chaplain in the prison has been evident from the church; as long as the state pays the subsidy, the chaplain will be there. 'For what purpose?' is a question that the church has not posed in a serious and critical way ... The church entertains and promotes the idea that it is reaching into areas of need, but little evaluation seems to have been done on whether this effort is in any way effective, or indeed valuable.[9]

For Macarthur, the answer to the silence that surrounds the crisis of the prison chaplain's exile is to hope for some return to prominence, centrality and influence. It is in spite of this exile that the chaplain remains within the prison. While I have conceptualized the crisis of chaplaincy in the NHS as a product of its multiple marginalities, it should not be assumed that this is in itself a disastrous situation. The advantage of belonging in different ways to different groups is that there is a potential wealth of support that can be mobilized in a time of crisis. In the case of Worcester, arguments used to defend chaplains called on their history (they have always been a part of the NHS), support from other professional groups in the same trade union (community health visitors), their professional claims written into guidance and legislation, the general public, and a variety of faith groups and churches. All this made a formidable and effective coalition. Since then, we can surmise that groups such as Stonewall and the Lesbian and Gay Christian Movement might have contributed to the debate given the very significant number of same-sex partnered clergy we now know to be serving in chaplaincy. The general crisis of chaplaincy's location and purpose focused by the Worcestershire debacle revealed its inter-relatedness with groups to which it was at once marginal but also – in a time of crisis – significant.

The need now is to turn the support of a moment into a dialogue that is both longer lasting and more open. The Theos report's evidence of the gradual reduction of chaplaincy posts reveals that behind the dramatic cuts in one Trust a quieter crisis continues across the NHS in England. For chaplains to enjoy the kind of supportive and critical partnerships that will develop their role the engagement by faith communities needs to move beyond the superficial. If fruitful communication is to begin, then Church authorities must show some recognition that the way they have related to many of the clergy who have become chaplains has fostered distrust. Chaplains have wanted to be open about their personal struggles, joys and doubts but have found a Church that appears fearful and defensive. The pastoral complexity of the chaplains' work, and its location in the public space of contemporary health care, means that chaplains are at the forefront of a ministry

---

[9]   Melvyn Macarthur, *From Armageddon to Babylon* (Sydney, 2006) p. 338.

that is far less orthodox than was once the case. It is a sadness that the experience of chaplains is not drawn on more extensively, and this may yet be redeemed if Church and chaplains can work more closely together in the conviction that a theology which is serviceable in the wards of a twenty-first-century hospital is likely to be a practical theology that will be of real help to people.

The Empty Handed Healer

Helen Orchard's King's Fund study of chaplaincy in London refers to one particularly illuminating, brief, but crucial reflection on the role of the chaplain:

> The 'all can deliver' approach works especially well if care-giving is grounded in an 'empty handed' ideology (or theology). Here, delivering spiritual care is not about *delivering* anything, but about being present while the other person works it out for him or herself ... And while a person can be an expert in matters of religion, the 'empty handed' approach requires no expertise; indeed it is not possible to be *the* expert on matters spiritual, as no one has the full facts, answers, or truth.[10]

This is without doubt a negative casting of the marginality and occupational resources of the twenty-first-century chaplain. As I have argued, in a culture where the production of new knowledge and skill is paramount, the chaplains are vulnerable to a creeping sense of occupational inferiority. However, I would contend that being alive to the ambiguities and 'emptiness' of spirituality in the face of suffering is in itself a vocational skill that has value in health care. Even the small amount of ethnographic material contained in Chapter 5 provides evidence for this. In conversation with a renal transplant surgeon, I quoted Harriet Mowat's reference to the attempt to define spirituality as being akin to finding oneself in a 'room with no doors'. His response was to say that he would find that 'terrifying'. Standing in the place where there are no answers, no quick exits to open, does not require the gifts of those whose hands are full. It is a situation that calls for great patience, compassion and faithfulness to the value of the human being in front of you. While some might assume that this kind of availability is simple, I would contend that it is in fact the product of considerable preparation, maturity and deep personal self-knowledge. Chaplains can develop these skills together but it is to be hoped that many faith communities will want to encourage and foster this kind of personal pastoral development. For only when the chaplain's hands are empty will wounded people dare to offer their stories and allow their most intimate shards of doubt and hope to be handled with love and honoured with insight. The primary task for chaplains in the twenty-first century is to communicate to the NHS and to faith communities the difference that this kind of care can make. If this can be

---

[10] Orchard (Sheffield, 2000) p. 139.

achieved then chaplains will remain open and available to the stories of those like themselves who dwell on the margins.

Bibliography

Adams, N. and Elliott, C., 'Ethnography is dogmatics: Making description central to systematic theology', *Scottish Journal of Theology* 53/3 (2000): 339–64.

Adhiyaman, V., Adhiyaman, S. and Sundaram, R., 'The Lazarus phenomenon', *JRSM* 100/12 (2007): 552.

Alvarez-Rosete, A. and Mays, N., 'Reconciling Two Conflicting Tales of the English Health Policy Process Since 1997', *British Politics* 3/2 (2008): 183.

Andrews, J., Briggs, A. and others, *The History of Bethlem* (London: Routledge, 1997).

Archivist, *St Thomas' Hospital: Historical Notes* (London: London Metropolitan Archives, 1957).

Atkinson, P., Coffey, A., Delamont, S. and others (eds), *Handbook of Ethnography* (London: Sage Publications, 2001).

Autton, N., *The Hospital Ministry* (London: Church Information Office, 1966).

——, *Pastoral Care in Hospital* (London: SPCK, 1968).

Ballard, P.H. and Pritchard, J., *Practical Theology in Action: Christian thinking in the service of Church and society* (London: SPCK, 2006).

Barber, B.R., *Con$umed: how markets corrupt children, infantilize adults, and swallow citizens whole* (New York: W.W. Norton & Co., 2007).

Becker, P.E. and Eiesland, N.L. (eds), *Contemporary American Religion: An Ethnographic Reader* (California:Walnut Creek and London: AltaMira Press, 1997).

Beckford, J.A., *Social theory and religion* (Cambridge: Cambridge University Press, 2003).

—— and Gilliat, S., *The Church of England and Other Faiths in a Multi-Faith Society* (Warwick: Department of Sociology, 1996).

Bender, C., *Heaven's kitchen: living religion at God's Love We Deliver* (Chicago and London: University of Chicago Press, 2003).

Berger, P.L., 'Reflections on the Sociology of Religion Today', *Sociology of Religion* 62/4 (2001): 443–54.

Bernard, G.W., *The King's Reformation: Henry VIII and the Remaking of the English Church* (New Haven: Yale University Press 2005).

Bernauer, J.W., *Michel Foucault's force of flight: towards an ethics for thought* (New Jersey and London: Humanities, 1990).

—— and Carrette, J.R., *Michel Foucault and theology: the politics of religious experience* (Aldershot: Ashgate, 2004).

Bird, J., 'Medicine for Body and Soul: Jacques de Vitry's advice to Hospitallers and their Charges', in P. Biller and J. Ziegler (eds), *Religion and Medicine in the Middle Ages*, (York: York Medieval Press, 2001).

Bloor, M. 'The Ethnography of Health and Medicine', in P. Atkinson, A. Coffey, S. Delamont and others (eds), *Handbook of Ethnography* (London, Sage Publications, 2001): p. 180.

Bouchard, D.F. (ed.), *Michel Foucault. Language, counter-memory, practice* (Ithaca, New York: Cornell University Press, 1980).

Bretherton, L., 'A New Establishment? Theological Politics and the Emerging Shape of Church–State Relations', *Political Theology* 7/3 (2006): 371–92.

Brewer, J.D., *Ethnography* (Milton Keynes: Open University Press, 2000).

Brigden, S., 'Religion and Social Obligation in Early Sixteenth-Century London', *Past and Present* 103 (1984): 67–112.

Brown, C.G., *The Death of Christian Britain* (London: Routledge, 2000).

Browning, D.S., *A fundamental practical theology: descriptive and strategic proposals* (Minneapolis: Fortress Press, 1991).

Bruce, S., *God is Dead* (Oxford: Blackwell, 2002).

Bury, Michael, 'Chronic Illness as biographical disruption', *Sociology of Health and Illness* 4/2 (1982): 167–82.

Campbell, A., 'The Nature of Practical Theology', in J. Woodward and S. Pattison (eds), *The Blackwell Reader in Pastoral and Practical Theology* (Oxford: Blackwell, 2000).

Carrette, J.R., *Foucault and religion: spiritual corporality and political spirituality* (London: Routledge, 2000).

—— and King, R., *Selling spirituality: the silent takeover of religion* (London: Routledge, 2004).

Chaplain, *Chaplain's Report Book* (Leeds, Workhouse & Infirmary, 1870).

Chaplains, *Chaplain's Report Book* (Leeds, St James's Hospital, 1927).

Charmaz, K. and Olesen, V., 'Ethnographic Research in Medical Sociology: Its Foci and Distinctive Contributions', *Sociological Methods and Research* 25/4 (1997): 452–94.

Charon, R., 'Narrative Medicine: Attention, Representation, Affiliation', *Narrative* 13 (2005): 261–70.

Clark-Kennedy, A., *The London: A Study in the Voluntary Hospital System* (London: Pitman Medical Publishing Ltd, 1962).

Clifford, J. and Marcus, G.E. (eds), *Writing Culture* (London, 1986): p. 123.

Cobb, M., 'The Location and Identity of Chaplains', *Scottish Journal of Healthcare Chaplaincy* 7/2 (2004): 10–15.

—— and Robshaw, V., *The spiritual challenge of health care* (Edinburgh and New York, Churchill Livingston, 1998).

College of Health Care Chaplains, *Questionnaire Newsletter* (London, CHCC, 2005).

Cox, J.G., *A Priest's Work in Hospital* (London: SPCK, 1955).

Crown (1546), *Indenture for the Re-Founding of St Bartholomew's Hospital* (St Bartholomew's Historical Archives).

Crowther, A., *The workhouse system, 1834–1929: the history of an English social institution* (London: Methuen, 1981).

Cupitt, Don, *Is Nothing Sacred? The Non-Realist Philosophy of Religion* (New York: Fordham University Press, 2002).

Curt, B., *Textuality and tectonics: troubling social and psychological science* (Milton Keynes: Open University Press, 1993).

Davie, G., 'Believing without Belonging: Is This the Future of Religion in Britain?', *Social Compass* 37/4 (1990): 455–69.

Dean, M., *Critical and Effective Histories: Foucault's Methods and Historical Sociology* (London: Routledge, 1994).

——, *Governmentality: Foucault, power and social structure* (Thousand Oaks, California and London: Sage, 1999).

Department of Health, *Standards for Better Health* (6405) (London: The Crown, 2004).

Engelhardt, H.T., 'The Dechristianization of Christian Hospital Chaplaincy: Some Bioethics Reflections on Professionalization, Ecumenization, and Secularization', *Christian Bioethics* 9/1 (2003): 139–60).

Faubion, J.D. (ed.), *Ethics: subjectivity and truth; the essential works of Michel Foucault, 1954–1984 volume 1* (London: Penguin Books, 2000).

——, *Michel Foucault: Power* (London: Allen Lane, The Penguin Press, 2001).

Field, C., 'Rendering unto Caesar?', *Journal of Anglican Studies* 5/1 (2007): 89–108.

Forrester, D.B., *Truthful Action: Explorations in Practical Theology* (Edinburgh: T. & T. Clark, 2000).

Foucault, M., *The Archaeology of Knowledge* (New York: Pantheon Books, 1972).

——, *Ceci n'est pas une pipe* JSTOR (1973).

——, 'Body/Power: interview with Quel Corps?' in C. Gordon (ed.), *Power/ Knowledge Selected Interviews and Other writings 1972–1977 Michel Foucault* (Harlow: Harvester Press Limited 1980) 55–62.

——, 'Intellectuals and Power', in Donald F. Bouchard (ed.), *Language, Counter-Memory, Practice* (New York: Cornell Paperbacks, 1980): 205–17.

——, 'Of Other Spaces', *Diacritics* 16/1 (1986): 22–7.

——, 'Christianity and Confession: The Politics of Truth', in S. Lothringer and L. Hochroth (eds), *The Politics of Truth* (New York: Semiotext(e), 1997): 199–236.

——, 'Interview with Michel Foucault by D. Trombadori', in J.D. Faubion (ed.), *Michel Foucault: Power*, (London: The Penguin Press, 2000).

——, *The Order of Things: An Archaeology of the Human Sciences* (London: Routledge, 2000).

Fox, N.J., *Beyond Health: Postmodernism and Embodiment* (London: Free Association, 1999).

——, 'Practice-based Evidence: Towards Collaborative and Transgressive Research', *Sociology* 37/1 (2003): 81.

Geertz, C., *The Interpretation of Cultures: selected essays* (London: Fontana Press, 1993).

Getz, Faye, *Medicine in the English Middle Ages* (Chichester: Princeton University Press, 1998).

Gilliat-Ray, S., '"Sacralising" Sacred Space in Public Institutions: A Case Study of the Prayer Space at the Millennium Dome', *Journal of Contemporary Religion* 20/3 (2005): 357–72.

Goffman, E., *Asylums: essays on the social situation of mental patients and other inmates* (New York: Doubleday, 1961).

Good, B., *Medicine, rationality, and experience: an anthropological perspective* (Cambridge: Cambridge University Press, 1994).

Goodliff, P., *Care in a confused climate: pastoral care and postmodern culture* (London: Darton Longman and Todd, 1998).

Graham, E., 'Pastoral theology in an age of uncertainty', *HTS: Theological Studies* 62/3 (2006): 845–65.

Gutierrez, G., *Power of the Poor in History: Selected Writings* (Maryknoll: Orbis Books, 1983).

Gutting, G., *The Cambridge Companion to Foucault* (Cambridge: Cambridge University Press, 1994).

Habermas, J., 'Religion in the Public Sphere', *European Journal of Philosophy* 14/1 (2006): 1–25.

Hancocks, G., Sherbourne J. and Swift, C., 'Are they Refugees? Why Church of England male clergy enter health care chaplaincy', *Practical Theology*, 1/2 (2008): 163–79.

Hastrup, K., 'Writing ethnography: state of the art', in J. Okely and H. Callaway (eds), *Anthropology and autobiography* (London: Routledge, 1992): 116–33.

Hay, D., 'The Spirituality of Adults in Britain – Recent Research', *Scottish Journal of Healthcare Chaplaincy* 5/1 (2002): 4–10.

Heelas, P. and Woodhead, L., *The spiritual revolution: why religion is giving way to spirituality*,(Malden, MA and Oxford: Blackwell, 2005).

Henery, N., 'Constructions of spirituality in contemporary nursing theory', *Journal of Advanced Nursing* 42/6 (2003): 550–57.

Herbert, C., 'Barnet General Hospital Address', *Journal of Health Care Chaplaincy* (1998): 25–7.

Hillesum, E., *An interrupted life: diaries and letters of Etty Hillesum 1941–1943* (London: Persephone, 1999).

Hopewell, J.F., *Congregation: stories and structures*, Barbara G. Wheeler (ed.), (Philadelphia: Fortress Press, 1987).

Hospital Chaplaincies Commission, *Hospital Chaplaincies Interim Report (CA 871)* (London: Church Information Office, 1948).

Hull, J.M., *Mission-Shaped Church: A Theological Response* (London: SCM Press Ltd., 2006); 36.

Humble, J. and Hansell, P., *Westminster Hospital 1716–1974* (London: Pitman Medical Publishing Co., 1974).

Hunt, K., 'Understanding the Spirituality of People who Do Not Go to Church', in G. Davie, P. Heelas and L. Woodhead (eds), *Predicting Religion: Christian, secular, and alternative futures* (Aldershot: Ashgate, 2003).

Jenkins, T., *Religion in English everyday life: an ethnographic approach* (New York and Oxford: Berghahn Books, 1999).

Johnson, C.P., 'Assessment tools: are they an effective approach to implementing spiritual health care within the NHS?', *Accident & Emergency Nursing* 9/3 (2001): 177–86.

King, M., *Submission to the Church of England's Listening Exercise on Human Sexuality* (London: Royal College of Psychiatrists, 2007).

King, M., Speck, P. and others, 'The Royal Free Interview for Religious and Spiritual Beliefs: Development and Standardization', *Psychological Medicine* 25/6 (1995): 1125.

Klein, R., 'The new model NHS: performance, perceptions and expectations', *British Medical Bulletin* (2007).

Koch, A., 'Interpreting God's truth: A postmodern interpretation of medieval epistemology', *International Social Science Review*, 75/:3 & 4 (2000): 47–60.

Liturgical Commission, *Transforming Worship: Living the New Creation (GS 1651)* (London: Church of England, 2007).

Louth, A., 'The Body in Western Catholic Christianity', in S. Coakley (ed.), *Religion and the Body* (Cambridge: Cambridge University Press, 1997): 111–30).

Lyall, D., *The integrity of pastoral care* (London: SPCK, 2001).

Macarthur, M.J., *From Armageddon to Babylon: A sociological-religious studies analysis of the decline of the Protestant prison chaplain as an institution with particular reference to the British and New South Wales prisons from the penitentiary to the present time* (Sydney: University of Sydney, 2006).

Manning, Peter K., 'The Challenges of Postmodernism', in J. Van Maanen (ed.), *Representation in ethnography*, (London: Sage Publications Inc., 1995).

Markham, I.S., *A theology of engagement*, (Oxford: Blackwell, 2003).

McSherry, W., 'Spiritual crisis? Call a nurse', in H.C. Orchard (ed.), *Spirituality in Health Care Contexts* (London: Jessica Kingsley, 2001).

McSherry, W. and Ross, L., 'Dilemmas of spiritual assessment: considerations for nursing practice', *Journal of Advanced Nursing* 38/5 (2002): 479–88.

Mellor, P.A. and Shilling, C., *Re-forming the body: religion, community and modernity* (London: Sage and California: Thousand Oaks, Sage 1997).

Miller, G., 'Toward ethnographies of institutional discourse', *Journal of Contemporary Ethnography* 23/3 (1994): 280–306.

Moore, N., *The History of St. Bartholomew's Hospital* (London: Arthur Pearson, 1918).

Mowat, H., *The potential for efficacy of healthcare chaplaincy and spiritual care provision in the NHS (UK)* (Aberdeen: Mowat Research, 2008).

National Institute for Clinical Excellence, *Improving supportive and palliative care for adults with cancer* (London: National Institute for Clinical Excellence, 2004).

Norwood, F., 'The Ambivalent Chaplain: Negotiating Structural and Ideological Difference on the Margins of Modern-Day Hospital Medicine', *Medical Anthropology* 25/1 (2006): 1–29.

Okely, J., Callaway, H. and others, *Anthropology and autobiography* (London: Routledge, 1992).

Orchard, H. *Hospital Chaplaincy Modern, Dependable?*, (Sheffield: Lincoln Theological Institute for the Study of Religion and Society, 2000).

—— (ed.), *Spirituality in Health Care Contexts* (London: Jessica Kingsley Publishers, 2001).

The ordre of the hospital of S. Bartholomewes (London: Richard Grafton, 1552).

The ordre of the Hospital of S. Bartholomowes in West-Smythfielde in London (London: The Hospital, 1997).

Orme, N. and Webster, M., 'The English Hospital, 1070–1570', *Bulletin of the History of Medicine* 71 (1995): 706–8.

Paley, J., 'Spirituality and nursing: a reductionist approach', *Nursing Philosophy* 9/1 (2008): 3–18.

Paley, J., 'Spirituality and secularization: nursing and the sociology of religion', *Journal of Clinical Nursing* 17/2 (2008): 175–86.

Pargament, K.I., *Spiritually integrated psychotherapy: understanding and addressing the sacred*, (New York and London: Guilford Press, 2007).

Park, K., 'The Life of the Corpse: Division and Dissection in Late Medieval Europe', *Journal of the History of Medicine and Allied Sciences* 50/1 (1995): 111–32.

—— and Henderson, J., '"The First Hospital Among Christians": The Ospedale di Santa Maria Nuova in Early Sixteenth-Century Florence', *Medical History* 35/2 (1991): 164–88.

Pattison, S., *Alive and kicking: towards a practical theology of illness and healing* (London: SCM, 1989).

——, 'Dumbing down the spirit', in H.C. Orchard (ed.), *Spirituality in Health Care Contexts* (London: Jessica Kingsley Publishers, 2001).

——,*The Challenge of Practical Theology: Selected Essays* (London: Jessica Kingsley Publishers, 2007).

——, 'Is pastoral care dead in a mission-led Church', *Practical Theology* 1/1 (2008): 7–10.

Percy, M., *Engaging with contemporary culture: Christianity, theology, and the concrete church* (Aldershot: Ashgate, 2005).

Principe, W., 'Toward defining spirituality', *Studies in Religion*, 12/2 (Toronto, 1983): 127–41.

Pullman, P., *The Amber Spyglass* (London: Scholastic Press, 1998).

Rawcliffe, C., *Medicine for the Soul* (Stroud: Sutton Publishing, 1999).

Reader, J., *Reconstructing Practical Theology: The Impact of Globalization* (Aldershot: Ashgate, 2008).

Reisz, M., 'Losing our religion?', *Times Higher Education*, 24 January 2008.

Rex, R. and Armstrong, C D.C., 'Henry VIII's Ecclesiastical and Collegiate Foundations', *Historical Research* 75/190 (2002): 390–407.

Risse, Guenter B., *Mending Bodies Saving Souls: A History of Hospitals* (New York: Oxford University Press, 1999).

Robinson, S., Kendrick, K. and others, *Spirituality and the practice of healthcare* (Basingstoke: Palgrave Macmillan, 2003).

Ross, L., 'The nurse's role in assessing and responding to patients' spiritual needs', *International Journal of Palliative Nursing* 3/1 (1997): 37–42.

Royal Commission on the Historic Medieval Hospital, *English Hospitals 1660–1948* (London: RCHMH, 1998).

Ryle, G., *Collected papers* (London: Hutchinson, 1971).

Scharen, C.B., '"Judicious narratives", or ethnography as ecclesiology', *Scottish Journal of Theology* 58/2 (2005): 125–42.

Schleiermacher, F., Duke, J.O. and Stone, H.W., *Christian caring: selections from Practical Theology* (Philadelphia: Fortress Press, 1988).

Sheikh, A., Gatrad, A.R. and others, 'The myth of multifaith chaplaincy: a national survey of hospital chaplaincy departments in England and Wales', *Diversity in Health and Social Care* 1/2 (2004): 93–8.

Sommerville, R., *The Savoy: Manor; Hospital; Chapel* (London: The Chancellor and Council of the Duchy of Lancaster, 1960).

South Yorkshire Workforce Development Confederation, *Caring for the Spirit: A strategy for the chaplaincy and spiritual healthcare workforce* (Sheffield: South Yorkshire WDC, 2003).

St Bartholomew's Hospital. *The Ordre of the Hofpital of S. Bartholomewes in Weft'fmythfielde in London* (Orpington: A.G. Bishop and Sons Ltd., 1997).

Staff Reporter, 'Chapel Opened' (Barnet: *Barnet Times*, 1922).

Stell, P.M., *Medical Practice in Medieval York* (York: Borthwick Institute of Historical Research, University of York, 1996).

Stewart, J., *Theological Considerations in Chaplaincy Development: Humanity, Modernity and Postmodernity*, CHCC Yorkshire Branch Annual Study Day, (Leeds, 2003).

Swift, C., 'Speaking of the Same Things Differently', in H.C. Orchard (ed.), *Spirituality in Health Care Contexts* (London: Jessica Kingsley, 2001): 96–106).

——, 'The Function of the Chaplain in the Government of the Sick in English Acute Hospitals', *School of Health and Related Research* (Sheffield: University of Sheffield, PhD thesis, 2005): 275.

——, 'The Political Awakening of Contemporary Chaplaincy', *Journal of Health Care Chaplaincy* 7/1 (2006): 57–63.

——, 'Cutting chaplains will cost the NHS', in *The Church Times*, 18 August 2006.

——, Calcutawalla, S. and others, 'Nursing attitudes towards recording of religious and spiritual data', *British Journal of Nursing* 16/20 (2007): 1279.

Tanner, A., 'A Troublesome Priest: A Victorian Workhouse Chaplain in the City of London', *London Journal* 23 (London: Longman, 1998): 15–31.

Tawney, R.H. and Power, E.E., *Tudor economic documents : being select documents illustrating the economic and social history of Tudor England* (London: Longmans, 1924).

Taylor, C., *A secular age* (Cambridge, MA and London: Belknap, 2007).

Theos, *NHS Chaplaincy Provision in England: Theos Research Paper (Interim Findings)*, (London, 2007).

Touraine, A. and Macey, D., *Critique of Modernity* (Oxford: Blackwell, 1995).

Tracy, D., *Analogical imagination: Christian theology and the culture of pluralism* (New York: Crossroad, 1981).

Tyler, Stephen, 'Post-Modern Ethnography: From Occult document to Document of the Occult', in J. Clifford and G.E. Marcus (eds), *Writing Culture* (London, 1986): 123.

Ulanov, A.B., 'The Space Between Pastoral Care and Global Terrorism', *Scottish Journal of Healthcare Chaplaincy*, 10/2 (2007): 3–8.

Van Maanen, J., *Representation in ethnography* (London: Sage Publications Inc., 1995).

——, 'An End to Innocence: The Ethnography of Ethnography', in J. Van Maanen (ed.), *Representation in ethnography* (London, Sage Publications Inc., 1995): 23.

Ven, J.A. van der, *Education for reflective ministry* (Louvain: Peeters, 1998).

Voas, D. and Crockett, A., 'Religion in Britain: Neither Believing nor Belonging', *Sociology* 39/1 (2005): 11–28.

Walton, H., 'Speaking in Signs: Narrative and Trauma in Pastoral Theology', *Scottish Journal of Healthcare Chaplaincy* 52 (2002): 2–5.

Willis, P., *The Ethnographic Imagination* (Gateshead: Athenaeum Press Ltd, 2000).

Wilson, A., 'The politics of medical improvement in early Hanoverian London', in A. Cunningham and R. French (eds), *The Medical Enlightenment of the Eighteenth Century* (Cambridge: Cambridge University Press, 1990).

Wilson, M., *The Hospital – A Place of Truth* (Birmingham: University of Birmingham, 1971).

Wilson, T., *The works of the Right Reverend Thomas Wilson, D.D. Lord Bishop of Sodor and Man* (Bath: Cruttwell, 1779).

Woodward, J., *To do the sick no harm: a study of the British voluntary hospital system to 1875* (London and Boston: Routledge and Kegan Paul, 1974).

——, *A Study of the Role of the Acute Health Care Chaplain in England* (Open University: School of Health and Social Welfare, 1998).

Woodward, J., Pattison, S. and Patton, J., *The Blackwell reader in pastoral and practical theology* (Oxford: Blackwell, 2000).

Wuthnow, R., 'The Cultural Turn: Stories, Logic, and the Quest for Identity in American Religion', in P.E. Becker and N.L Eiesland (eds), *Contemporary American Religion: An Ethnographic Reader* (London: Sage Publications Ltd, 1997).

Young, R.K. and Meiburg, A.L., *Spiritual Therapy: How the Physician, Psychiatrist and Minister Collaborate in Healing* (London: Harper, 1961).

Index